TRUTH&
HONOUR

THE DEATH OF RICHARD OLAND
AND THE TRIAL OF DENNIS OLAND

GREG MARQUIS

NIMBUS
PUBLISHING

Nimbus Publishing Limited
3731 Mackintosh St, Halifax, NS, B3K 5A5
(902) 455-4286 nimbus.ca

Printed and bound in Canada

NB1272

Cover photo: Canadian Press
Cover and interior design: Jenn Embree

Library and Archives Canada Cataloguing in Publication

    Marquis, Greg, author
    Truth and honour : the death of Richard Oland and the trial of
    Dennis Oland/ Greg Marquis.
    Issued in print and electronic formats.
    ISBN 978-1-77108-425-3 (hardcover).
    ISBN 978-1-77108-426-0 (html)

1. Oland, Dennis—Trials, litigation, etc. 2. Oland, Richard—Death and burial. 3. Trials (Murder)—New Brunswick—Saint John. 4. Murder—New Brunswick—Saint John. I. Title.

HV6535.C33S3532 2016   364.152'30971532   C2016-903753-3
                                                 C2016-903754-1

Canada Council Conseil des arts
for the Arts   du Canada

Nimbus Publishing acknowledges the financial support for its publishing activities from the Government of Canada through the Canada Book Fund (CBF) and the Canada Council for the Arts, and from the Province of Nova Scotia. We are pleased to work in partnership with the Province of Nova Scotia to develop and promote our creative industries for the benefit of all Nova Scotians.

This book is dedicated to D. Gordon Willett, a well-respected Saint John barrister and community volunteer, who in February 1975 was robbed and brutally beaten in his Fredericton hotel room. Michael Alward and Raymond Mooney were arrested and charged with robbery, but when the diminutive eighty-year-old victim died of his injuries, they were prosecuted for murder. The attackers stole $120 in cash and a wristwatch, which one of the accused sold to the other for $5. That watch, when its serial number was matched to a bill of sale, helped send the two men to penitentiary. Mr. Willet, who at the time of his death had been a lawyer for more than fifty years, was the partner of my late father, Henry J. Marquis, Q.C.

TABLE OF CONTENTS

ACKNOWLEDGEMENTS

I wish to thank my wife, Donna, who lived with this project for two years, and my colleagues Professor Nicole O'Byrne and Professor Mary Ann Campbell of the University of New Brunswick, lawyer David Lutz, Q.C., and Saint John Chief of Police John Bates, who consented to be interviewed for this project. John Henderson generously provided advice on criminal law and procedure. I need to recognize the special assistance of Christine Robson, administrative assistant for the Department of History and Politics at the University of New Brunswick Saint John, the staff at the Saint John Law Courts, and the helpful people at the Saint John Free Public Library. For photographs I am indebted to Kâté Braydon, Sail Canada, and Canadian Press photographer Andrew Vaughan. Artist Carol Taylor of Rothesay provided courtroom sketches. My sincere thanks to Jim Turnbull for his advice and research. Jim also contributed detailed drone aerial photography. Thanks to regular court attendees Judith Meinert and Alan Heward as well as to those members of the media with whom I shared the long days in court. UNB Saint John Dean of Arts Joanna Everitt allowed me to adjust my 2016 teaching term so that I could devote more time to writing. And special thanks to Whitney Moran and the staff at Nimbus Publishing and editor Elaine McCluskey for helping to make this project happen.

A NOTE ON SOURCES

Court records often contain inaccurate, uncorroborated, and contradictory information. For the most part, this book is based on evidence presented at the 2015 trial of Dennis Oland and the preliminary inquiry that preceded it in 2014. I was limited to exhibits and other evidence presented in court and did not have access to full disclosure in this case.

INTRODUCTION

July 6, 2011, was a typical summer night in uptown Saint John, New Brunswick, one of the oldest cities in Canada. The central business district was nearly deserted, but on the Market Square boardwalk near the waterfront people were gathering for a popular talent contest. Two blocks to the east, with the exception of a few customers leaving or entering Thandi's restaurant, things were quiet on Canterbury Street. At some point that evening, a brutal murder was committed in a second-storey office across the street from the restaurant. This was a particularly vicious attack. The medical examiner would detect a total of forty-five sharp- and blunt-force blows to the head, neck, and hands, with fourteen of them penetrating the skull. For a criminal profiler, this was an example of "overkill": an excessively violent assault motivated by rage or revenge, sadly typical of many intimate-partner homicides. The victim, who likely died within minutes, lay on the floor possibly for more than fourteen hours before his body was discovered face down in a pool of blood. He was one of the richest individuals in the province, a recipient of the Order of Canada, and a man with an active and adventurous lifestyle. He also had a wife, a son and two daughters, and a brother and sister who lived in the area. Yet when he failed to return home that evening, no family member appears to have attempted to contact Richard Henry Oland by telephone, text message, or email. Statistically speaking, the odds were high that the murder had been committed by a relative, friend, or acquaintance. The odds were also quite high that the killer would be discovered and successfully prosecuted.[1]

One journalist summed up the Oland case as "a miasma of rumour and prurient fascination," fuelled by "sex, class and family discord" and characterized by "a series of maddeningly unanswered questions."[2] Responses to the murder, investigation, and subsequent trial suggested class tensions in a city that is experiencing an economic downturn. The size of the community and the need for police to protect the investigation from public scrutiny resulted in intense levels of gossip and rumour, enhanced by social media and unprecedented media attention, which included live tweeting from the courtroom. Although the victim was a member of the elite, the social profile of the accused, Richard's only son, Dennis Oland, evoked a fatalistic response from many who doubted that he would ever be convicted. The outward solidarity the accused's family was interpreted by some not as normal loyalty but an exercise in protecting the Oland family brand, which is linked to Moosehead Breweries. It was almost if an entire social class was on trial.

This turned into a case where the police chief controlled all statements to the media and where the police struggled to carry out their normal duties in the face of mounting criticism over the lack of an arrest. Although the Saint John Police Force (SJPF) in public described this as just another case of homicide, the chief acknowledged that the victim, Richard Oland, was well known locally, provincially, and nationally. The victim, it gradually became known, was overbearing, narcissistic, ruthless in business, stingy towards his own family, and an adulterer. Despite his reputation as a savvy businessman, much, possibly most, of his considerable fortune was inherited from his own father. The person charged with the murder, in contrast, was described by family and friends as polite, compassionate, kind, a loving husband, and an involved father, the quintessential nice guy. Dennis Oland, a divorced father of three who had recently remarried, lived in a heritage home in the upscale community of Rothesay but was struggling to earn a basic middle-class income. Caught in the squeeze between his lifestyle and income, he was charged and convicted of second-degree murder. Parricide, the killing of a parent, is a crime vilified throughout the ages as the ultimate act of betrayal. According to criminological literature, the typical child who kills a parent is an abused or severely anti-social adolescent or youth who suffers from conduct disorders.

The Oland murder, which many regard as a double tragedy, is intriguing not only because of the prominence of the victim and the accused, but also because of its unprecedented visibility, which included pretrial exposure of many investigatory details in the media.

But the most compelling aspect to this story is that the murder was not an open-and-shut case and many in the community remain unconvinced of the son's guilt. The diversity of opinion can be summed up as follows: (1) those who believe that Dennis Oland is innocent and is the victim of factors such as police tunnel vision, a poorly planned and executed defence, class resentment, or plain bad luck; (2) those who feel that he is guilty, that the police investigation, although not perfect, was adequate and that the Crown met the burden of proof; (3) those who believe that Dennis probably killed his father, but that the evidence against him was thin and he should have been acquitted based on the principle of reasonable doubt. The overall impact of the case, for many, was to put the justice system itself, including the police, the institution of the jury, and so-called legal dream teams, on trial. Rarely has a Canadian trial jury, which, according to one author, reflects a community's "weaknesses and strengths," been subjected to so much critical commentary—much of it based on a limited understanding of the role of the jury in our justice system.[3]

The high visibility of this case and its complex interconnections in the community were reflected in what was the largest jury pool in Canadian history: more than five-thousand potential jurors were contacted. Other than Saint John's small size and the web of connections with the Olands, another reason that explains the intense public interest in the case is the increasing trend in North America for people to play detective. We are inundated with forensics-driven crime dramas on television such as *CSI*. More recent phenomena are the American public radio series and podcast *Serial*, about a Baltimore murder case dating from 1999, and the 2015 Netflix series *Making a Murderer*.

The murder of Richard Oland, the subsequent investigation—with attempts by media outlets to publicize investigatory information a judge had sealed—and the arrest and prosecution of his son, all add up to New Brunswick's most fascinating crime story since the reign of terror conducted by Allan Legere in 1989. This convicted murderer escaped custody while on a visit to a Moncton hospital. Over a seven-month period, "the monster of the Miramichi" eluded police, terrorized northern New Brunswick's Miramichi region, and murdered four people: seventy-five-year-old shopkeeper Annie Flam, sisters

Linda and Donna Daughney, and sixty-nine-year-old Roman Catholic priest Father James Smith. He also seriously injured and sexually assaulted a fourth woman. The sisters had been sexually assaulted, and all victims had been brutally beaten. Legere was arrested in dramatic circumstances in late 1989 and convicted of four counts of murder in 1991.[4] The Legere case was recently overshadowed in New Brunswick by another violent incident that captured national and international headlines: the murder of three RCMP officers and the wounding of two others by twenty-four-year-old Justin Bourque. A young man characterized by substance abuse, paranoia, and a love of firearms, Bourque had no criminal record. His Facebook page was full of pro-gun and anti-police posts. In June of 2014, wearing camouflaged clothing, he went on an anti-police rampage armed with a shotgun, a semi-automatic rifle, and a crossbow. Until his arrest, entire neighbourhoods of Moncton were on lockdown, with people advised to stay in their basements. The sacrifice of the members of the Codiac RCMP detachment, who left behind wives and children, prompted a massive outpouring of grief and support for the police by the citizens of Moncton and beyond, something that far surpassed similar public displays of grief for the four victims of Allan Legere.

Why was I drawn to this tragic story of Richard Oland? First of all, I am an academic historian who specializes in the history of crime and policing. I grew up in a legal family and I have been researching the histories of Saint John and the Canadian legal system since the early 1980s. Years of research have suggested that an examination of a prominent crime offers the historian an evocative window into a community at a specific time in its history.[5] I was born and raised in Saint John (near the Moosehead Brewery), I have lived in Rothesay, home to many of the Olands, and currently live in the neighbouring community of Quispamsis. I have taught classes in Philip Oland Hall at the University of New Brunswick Saint John and organized events in the Mary Oland Theatre at the New Brunswick Museum. I drive past the grave of Richard Oland on a daily basis. And over the years, I have consumed my share of Moosehead beer.

In a nation with many high-profile criminal cases, there are several reasons why the Oland case is so exceptional. In a city where most victims and perpetrators of major crime are poor, both the victim and the chief suspect were members of one of province's most prominent families. Right or wrong, celebrity crimes such as the 1973 murder of model Christine Demeter in Toronto and the 1983 murder of JoAnn Wilson, ex-wife of controversial politician Colin Thatcher, in Saskatchewan, draw media and public attention.[6] Murder and adultery always make for good copy—especially in the Maritimes, where society supposedly is more conservative. (Extramarital affairs are a fact of life in modern society but they appear to be more rare, according to surveys, in New Brunswick than elsewhere in Canada. According to the online dating service Ashley Madison, as of 2013, Saint John definitely was not considered one of the nation's top twelve "infidelity cities."[7]) This created complications for journalists and writers covering the case, as the New Brunswick business elite not only values its privacy, but it is also protected by a web of complex business, personal, and social ties that makes many people unwilling or unable to go on the record. When Dennis Oland was convicted of murdering his father, not a single prominent New Brunswicker stated in public that justice had been served. Similarly, there were no editorials in provincial newspapers and even the victorious Crown attorneys refrained from any statements that could be interpreted as self-congratulatory. In New Brunswick, the business elite exercises a disproportionate share of economic, political, and social power. Partly because of the control of the province's print media by the Irving interests, the public constantly hears of, and local politicians channel, business perspectives on education, economic development, poverty reduction, energy policy, urban planning, municipal services, and even policing.[8]

The Olands are not the Irvings or the McCains, but they are clearly not an average New Brunswick family. When a working-class mother of four children was killed by her husband the same year Richard Oland was murdered, the mayor did not order municipal flags to be flown at half-mast, and the media did not describe her loss as "a heavy blow" to the community.[9] Paul Zed, a Saint John lawyer and former Member of Parliament who once was married into one of those families (the Irvings), explained in 2011 that it was the celebrity factor that was drawing public interest in the case.[10] Identified with Moosehead beer outside of the community, in the Saint John area the Olands are also identified with Rothesay, an upscale, well-educated, and socially homogenous town that has its own associations: people who golf, sail, play tennis, live in nice houses, and send their children to private school and the best universities. (Rothesay, for example, is one of the few communities in Canada to say no to the American retail giant Walmart.) Yet until the crime, the Olands were relatively low-profile celebrities and the victim's controversial reputation was not common press fodder. Dennis, for example, drove a VW Golf and although his residence was in the tradition of a Rothesay blueblood, he lived the lifestyle of a suburban husband and dad. The Saint John Olands, compared to their Halifax cousins, were supposedly down to earth. According to writer Harvey Sawler, author of *Last Canadian Beer: The Moosehead Story* (2008), in contrast with the Irvings and the McCains, the Olands have not polarized public opinion in New Brunswick. In Sawler's words, the public sees the family "in a positive light," with their beer company being associated with "social interaction, conviviality, and the sharing of happy times."[11]

The investigation and trial revealed evidence of adultery, family tensions, and a less-than-flattering image of the victim, who was described in family statements to the police as a self-centred, selfish bully who was obsessively tight with his money. The Olands are accustomed to a certain lifestyle and many, particularly investigating officers, believed this lifestyle was a factor in Richard's demise. In 2011, the median annual family income in Rothesay was a third higher than the New Brunswick average. Saint John, where the Oland trial was held (and from where part of the jury was drawn) in 2012 had a poverty rate of 18.8 percent, one of the highest child-poverty rates in Canada, a teen-pregnancy rate double the national average, and a large minority of families headed by a single parent. As Dennis Oland would be told during his first police interview, the SJPF was accustomed to investigating suspects who were poor and had criminal records. In fact, in the period 2010 to 2015, only one other murder or manslaughter case in the Saint John area involved a victim or accused who was middle class.

Another factor that distinguished this case is the length of time between the discovery of the crime and the laying of a murder charge—more than two years—despite early police assurances that they had identified a lone suspect. This caused many in the community to speculate that the case for the prosecution was weak and the accused would go free. Next, given the lack of eyewitness testimony, is the key role of forensic evidence in a murder prosecution taking place in a city where most serious crimes are solved by old-fashioned techniques and confessions. Since the 1994–95 O. J. Simpson case, where forensic science failed to secure a conviction, the public and media have been fascinated with DNA typing and other tools of forensic investigation. In the Oland case, the most contested evidence was bloodstain and DNA evidence. Video-surveillance footage, cellphone and cell-tower data, and records of computer usage were important for both the prosecution and the defence. A further reason why this case is noteworthy is the size and reputation of the defence team which was presumably bankrolled by the Oland family—blood relatives of the victim. It included one of Canada's leading defence lawyers, who specializes in discrediting "junk science." Another intriguing factor is the Oland family's continued public insistence, despite circumstantial evidence, that Dennis Oland is innocent. This is backed up by their considerable financial resources in a case that has probably cost them millions of dollars. This outward solidarity appears so strong that it strikes many that the family views the now convicted defendant, not his dead father, as the real victim of the tragedy. At the time of writing, the family is supporting not only an appeal of Dennis's conviction, but an appeal all the way to the Supreme Court of Canada to allow his release on bail, which is set to be argued on October 31, 2016.

In addition to the personal tragedy, the Oland murder was not good for Saint John's soul. Both the city's morale and outside reputation, never totally positive, suffered a heavy blow with the unsolved murder of one of its most prominent citizens. Both the economy and population were in decline, the city government's fiscal situation was grave, little construction was taking place, and the office-vacancy rate was high. Fires and the demolition of derelict buildings, such as the once-iconic Paramount Theatre on King's Square, left behind piles of rubble or empty lots, which were converted to parking spaces. The young and many middle-aged people were leaving in droves, often for the greener pastures of Alberta. Richard Oland's violent death, the silence of the police and the Oland family, and the lack of an arrest were depressing enough, but these developments were topped off by more shocking revelations.

In 2012, new allegations surfaced regarding Kenneth Estabrooks, a Saint John police officer who had died in 2005. In 1999, he had been convicted of molesting four boys during the period 1957 to 1982. Estabrooks had been investigated in 1975 following a complaint but had not been charged, only moved to a new job in another city department, from where he continued to molest children. In 2012, a private investigator working on behalf of the municipal government identified at least fifty possible victims and estimated that the total might exceed two hundred and sixty. In 2013, a Nova Scotia lawyer launched a class-action suit against the SJPF, the City of Saint John, and the police commission. In early 2013, before an arrest was made in the Oland case, police apprehended Donnie Snook, a popular common councillor and youth worker, for sexual offences against minors and child pornography. He pleaded guilty to forty-eight charges and received eighteen years in penitentiary for his crimes.[12]

NOTES: INTRODUCTION

1. Adam Cotter, *Homicide in Canada, 2013* (Ottawa: Statistics Canada, 2013).
2. Eric Andrew-Gee, "Sex, class, family discord fuel Saint John's fascination with Oland trial," *Globe and Mail*, Dec. 13, 2015.
3. Stephen J. Adler, *The Jury: Trial and Error in the American Courtroom* (New York: Crown Publishing Group, 1994), 39.
4. Rick MacLean and Andre Veniot, *Terror: Murder and Panic in New Brunswick May–November 1990* (Toronto: McClelland and Stewart, 1990).
5. See for example Charlotte Gray's fine study of the 1915 Massey murder in Toronto: *The Massey Murder: A Maid, Her Master and the Trial That Shocked a Country* (Toronto: HarperCollins, 2013).
6. Demeter's husband, Peter, was convicted of her murder, and in the case of Wilson, it was her ex-husband, the businessman and politician Colin Thatcher. In both cases, the suspects had accomplices and wiretap or body-pack tape recordings had been key in securing a conviction.
7. Richard Johnson, "The demography of adultery," *National Post*, Nov. 16, 2012.
8. John DeMont, *Citizens Irving: K. C. Irving and His Legacy* (Toronto: Doubleday Canada First Editions, 1991); Jacques Poitras, *Irving vs. Irving: Canada's Feuding Billionaires and the Stories They Won't Tell* (Toronto: Viking, 2014).
9. Oliver Moore, "Oland's killing a heavy blow to Maritime community," *Globe and Mail*, July 12, 2011.
10. Julian Sher, "The inscrutable murder of a magnate," *Globe and Mail*, Oct. 15, 2011.
11. Harvey Sawler, *Last Canadian Beer: The Moosehead Story* (Halifax: Nimbus Publishing, 2009), 3.
12. "Scandal and suffering," CTV Atlantic News, Nov. 7, 2012; "Ken Estabrooks may have had more than 260 victims: investigators," CTV Atlantic News, Sept. 30, 2012; "Ken Estabrooks sex abuse victims file for class action suit," CBC News New Brunswick,

Dec. 04, 2013; April Cunningham, "Snook sentenced to 18 years," *Telegraph-Journal*, Oct. 11, 2013, A1; "Donnie Snook Sentenced to 3 Months for N.L. Sex Crimes," CBC News, Dec. 17, 2013.

CHAPTER 1

DISCOVERY OF THE CRIME

July 6–7, 2011

On July 7, 2011, Richard Oland's long-serving secretary, Maureen Adamson, arrived for work at 52 Canterbury Street at approximately 8:45 A.M. to find the ground-floor door unlocked. This was not unusual, as both Oland and his employee had keys to this side of the building. She was carrying cups of coffee and paperwork. Reaching the top of the stairs, she noticed the door that opened up into a lobby on the second floor was partially open. Normally, the door was locked at this time of day. As she passed through the lobby into the office of Far End Corporation, Oland's investment firm, she immediately noticed four things: the lights and air conditioner had been left on, the blinds were drawn, and a foul stench filled the air. A television monitor that habitually displayed the CNBC channel was on, but the sound was down. Advancing further into the office, she spotted two legs on the floor near her boss's desk. Adamson immediately ran down to seek assistance from Printing Plus, the commercial printing business the occupied most of the building's ground floor.

Fifty-two Canterbury Street is a late-Victorian three-storey building located in a relatively quiet block of Saint John's central business district, opposite a popular restaurant, Thandi's, and, in 2011, was next to a former garage turned storage space. The area, part of the Trinity Royal Heritage Conservation Area, continues to slowly gentrify. The other suite on the second floor was unoccupied. The third floor was used from time to time by rock bands as a practice space. Far End Corporation had its own set of stairs that led from the ground floor, and its own entrance on Canterbury Street, although the entrance was accessible from the printing establishment on the ground floor. This block, located near a number of other restaurants and bars, had been moderately busy with traffic and pedestrians the previous evening. Some of that activity was caught on nearby security cameras, such as two on the exterior of Thandi's restaurant, across the street from the crime scene. The building itself had no internal security camera, and no camera on Canterbury provided a view of the main entrance.

Reaching the Printing Plus office, located on the south end of the building, Adamson called out for help and was answered by Preston Chiasson, a friend of business owner John Ainsworth, who also owned the building. Richard Oland had run Far End and his real-estate company, Kingshurst Estates Ltd., from the second floor since 2005. Ironically, he was planning to move his office to nearby Brunswick Square, an office tower whose entrances are monitored by security cameras. Chiasson proceeded upstairs, saw the body, and called 911 at 8:54 A.M. with a report that a male "was not breathing." The call was relayed from the Public Safety Communications Centre to the SJPF. Constables Don Shannon and Duane Squires, together with cadet Trinda Fanjoy, responded within minutes, unaware they were entering a crime scene. At 9:00 A.M., paramedics Phil Comeau and Chris Wall, whose ambulance had been parked nearby, arrived.[1] They were told not to bother to bring up special equipment, meaning that the person was now deceased. The paramedics were in the room for only a minute; Comeau pushed down on the body and determined that rigor mortis had set in. The officers checked the rest of the office, and then Shannon went down to speak to Chiasson who was experiencing some distress. The paramedics were called back to check Chiasson's vital signs. Others, including John Ainsworth, the coroner, and Major Crime Unit (MCU) members, continued to arrive at the scene.

When Oland was attacked, he was probably reading or thinking about his real passion, competitive sailing. On his desk, face down, was a 2010 book from the New York Yacht Club, an organization he was hoping to join. Nearby was a memo on electronic gear for his new sailboat being built in Spain, and a printed copy of a weekly investment advice newsletter. On his wrist was a Rolex watch, likely the engraved Yacht-Master model he had been presented during the New York Yacht Club's race week at Newport, Rhode Island. The police only confirmed the identity of the victim when they checked his wallet, which was still in the pocket of his pants. A healthy man who was nearly six feet tall, the victim appeared to have been killed at his desk; his body was found face down in a pool of blood, an ugly gash in the back of his skull. Crime-scene photos revealed a gory scene, yet there was surprisingly little trace blood evidence beyond the immediate vicinity of the body. There were no signs of a forced entry or robbery. The office contained several computers, cameras, an iPad, and other devices, all untouched. The victim's wallet, credit cards, watch, and car keys, as well as petty cash and an envelope containing cash for the family gardener, were also safe. According to Adamson, she, the victim, co-worker Robert McFadden, and Ainsworth held the only keys to the building. (Ainsworth later stated that the musicians who periodically used the third floor had a key and may have made copies.) In addition, there was no evidence of a murder weapon or a cleanup at the scene. The autopsy would reveal that the victim did try to defend himself from the assailant or assailants, but had been overwhelmed by the ferocity of the assault. The public would not learn the details of Richard Oland's injuries for more than four years.[2]

If most semi-retired men do not come home at night, their family worries. Although he still lived at home on secluded Almon Lane in Rothesay, Richard Oland was not necessarily missed by his wife, Constance. She later explained in a character-reference letter for her son that she believed her husband had travelled to nearby St. Stephen on the evening of July 6 to attend a meeting of the board of Ganong Brothers, the candy manufacturer. A former mayor of Saint John explained to the media that given Oland's work ethic, he could have been at his office all night. Yet the building owner later testified that Oland rarely stayed beyond the early evening as the musicians practising on the third floor were unpredictable with their schedule. The reality was that Richard and Constance Oland, married for more than four decades, appeared to be estranged. Richard often was away for weeks at a time and had been involved with a mistress for several years.

According to one of the victim's daughters, her parents lived "separate lives" but had refused to divorce out of consideration for their children. Oland had just returned from a salmon-fishing trip on New Brunswick's Miramichi River. Upon his arrival home, Constance was hosting her brother Jack Connell, who was visiting from Toronto. When Oland left Almon Lane on the morning of July 6, 2011, it was the last time his wife would see him alive.[3]

In April, Oland had travelled to Spain in connection with a new sailboat project. He spent most of the month of May in the Saint John area. On June 8, he flew to Providence, Rhode Island, accompanied by a sailing friend, Jamie McCormick, to take part in the New York Yacht Club Annual. His yacht, *Vela Veloce*, raced in the annual regatta at Newport from June 8 to 12. Oland next travelled to Connecticut and took a ferry from New London to Block Island, Rhode Island, to compete in the IRC division during the June 20–24 race week. Oland flew back to New Brunswick on a Grand Manan–based charter plane to attend a family gathering, the one-hundredth birthday celebration of a relative in Rothesay. On June 26, he left for a fishing trip at the Miramichi Fish and Game Club (founded by Americans in the 1890s), which is located on the Northwest branch of the Miramichi. Oland was a member of the lodge and had also served on the executive of the Miramichi Salmon Association. He returned from the fishing trip on July 4 and had a meeting with Roman Catholic Bishop Robert Harris on a major fundraising project. July 6 was his first full day back in the office and, according to his secretary, his inbox was full.

At 9:08 A.M. on July 6, Richard, from his home in Rothesay, sent realtor Diana Sedlacek a text message regarding a planned trip to Portland, Maine. As the public would find out in subsequent months, Sedlacek, who was younger than Oland, had been his mistress for several years. At 9:50 A.M., he was telephoned by his secretary, Maureen, with a reminder about a scheduled meeting at his office. Driving in from Rothesay in his 2009 BMW, Oland tried without success to call Sedlacek who was in a spin class at Quispamsis, outside of Saint John. After arriving at his office, Oland met with his employee Robert McFadden and financial advisers Gordon Graham and Barry Prosser to discuss life insurance. McFadden's son Galen was also working in the office that day. Oland's last meal appeared to have been a takeout pizza from Pizza Hut on nearby King Street. There is no evidence that he left the office that day.

It was a busy day, with Oland reading investment reports and attending to other matters. At 12:01 P.M., he sent his last text, from his iPhone 4, to Diana Sedlacek, relative to their trip to Maine. His last outgoing call or text message was sent at 12:57 P.M. Computer records indicate that Richard last backed up his cellphone at 4:44 P.M. Sedlacek's final attempt to contact him during office hours was at 1:57 P.M., when she was working at an open house in East Saint John. Adamson told investigators that when she finished work, Oland was having his final meeting of the day, with his son, Dennis, who had shown up unannounced after 5:30 P.M.[4] Adamson later told police that as she began her winding-down routine her employer advised her: "I will be here for a while." The scanning of a camp logbook belonging to the Connell family, which Richard had borrowed for a year, was complete, so Maureen laid it aside for her employer (although exactly where was not clear in hindsight). Entitled "The Island Camp," this was a record of several generations of visitors to a camp once owned by the Connell family. Sometime after 5:30 P.M., Dennis dropped in and briefly chatted with Adamson. She thought his brown sports coat was an odd choice on such a hot day. Richard greeted his son in a friendly fashion, and the two were soon absorbed in family-history talk, aided by the materials Dennis had gathered on a recent trip to England. At approximately 5:45 P.M., Maureen reached her vehicle and told her husband that Dennis had stopped by to discuss geneal-ogy with her boss. She was fairly sure of the time as she had printed a document just prior to leaving.

Given the significance of Dennis Oland to the case, it is worth reconstructing his day for July 6, 2011. From 6:67 A.M. that day to 1:28 P.M. on July 7, he sent or received dozens of text messages and emails from his BlackBerry, as well as a number of phone calls. Most of these communications were with his immediate family or friends, but a number were work related and two were with his father. Dennis was at his office in Brunswick House at the foot of King Street most of that day. At 12:45 P.M., he reminded his daughter to phone her Grandfather Richard to thank him for a donation he made to her sports team. At 2:41 and 2:51 P.M., he sent emails to Richard on a stock split and a Registered Retirement Income Fund matter. To no great surprise for a busy father of three children and a stepson, most of his messages dealt with family matters such as the behaviour of one daughter, his son's trip to the beach, or his other daughter's orthodontic appointment. Between 5:08 and 5:10 P.M., Dennis was captured on security cameras leaving Brunswick House and entering the Brunswick Square Shopping Centre, wearing a dark brown blazer and carrying a number of books. He headed to the parking garage and a few minutes later a silver vehicle (presumably his VW Golf) was captured driving east up King Street in the direction of Canterbury Street. Seven minutes later, at approximately 5:22 P.M., the car reappeared, driving up lower King Street in the same pattern. According to the Thandi's parking-lot camera, a light-coloured car parked on the west side of Canterbury Street near the Far End Corporation office at approximately 5:26 P.M.[5]

A Thandi's restaurant camera captured Maureen Adamson joining her husband at their vehicle at 5:44 P.M. (time stamps can vary slightly from device to another). After she left, we have only Dennis Oland's account of what happened in the Far End Corporation office during the next forty-five minutes or so. Cellphone and computer-usage data and street security cameras offer some clues. At 5:39 P.M., Richard opened a file on a yacht-racing program on his main computer. Evidence would be entered at trial to suggest that all human-induced computer activity ceased after the son's arrival and there is no evidence that Richard used his iPhone or office line. At 6:12 P.M., Dennis mistakenly sent a text message to his sister Lisa (Oland) Bustin instead of his wife, Lisa (Andrik) Oland, explaining that he was at his father's office doing "history stuff" and would be home shortly. At this point, Dennis must have been on the street because within seconds he was captured on security camera walking along the west side of Canterbury, carrying a red shopping bag. When he disappears from the camera's view, he is crossing the street in the direction of 52 Canterbury. Soon after, he appeared at his vehicle on the west side of the street, opening its rear hatch. At approximately 6:14 P.M., a silver car headed south past Thandi's. A few minutes later, the same car was detected by a camera on lower King Street, apparently making the same loop it had earlier. The Thandi's parking-lot and restaurant cameras captured the vehicle heading south for the last time that evening, at roughly 6:21 P.M. Three minutes later, a call from his wife went to Dennis's voice mail, suggesting that either the ringer was turned off or that he was still driving or did not have his BlackBerry on his person.

At 6:36 P.M., Lisa called from home to her husband's BlackBerry and spoke with him for forty-one seconds. At this point, Dennis presumably was on his way home to Rothesay, a trip that normally takes twenty to twenty-five minutes. Eight minutes later, Richard's iPhone received a text from Diana—"Are you there?"—which was not answered. Diana, home with her husband on Darlings Island and increasingly frustrated, tried to reach Richard by phone five times in the next half hour and sent another text at 7:19 P.M. This and all subsequent texts failed to reach his phone, and a dozen or so unanswered calls went directly to voice mail. She also rang the Far End office phone at 7:15 and 8:01 P.M. At one point Diana threatened, "I will call your house." Her unanswered 6:44 P.M. text message would become one of the key factors in the investigation.

Following the 6:36 P.M. call from his wife, the next activity on Dennis's cellphone was an email response at 7:24 to a message from a family friend. Cellphone records indicate that between 7:24 and 7:28 P.M., Dennis and Lisa, both at home, called each other a number of times until they finally connected. Ten minutes later, according to security video, they were at Kennebecasis Drugs in Rothesay. Their next stop was nearby Cochran's Country Market where they encountered Dennis's aunt Jane Toward, Richard's sister. The security camera shows Dennis, who has changed out of his formal work clothes into a golf shirt and shorts, paying for items at the counter and then departing. Between 8:09 and 9:16 P.M., he exchanged email messages with a client, and between 8:19 and 10:01 P.M. there was a phone conversation with Mary Beth Watt, who, with his wife, co-owned the sailboat *Loki*, and text messages from a friend.

The final security-camera documentation of Dennis that evening is at around 10:30 P.M. when he is buying milk at the Irving convenience store on the Marr Road in Rothesay, a short drive from his residence.

The next morning, Diana, who still had not heard from Richard, drove in to Saint John. At 9:37 A.M., parking her car near his office, she texted: "What the hell is going on?" She also tried his cell and office phones, with no luck. On her way to a hair appointment, she saw his green BMW in his parking spot, uncharacteristically early, and grew alarmed. As she approached 52 Canterbury Street, she saw police officers on the street and once again tried texting Richard. Sensing that there was a problem, she tied to bluff her way past the police, telling them that she had an appointment. Told that there was no access to the building (and not much else), Diana returned to her car and sent more emails or texts. In court more than four years later, she could not remember exactly when she realized her lover was dead, but recalled the sense of foreboding when she saw his car being towed away (it was taken to the police garage at 1:10 P.M.). At some point later that morning, in an emotional state, Diana called Richard's home and spoke to his wife, Constance. For the victim's wife, this was the first inkling that something was wrong.

Meanwhile, the victim's son, Dennis, was having an errand-filled morning that had little to do with investments. As he would explain in court, his mission that day was to repair the throttle cable on the sailboat *Loki*, berthed at the Royal Kennebecasis Yacht Club (RKYC). At 8:08 A.M., he stopped at the Kent Building Supply store in Rothesay where he remained until 8:23 A.M. At 8:47 A.M., Dennis purchased a sail cover from the Estey Group on City Road in Saint John, and then continued on to the RKYC in the Millidgeville area of Saint John. On the way, he stopped to buy gas (9:22–9:25 A.M.) at an Irving station on Millidge Avenue. Between 9:35 and 10:02 A.M., he had email exchanges with his assistant at investment company CIBC Wood Gundy, Ethel Harrison, and a client. Dennis told Harrison that he would not be coming in to work that day as he was working on a boat. In the period 10:10–11:57 A.M., he exchanged emails with his uncle Jack Connell concerning the family camp logbook and invest-ment issues. These overlapped with a visit to the Canadian Tire store in East Saint John (10:32–11:09 A.M.). Between then and noon, Dennis received phone calls from his wife and stepson and exchanged more email messages with Connell. By this point, neither Dennis nor anyone else in his family had been informed of his father's death. This changed after Diana called the Oland residence and spoke to Constance. Between 12:20 and 12:34 P.M., there were six calls between Dennis and his mother. Constance found out about her husband's demise not from the SJPF but from Robert McFadden, whom she had called. Dennis was contacted and told to return to his parents' residence as soon as possible. In the period 1:21–28 P.M., he also was called by his ex-wife, Lesley, and tried to reach his sister Jacqueline Walsh. Dennis later testified that he first feared something had happened to one of his children.

At approximately 2:00 P.M., Constables Stephen Davidson and Tony Gilbert, and Mary Ellen Martin of victim services arrived at the victim's home in Rothesay to inform the family of his death. Constance, Dennis, his wife, sister Lisa (Oland) Bustin, and uncle Jack Connell were present. With the investigation only beginning, the police offered few details. At 2:30 P.M., the officers left Rothesay after asking family members to attend the SJPF headquarters to be interviewed by investigators. The family members, joined by Richard's second daughter, Jacqueline (Oland) Walsh, agreed and headed in to the cramped quarters of the police station, then located in Saint John's city hall building. Between interviews with witnesses at the scene and with the victim's family, the MCU hoped to be able to gather information on the victim, including his routine and associates, and whether he had any known enemies. The other purpose of the interviews was to exclude individuals as potential suspects.

Accountant Robert McFadden, who had known the victim since the 1980s, was interviewed just before noon on July 7. He told police that he and his son had left work at roughly 5:30 P.M. the previous day. On the street outside 52 Canterbury they saw and acknowledged William Adamson who was waiting for his wife in his parked car. This was corroborated by Adamson, who recalled viewing a man in a brown sports coat entering the ground-floor door of Far End Corporation. Because of the angle, he had been unable to see the man's face, but he remembered that the person carried a red, reusable grocery bag "not empty but not overly full or heavy." He would later tell police that he thought the person was Dennis Oland.

Important testimony came from Anthony Shaw and Printing Plus owner John Ainsworth, who had been working on the ground floor of the building possibly during the time of the murder. At roughly 6:00 P.M., Shaw, a former employee, popped in to see his friend Ainsworth and was enlisted to help him with a tricky computer program. The two men would remain on-site for approximately three hours, including part of the period during which Dennis claimed he was visiting his father. They heard "loud, quick pounding thumps," similar to "banging on a wall," and shuffling sounds emanating from upstairs, from the direction of Oland's office. They noted the time as they scanned a document and sent it by email on behalf of an after-hours customer, who appeared to be from the Middle East, at 8:11 P.M. Although Ainsworth owned the building, neither man was sufficiently concerned to check upstairs.[6] Shaw thought that the noises were heard sometime between 7:30 and 8:00 P.M. Ainsworth, unlike Shaw, had been in the Far End Corporation office many times and said he could pinpoint the sounds geographically. In his initial statement to police, he concurred with the 7:30–8:00 P.M. time frame, but as time passed, he would become less certain. The men, who noticed nothing suspicious on the street, left Printing Plus at 9:00 P.M.

In any criminal investigation where adultery is involved, a mistress is an obvious person of interest. Diana Sedlacek, following the terrible news, had gone to Moncton, probably to see her son. She returned at the request of the SJPF and was interviewed late on the evening of July 7 by Constable Charles Breen. She told the police that she contacted Richard every evening on his cellphone at 6:30 P.M. She claimed they had been in a "romantic relationship" for eight years and she felt that most of his family knew about the affair. She described it as "very unusual" that he did not respond to her 6:44 and 7:19 P.M. texts. Diana would also claim that her lover was disappointed in his son. Sedlacek would be interviewed again on July 8 and 13. During one of these meetings, or on another occasion, she agreed to submit to a lie-detector test.

In her video statement to Constable Stacy Humphrey, Lisa Oland explained that she and Dennis had been together for more than four years and married for two. She alleged that Dennis had tried to win his father's respect and found it difficult to do so, but felt that the shared interest in genealogy was a way to improve their relationship. Her explanation as to what the couple did after Dennis arrived home the previous evening matched her husband's timeline.[7] She told Humphrey that she had felt ill and had been lying down when her husband arrived home after 7:00. Before she saw him, he had gone to the master bedroom to change into casual clothes. She explained that Dennis had spoken of his visit with his father as being "really nice," with the two men discussing family history. After this, the couple went to Cochran's Country Market for bananas and Kennebecasis Drugs for medicine. After they returned home, they watched television before turning in for the night.

Constance Oland, according to her police statement, appeared to have no knowledge of her spouse's or her son's finances, or of any assistance provided by Richard to Dennis. She described Sedlacek as her husband's "friend." She told police that it was not unusual for her husband not to return home at night and that his principal mode of communication was text messaging. The image of the victim derived from the interviews of Constance and her daughters was that he was an extremely volatile and difficult person and was obsessive-compulsive about money. Constance told police that her late husband was "strong and controlling" and was not above emotionally and verbally abusing his three children. Dennis, as the only son, supposedly suffered the most from his father's high expectations and brittle personality. Yet, she did not think he was capable of hurting his father. Lisa (Oland) Bustin told police that her parents, who had been married for more than forty years, had grown apart and that Richard's aggressive business style meant that he could have "anyone for an enemy."[8]

Sergeant Mark Smith, a forensic identification officer, arrived at the crime scene just after 10 A.M. Smith, who had worked on fifteen homicide investigations, ten in the lead capacity, went back to headquarters to get his equipment and then returned to start processing the scene. He later testified that he gave the patrol officers at the scene no special instructions but expected the area to be made secure. He did supervise quick visits by various officers into the inner office to view the body. That morning, Smith took more than three hundred photos of the body and other exhibits. His work was only beginning. His next major task was directing, under the eyes of Coroner Andrew Cavanagh, the removal of the victim to the morgue. There the body and clothing would be minutely examined by forensic officers before a pathologist performed an autopsy. Removing the body was not an easy task. The corpse of a one-hundred-and-ninety-pound man had to be picked up with as little disturbance as possible, which meant it had to be lifted and placed in a body bag face down on the stretcher. It also had to be carried out of the office without compromising blood and other evidence. Once Sharlene MacDonald and Adam Holly, two funeral-home employees, arrived with their folding stretcher, Smith directed Const. Squires (who incidentally was too big to fit into a crime-scene suit) to assist him in rolling the body onto a sheet, which was used as a sling to place it in a body bag on the stretcher. Holly and three officers then carried the body down the narrow staircase to the ground floor. Smith removed his protective gear before he went down.

It is interesting to note that the police and funeral directors, despite the existence of a nearby exit door, chose to carry the body down the stairs and out through the front door to the funeral-home vehicle on Canterbury Street. The back door gave access to an alley that was big enough to park a number of vehicles and which had access to Grannan Street, which runs from east to west between Canterbury and Germain Streets. For people familiar with the building, this would have been the logical way to take the body to the vehicle. (The back door would take on a larger significance during the preliminary inquiry and the trial.) The three-vehicle convoy consisting of the coroner, the police forensic van, and the funeral-home van, drove to the emergency department of the Saint John Regional Hospital, where a doctor pronounced the victim deceased at 3:03 P.M. Oland's body was then put in the police locker in the morgue to await the next day's autopsy. By 3:40 P.M., Smith had returned to 52 Canterbury to continue to process the scene.

Dennis Oland was the last member of the family to be interviewed, starting at roughly 6:00 P.M. At this point, investigators, who had been taking statements and obtaining and viewing security-camera footage, still lacked a lot of basic information. The crime scene itself had not been fully processed; the forensic examination of the clothing and the victim's body at the regional hospital and the autopsy had yet to take place; cellphone data had yet to be secured, and hours of footage from several security cameras had yet to be viewed. RCMP technical-crime experts had yet to seize the hard drives of the several computers in the Far End Corporation office, and the financial and phone records of Oland's son had not been requested. Despite this, a combination of training, experience, and intuition convinced the MCU officers conducting and monitoring Dennis's interview that he was their suspect. In this situation, in contrast to high-profile cases like that of Colonel Russell Williams (the Royal Canadian Air Force officer who confessed to two counts of first-degree murder and two counts of sexual assault in 2010[9]), police did not have much time to study their subject and present examples of incriminating evidence against him.

At 6:01 P.M., Const. Davidson, who had been on the force since 1999, started the interview. This would prove to be the tipping point in the investigation. Dennis Oland was not told on camera that the interview would be recorded (although he may have been informed of this before he entered the room). Also, he was not informed that he was free to leave at any point. The goal of these interviews is to elicit information about the victim that helps investigators to develop a theory of the crime, further leads, or identify a potential suspect. If the person being interviewed, either because of new evidence coming in, their behaviour, or their answers, arouses suspicion of involvement, then the goal may be to secure a confession. Davidson previously had interviewed Robert McFadden and Jacqueline Walsh. The monitoring officer for this interview, who took notes and helped develop strategy, was Keith Copeland. Although he allegedly had been impatient earlier and complained of misplacing some cash on the way to the police station, Dennis appeared polite and relaxed.[10]

In 2010, the Supreme Court of Canada, ruling on three different cases, confirmed that suspects have no right to counsel during
a police interrogation. Five of the justices held that Section 10 (b)
of the Canadian Charter of Rights and Freedoms did not trump the
status quo in terms of police questioning suspects. In other words,
the court refused to import American-style Miranda rights into
Canada. A minority disagreed, and the president of the Criminal
Lawyers Association protested against police "holding people hos-
tage" through extended, late-night interrogations where they are
intimidated and especially vulnerable. Justice Ian Binnie objected to
"an endurance contest in which the police interrogators, taking turns
with one another, hold all the important legal cards."[11] Citizens being
interviewed by police in Canada (in contrast to the stereotypical scene
in American crime dramas) are on their own, unless they are legal
minors, in which case a parent can be present. They are free to use
the washroom, are offered water or coffee and even food depending
on the circumstances and length of the interview, and can make a
call to legal counsel. Interestingly, although anyone who is not under
arrest is free to leave at any point, Canadians will endure hours of
often-intense questioning by experienced and trained interrogators.
Perhaps they do not want to appear guilty (especially to a jury later
watching the video record) or they want to co-operate with the police.

The interview started with a friendly request for Dennis to write
a pure version statement (uncontaminated by police questioning) of
his activities and whereabouts on the day and evening of the murder.
Investigators are trained to check these statements for potential clues
and alibis and for insights into witness credibility. Although research
does not back up the theory, police are instructed to detect potential
deception by studying word usage and other aspects of the statement, according to psychology professor Mary Ann Campbell. People
who view Oland's posture during the interview may have opinions
on its significance, but Campbell warns that there is little research
indicating a connection between body language and deception. She
makes the same point regarding police theories about a person's eye
movements.[12] Police may ask a witness, a suspect, or even a victim
for a written account of the event or a summary of their activities

during the last day or some other time period. The statement is then subjected to a form of analysis known as SCAN (Scientific Content Analysis) which aims to help investigators develop leads by sorting out imaginary details from facts. Although a popular investigative tool, SCAN does have its critics. It is not known, without having access to the case's full disclosure, if other members of the family had been asked to write their statements, but it is probable.[13]

In his written statement, Dennis claimed he awoke at 8:15 A.M., drove to work, and stopped for coffee before heading to the CIBC Wood Gundy office in Brunswick House. He spent most of the day at work, grabbing lunch at Tim Hortons in the Brunswick Square pedway. He spoke to his father a few times on the telephone as "we were selling a stock that he owned." After work, Dennis wrote, "I went (drove) to my father's office to go over family history stuff and to give him my copies of documents that I had." He recalled that he went to his office two times: "On the first try I got into the office foyer and realized I forgot some family history papers so I left and headed back to my office to get them." He then claimed that he realized he did not have after-hours access to the CIBC Wood Gundy elevator so he returned to his father's office. Dennis recalled that he had arrived at the office around 5:30 P.M. and that "Maureen left about 5–10 min after I arrived." He wrote that he stayed at 52 Canterbury Street until about 6:30 and that he spoke with Richard about family history and in particular a research report on an old will from England. After he left "dad's office," he headed for Brunswick Square "to get meds for my knee but my wife Lisa called me and was ill so I headed for home." He wrote that he drove "straight home with the exception of a quick stop at Renforth Wharf/beach to see if my kids were there swimming. They were not." After returning home, he changed and went to the drugstore "to get cold meds" and then to Cochran's "for dinner food." Later, he and his wife watched a movie and he went back out to an Irving convenience store in Rothesay for milk. Returning home, he did chores such as putting his chickens away for the night and retired to bed around 11:00 P.M.[14]

During the first hour, the investigator and Dennis have a fairly friendly chat about the victim and his relationship to the rest of the family. Then the questions turn to the whereabouts of Dennis prior to his meeting with his father. Another curious feature of the interview is its subject's apparent lack of emotion or concern despite the fact that his father had met his death by means of some type of undisclosed foul play. In a matter-of-fact and emotionless fashion, Dennis speculates that a "crackhead" had perpetrated the deed during a robbery, but does not ask if any arrest had been made or even how his father had been killed. Davidson initially adopts a friendly, professional, and non-accusatory tone. In this initial stage, the suspect does most of the talking. This part of the interview stressed the negative aspects of Richard's personality and the difficulties this posed for the family and especially its only son. Oland offered some perspective on his father's nature, claiming that things had gotten worse after Richard was denied being made head of Moosehead Breweries back in the 1980s and that he probably suffered from a personality disorder. The narrative was not entirely negative, as Dennis revealed how his father, of his own volition, had helped him financially through his divorce. The amount was $500–600,000 and Richard's intervention was portrayed as a spontaneous and generous act. The reality, as would be heard at trial, was more complex. And these financial issues would became a central theme of the Crown's case against Dennis.

When asked by Davidson if he had any involvement in the crime, Dennis replied that he had "no reason" to kill his father. This was delivered with little emotion—a factor, which, based on the example of other cases, can complicate things for both the innocent and the guilty.[15] When asked to name a possible suspect, Dennis replied: "He's pissed a lot of people off." Then he became more specific, mentioning his father's mistress, whom he discussed in negative terms as a "bitch," a "dragon lady," and possibly "that fatal attraction kind of person." This detail and the emotion behind it appeared to convince investigators that resentment towards Richard's affair was part of the motive behind his death. (Sedlacek, incidentally, would also be interviewed that night.) In addition, they were now hearing from a fourth family member that the deceased was a difficult person to deal with, a man whose judgmental nature and short fuse could ruin a sailing race, a family Christmas dinner, or the wedding of a family friend. Dennis explained that his father was a product of his generation and had suffered from a poor relationship with his own father.

In police interviews, details are significant not only in themselves but also because investigators are trained to look for inconsistencies as indicators of deception. Yet the police can use deception, although they are not permitted to invent evidence in order to secure a confession. This pressure tactic was utilized by Davidson when he asked Dennis about his visit to 52 Canterbury Street and added the false claim that the office was monitored by security cameras. Another statement that may not have been true is when Dennis was told that investigators had noticed that none of the family seemed particularly upset by the news of Richard's death.

The full interview would be played at Dennis Oland's preliminary inquiry but not at the second-degree-murder trial. Dennis, like most people in police interviews, remained in the small room for several hours. He was occasionally impatient, but never rude. He allegedly had avoided telling his mother about the affair and relied on his sister and Robert McFadden to speak to his father on the matter, which suggests a non-confrontational personality. When things became more intense, Dennis turned partly away from the interrogator, and when he spoke, which was rarely, he was low key, almost childlike. He adopted a passive, defensive posture, and at one point closed his eyes while being harangued by the interrogator. A more forceful response or demeanour may have helped him in the long run, as police officers often believe that the innocent display more emotion during interviews.[16]

When questioned in detail about his exact movements, Dennis appeared confused, telling Davidson that he had arrived outside 52 Canterbury at 5:15 P.M. but did not enter his father's office because he had forgotten family-history materials at Wood Gundy. He claimed to have climbed the stairs to the foyer, possibly used the bathroom, and then left. Dennis explained that he parked his car in three different places after leaving work: in the same lot as his father's car, in the gravel parking lot at the intersection of Canterbury and Princess, and on the street near the Thandi's parking lot. After he left the Far End entrance, he returned to his vehicle and thought about returning to his office at Brunswick House, visiting his father anyway, or simply driving home to Rothesay. At one point, he recalled, he contemplated stopping first at a nearby drugstore at Brunswick Square for pain medication for a sore knee (which he is seen favouring in the video of the interview). Allegedly, he sat in his car checking text messages for a few min-, utes. Remembering that he lacked a pass card to access CIBC Wood Gundy, he explained that he decided to return to 52 Canterbury and parked his car on the street nearby at roughly 5:30 P.M. His visit with his father ended at around 6:30 P.M. When Davidson pressed Oland for his exact route, he replied: "What I believe I did was leave my office and drive down Chipman Hill, drive up King Street, park in the parking lot, go up to the top of the stairs, down the stairs, leave… drive somewhere…being challenged of whether to go home or go back to my office or go back to dad's office…um…going back and parking on Canterbury Street, ah, sitting in the car for a while." After pondering the question further, he stated: "You have intimidated me now, so now I'm getting a mental block."

Dennis's inconsistent and convoluted tale of his visits to his father's office and his movements in general were a trigger, and subsequent video-camera evidence of his vehicle circling the block only added to police perception that he was acting suspiciously. Near the end of the portion of the video viewed in court in 2015, Oland is alone in the small interview room. Speaking to himself in a low voice, he tries retracing in his mind where he drove, parked, and walked just over twenty-four hours earlier. More than two hours into questioning, the small inconsistencies in his story prompted investigators to decide that he was no longer simply a person of interest but a suspect in his father's murder. Davidson cautioned Oland against making incriminating statements and advised him that he had the right to call a lawyer. Oland was given a secondary Charter of Rights caution to sign. He was not under arrest, yet he was not told that he was free to depart. Oland did leave the room to speak to his counsel, Bill Teed, by phone, and then returned to a decidedly different atmosphere. At 8:25 P.M., Davidson (later dismissed by Oland's defence as a "rookie homicide investigator") was replaced by seasoned veteran Keith Copeland.

Citizens in the hands of the police in Canada but who are not yet arrested are often subjected to a widespread but controversial interrogation technique known as the Reid method, named after the American company that trains police investigators across North America. It is taught by the RCMP at the Canadian Police College. Its critics have included judges and academics. The approach is manipulative, blunt, and accusatory, and often suggests that if the suspect can convince the interrogator that they are basically a good person, the penalty for the crime in question may be less severe. The object of the Reid Technique is to obtain a confession.[17] Media reports in recent years have suggested that the method can produce false testimony and confessions and violate legal rights. According to Canadian criminologist Brent Snook, the Reid approach can lead to police tunnel vision; by being overly confident and aggressive, interrogators also risk forcing subjects to go mute. Snook and other critics see the Reid Technique as a projection of traditional police culture with its emphasis on intuition, and warn that it is not backed up by empirical research. Another abuse of the technique, featured on the CBC program *The Fifth Estate* in 2014, is to induce witnesses to change their testimony.[18] In contrast, the PEACE (Planning, Engage, Account, Closure, Evaluate) method, as employed in Britain, aims not at manipulating a subject into a confession but at uncovering the truth.[19] The goal of the interrogation is "to peel away the layers" and, ideally, extract a confession. Being non-confrontational and rational, according to Snook, is the key to a professional and successful interrogation.[20]

With the arrival of the more intense and accusatory Copeland, Dennis's interview became an interrogation. According to Reid training, the interrogator acts as the bad cop, declares that the suspect is guilty of the offence, and ignores claims of innocence. This is called the "positive confrontation."[21] Yet, in this case, the officer revealed no details of the event; Dennis had not been informed of the method of death or the circumstances of the crime. Instead, Copeland relied on "theme development," where the interrogator suggests why the crime was carried out. Later, the bad cop may try minimization tactics: they attempt to build a rapport with the interviewee, encourage them to get things off their chest, and offer them the best deal possible. This stage can include a "moral justification" or "a better justification" for the offence.[22]

Copeland employed various strategies to uncover information and to elicit a reaction. One was to appeal to Oland's education and social status, by telling him that he did not match the profile of the typical suspect in a violent crime, who usually sat "picking their scabs." (The low socio-economic status of the typical violent offender is not a phenomenon unique to Saint John; criminology studies suggest risk factors for perpetrators of homicide include involvement in drug trafficking, peer delinquency, conduct disorder, poverty, and violent surroundings.) He also appealed to Dennis as a parent, a son, and a husband, and attempted to get a response by asking if his wife was involved in the crime. Another minimization tactic used was when Copeland stated that he did not view Dennis as a calculating, cold-blooded killer. Rather, he was a normal guy under tremendous pressure who just snapped.[23]

According to Reid training, one goal is to employ questions to provoke certain responses from the suspect and watch for non-verbal cues. During the interrogation phase, the tone was accusatory, with the officer doing most of the talking and sitting very close to the suspect. Copeland tried minimization, suggesting that the deceased was "a mean son of a bitch" who "controlled every penny" and disrespected his wife and his entire family. Drawing on the interviews with other members of the family, and the first hour or so of Dennis's interview, Copeland portrayed the victim as a selfish, mean-spirited adulterer who pinched pennies with his own family while fulfilling his own indulgences. Richard supposedly sat in judgment of his long-suffering son while spending money inherited from his own father, money that rightly belonged to the younger generation. Copeland had observed Dennis's earlier comment that his father was one of his investment clients but in reality had treated his son like "an order taker" not an adviser. Another possible cause of resentment was that the wealthy victim had been making his daughter Jacqueline, who had health problems, pay rent for use of a farm property. At one point, Copeland described Richard's death as beneficial to the family: "The tyranny is over."

Like Davidson, Copeland explained that he was trying to help Oland, and declared that he was a "fair cop." On first view, this attempt to establish a rapport with the suspect, however rough around the edges, appeared to be genuine. Copeland claims that he understood the Oland family's lack of remorse over news of Richard's violent death because he, too, had experienced a difficult childhood. He tells Dennis that his father left after he was born and that his mother was an extremely difficult parent with whom he felt no bond. The tale initially is plausible, but Copeland later goes too far with a claim that he had been sitting in an unmarked police car at Renforth Wharf on the evening of the murder, catching up on paperwork, when the suspect appeared at the scene on his way home. At this point Oland, who had been relatively silent, protests in an almost childlike voice, "You're sneaky," signalling that he neither trusts nor believes the officer. Copeland and other monitoring officers had probably read the pure version statement and heard Dennis's explanation about stopping at the wharf on the Kennebecasis River despite the fact that, as he had told Davidson, his wife was sick and mad at him for running late. A detective would view this stop as a chance to dispose of evidence, and that night an officer was sent to the wharf to conduct an initial search. As an educated professional, and personal friend of Bill Teed, Oland, despite his quiet demeanour, probably did not appreciate Copeland's observation that he should not trust a lawyer's advice. Yet at no time during the five-hour session did Dennis express any outrage at the allegation that he had killed his father, protest his innocence, or attempt to establish an alibi. Reid trainers usually state that innocent parties tend to actively protest their innocence, so Oland's silence, which he justified on the grounds of following his lawyer's advice, may have been misconstrued. Copeland also repeated Davidson's earlier bluff, suggesting that Richard's Oland's office had hidden video cameras and that the police would be checking the digital imagery. In reality, there were no security cameras at the building but the police had already started to review video surveillance from the restaurant across the street, a nearby parking lot, and other businesses. Soon after Dennis's realization that the officer had been misleading him, the interrogation, which yielded no information after the suspect was read his rights, ended. Oland had followed the advice of his lawyer, and on this important level the interview failed.

The complete interview, including the part not made available to the jury, can be watched on YouTube and various media websites. It does raise a number of important questions: Should the police have been so quick to show their hand? Was Dennis acting like the son of a person who had just been murdered? Why was he not more upset? Did other family members show any emotion when they were interviewed? Did Dennis's demeanour encourage investigators to prematurely construct a theory of the crime that was marked by tunnel vision? How did his responses influence the trial jury, both in terms of their substance and perceptions of his character and credibility? Although it is logical to view individuals in these situations as acting suspiciously or at least abnormally, police perceptions of a lack of empathy can lead to bad investigations and wrongful convictions.[24]

The suspect, whose faithful mother was waiting for him outside, had been in the small interview room for five hours. In hindsight, one major gaffe in the investigation was to tell Oland that he was suspected of killing his father, but then fail to ask him to voluntarily surrender his brown shoes and khaki pants, which he claimed to have been wearing the day of Richard's death. Once details of the case became known to the public, many in the community faulted the SJPF for not acting more swiftly to secure warrants to authorize searches of the residence, vehicle, and workplace of the accused. Especially after they made the threat (or warning) during the interrogation that a search warrant would be forthcoming. Yet a week would elapse before warrants were executed. The statement and delay can be explained: the SJPF needed time to gather more probable-cause evidence to satisfy a provincial court judge. What Dennis was not told was that starting that night, and for several days, he would be under police surveillance. Viewers of the A&E television series *The First 48* are continually reminded that the first two days following the discovery of a crime are critical to the closing of the case. While it is true that SJPF investigators believed they had identified their suspect less than eleven hours after the victim's body had been found, at first they appeared to be operating more on intuition than fact.

NOTES: CHAPTER 1

1. Jennifer Pritchett, "Final day of Richard Oland's life," *Telegraph-Journal*, Oct. 6, 2012, A1.
2. Nicholas Köhler, "Murder and a maritime dynasty," Macleans. ca, July 28, 2011, http://www.macleans.ca/news/canada/murder-and-a-maritime-dynasty/.
3. Chris Morris, "Inside the Oland murder investigation," *Daily Gleaner*, Sept. 14, 2013, A3.
4. Pritchett, "Final day of Richard Oland's life."
5. The details for July 6 and 7 are taken from *R. v. Dennis James Oland*, Exhibit #D-80 (Timeline), July 6–7, 2011.
6. Her Majesty the Queen v. Dennis Oland, Ruling following a preliminary inquiry by the Honourable Ronald LeBlanc, judge of the Provincial Court, in Saint John, New Brunswick, Dec. 12, 2014, 40–41.
7. The author did not have access to any of the family video statements; the relevant if partial information was obtained from ITOs prepared as part of applying for search warrants.
8. Stephen Kimber, "Spilled secrets: The Richard Oland murder mystery." *Atlantic Business*, Dec. 19, 2013.
9. CTV News, "A deeper look into the interrogation of Russell Williams," Oct. 22, 2012.
10. Interview of Dennis Oland, July 7, 2011: http://atlantic.ctvnews.ca/video?clipId=732471.
11. Kirk Makin, "No right to counsel during interrogation: top court," *Globe and Mail* online, Oct. 8, 2010.
12. Interview with Mary Ann Campbell, March 14, 2016.
13. Susan H. Adams, "Statement Analysis: What Do Suspects' Words Really Reveal?" *FBI Law Enforcement Bulletin*, 65 (10) (October 1996): 12–20.
14. *R. v. Dennis James Oland*, Exhibit P-78, Oct. 21, 2015.
15. Vincent Bugliosi, *Outrage: The Five Reasons Why O. J. Simpson Got Away with Murder* (New York: W. W. Norton & Co., 1996), 104.
16. Interview with Mary Ann Campbell, March 14, 2016.

17. Timothy Appleby, *A New Kind of Monster: The Secret Life and Chilling Crimes of Colonel Russell Williams* (Toronto: Vintage Canada, 2011); Joseph Brean, "Famed detective Jim Smyth's interrogation techniques derail murder case," *National Post*, Oct. 24, 2011.

18. CBC, "The Interrogation Room," *The Fifth Estate*, Nov. 21, 2014.

19. Joseph Brean, "You're guilty, now confess: False admissions put police's favourite interrogation tactic under scrutiny," *National Post*, Nov. 25, 2011; Douglas Quinn, "Alberta judge slams use of 'Reid' interrogation technique in Calgary police investigation," *Calgary Herald*, Sept. 11, 2012.

20. CTV News, "A deeper look into the interrogation of Russell Williams," Oct. 22, 2012.

21. James Orlando, "Interrogation Techniques," Connecticut Office of Legislative Research, Report, March 12, 2014: https://www.cga.ct.gov/2014/rpt/pdf/2014-R-0071.pdf.

22. *Ibid.*

23. Curt R. Bartol and Ann M. Bartol, *Criminal Behaviour: A Psychological Approach, 10th Edition* (Toronto: Pearson, 2012), 256.

24. Julian Sher, *"Until You Are Dead": Steven Truscott's Long Ride into History* (Toronto: Vintage Canada, 2002).

CHAPTER 2

THE OLAND CLAN

I n 2012, Derek Oland marked his fiftieth year with Moosehead. At a celebratory lunch at the Opera Bistro, a five-minute walk from the scene of his brother's murder fourteen months earlier, he stated, "Dick was my brother and what happened to him was a family tragedy." The last time Derek saw his brother alive was in spring 2011, at lunch at the Union Club, which is one street away from 52 Canterbury, and where the city's lawyers, business types, and other professionals had traditionally socialized.[1]

Moosehead Breweries, based in Saint John, is a Canadian success story. In 2014, it employed 250 people in Saint John and another 150 in the United States and elsewhere in Canada. Its plant was capable of producing 600-million bottles of beer each year. Since then, the brewery's workforce has shrunk. In contrast to modern businesses, where corporate executives are selected from outside and report to shareholders, the business is family owned and operated. By the early twenty-first century, Moosehead, a minor player in the national beer business, found itself the largest Canadian-owned brewery.[2] Although Richard Oland stopped working directly with the family business in the 1980s, he continued to benefit from his family connection both before and after the death of his father, Philip W. Oland. His son, Dennis, did not work in the family business but ended up owning his grandfather's Rothesay residence.

If the history of Moosehead Breweries had played out differently, Dennis Oland, rather than sitting in a federal penitentiary convicted of killing his own father, may have been running, or helping to run, the largest independent brewery in Canada. Although a minor player nationally, the company has done well in the United States in recent decades, and has been making inroads in markets such as Ontario.[3] Yet, the path has not always been smooth.

In New Brunswick, big business, especially family-owned enterprise, enjoys economic power, political influence, and social status rare in the rest of Canada. The Irvings in 2015, for example, were described as the second-richest person or family in Canada. The exact number of Irving-owned companies is not known, but they may total more than two hundred and employ an estimated one in twelve New Brunswickers. Power brings privacy and a lack of public scrutiny and criticism. In 2016, a journalist working on the Irvings discovered that "former premiers and other politicians, academics, businesspeople and family friends" refused to be interviewed.[4] The Olands are not in the same class as the Irvings, but they clearly are not the typical New Brunswick family.

Moosehead lore and public relations often refers to the Halifax Olands as opposed to the Saint John Olands, but the reality is more complex, as there were really two branches of the family running breweries in New Brunswick for several decades. The family brewing business can be traced back to Dartmouth, Nova Scotia, in 1867, the year of Confederation. That year, English immigrant John James Oland became a partner in a brewery located at Turtle Cove. According to family tradition, his wife, Susannah (Culverwell) Oland, was the active force in the enterprise, which was based on her recipe for brown ale. When John died a new investor became involved and the firm was known as Fraser, Oland and Co. (and sometimes the Army and Navy Brewery). After inheriting money in the late 1870s, Susannah bought out Fraser and the company became S. Oland and Sons, a rarity in an era when business owners and partners tended to be men. After Susannah's death, son George W. C. Oland operated the business as the Maritime Brewing and Malting Company. A few years later, it was purchased by a syndicate, Halifax Breweries Limited. Brothers George and John C. Oland worked with that firm until 1909. George W. C. and his son Sydney purchased another brewery and renamed it Oland and Sons Limited.

George W. C.'s son George B. took part in the South African War, then returned to Nova Scotia where he gained experience in the family trade. He served in the First World War, during which the Dartmouth plant was levelled in the Halifax Explosion of 1917. Following that disaster, the Olands expanded into neighbouring New Brunswick. George W. C. and George B. purchased the Red Ball Brewery, located in Saint John.[5] Four years later, Red Ball was advertised under the name of George W. C. Oland, "successor to Simeon Jones Limited" and marketed as a low-alcohol (2 percent) prohibition beverage."[6] In contrast with his flamboyant brother, Sid, who ran the Oland brewery in Halifax and who purchased the Alexander Keith brewery there in 1928, George B. lived a low-profile existence in New Brunswick. One of his seven children, Philip W., began working in the family business at age eighteen. P. W. attended the University of New Brunswick, then studied brewing in England and at the Carlsberg and Tuborg breweries in Europe. In 1928, George W. C. purchased the James Ready brewery, located in Lancaster, a municipality west of Saint John. Run by son George B., it was later renamed New Brunswick Breweries.[7] Provincial prohibition had just ended and the two Oland breweries in Saint John enjoyed a special place in the new system of government liquor stores that began to spread across the province. Later, they were joined by taverns and licensed dining rooms.

In 1933, family patriarch George W. C. died and his estate left two breweries in Halifax, Saint John's Red Ball Brewery, and 20 percent of the Lancaster brewery to his son Sydney. George B. was given the controlling shares of the Lancaster operation (renamed Moosehead Breweries Ltd. in 1947).[8] The years between the end of the Second World War and the 1960s were those of steady growth. In the late 1950s, P. W. Oland claimed that Moosehead was responsible for more than three-quarters of the market in New Brunswick.[9] In 1962, P. W. became president and chief executive officer of Moosehead; the next year he was named chair of the board. In 1963, in response to New Brunswick's liberalized liquor laws, which allowed brewers with plants in the province to sell draft and bottled beer in now-legal taverns, Victor Oland of Halifax decided to build a new plant in Lancaster, home of rival Moosehead Breweries, and closed down the old brewery in Saint John. Like Moosehead, the market for this brewery was limited to New Brunswick and Prince Edward Island. The new, partially automated Oland brewery officially opened in the fall of 1964. In response, Moosehead built a new plant in Dartmouth to compete with Oland's in Nova Scotia.

P. W. was heavily embedded in the community as a business leader and philanthropist. During the Second World War, he served in the Canadian artillery and after the war was involved with the militia, retiring as a brigadier in 1961. He was also involved in many charity and community organizations, such as the UNB Board of Governors, the New Brunswick Youth Orchestra, the United Way, the Saint John Board of Trade, the Confederation Centre of the Arts in Charlottetown, PEI, and the Saint John Foundation. A major promoter of the establishment and expansion of the Saint John branch of UNB in the 1960s and 1970s, his honours included the Order of Canada and honourary degrees. P. W. was regarded as a prestigious and trustworthy public figure, serving with the Atlantic Development Council and the Saint John Port Development Commission.

Described as a hard-working but modest and down-to-earth man, P. W. dressed conservatively and enjoyed golf, curling, and cruising in his boat on the St. John and Kennebecasis Rivers. In a 1992 interview, he made an oblique reference to his own father's parenting style when a reporter asked him if photographs on display at Moosehead brought back any memories: "Yes. Like a big bump on the head."[10] There are hints that life was not perfect in the household of this apparently benign patriarch. In her 2016 letter to the court on behalf of her son, Constance Oland alleged that her late husband, Richard, had been raised by one or more parents who resorted to yelling at and belittling their children. When P. W. made his will in 1992, son Derek and daughter Jane were named executors. Under the terms of the will, Derek, Jane, and second son, Richard, would split a trust fund of $1.5 million. Each grandchild, including Dennis Oland, would receive $50,000 when of age. In terms of the brewery, P. W. left 53 percent of the company to Derek, 33 percent to Richard, and 14 percent to Jane.[11] Jane, who later moved back to Rothesay from Montreal, was reportedly very close to Richard.

Born in 1939, Derek graduated with a business degree from the University of New Brunswick in 1962. He started working at Moosehead when the province's liquor laws and social attitudes were being liberalized.[12] In 1964, Derek met his future wife, Jacqueline Evans, a veterinarian newly arrived from Britain.[13] Around this time, he moved to Nova Scotia to oversee the new Moosehead brewery, competing head to head with his cousins. By the early 1970s, Moosehead, with a small share of the national beer market, was the largest in the Maritime provinces. Looking back nearly two decades later on the sale of the Halifax brewery, Oland's, to John Labatt's of London, Ontario, in 1971, Derek commented: "I guess maybe we pushed them [the Halifax Olands] too hard."[14] The next year, the New Brunswick Olands finally acquired full control of Moosehead.[15] One reason the company survived in an era of corporate mergers and takeovers by multinationals was the decision in the late 1970s to diversify into the American market. The export strategy was a success: Moosehead captured up to 30 percent of the import market south of the border and went on to be marketed in Britain and Australia.[16] In comparison, interprovincial trade barriers, the sort that had allowed Moosehead to dominate the New Brunswick market starting in 1927, were an impediment to significant expansion within Canada.[17]

One of the vexing questions for family-owned enterprises is that of succession. In 1992, a *Financial Post* examination of the Oland clan said that Derek would not be replaced by a family member when he retired. At the time, his son Andrew was working at the Halifax-Dartmouth Industries Limited shipyard. Asked if he would ever join the family business, he suggested that if he did, it would be on the basis of merit, not bloodline.[18] By 1999, the press was reporting that both Andrew and his younger brother Patrick were working for the company. Andrew, then thirty-two, held a MBA from Harvard and was described as having a detailed knowledge of brewery operations. Patrick, who had worked in the food business and was more interested in marketing, was a manager of export sales. They were the sixth generation in the business. Brothers Matthew, twenty-eight, and Giles, twenty-five, worked for Colgate in Ontario and Maritime Steel in Nova Scotia in the information-technology division.[19]

The new century brought a number of challenges which involved Moosehead in public disputes with the municipal and provincial governments, something that was common for Irving companies but rare for the Olands. One of these was the rate charged by the City of Saint John to industrial water customers. In 2003, Derek hinted that the brewery might relocate, but soon confirmed that Moosehead would remain in Saint John.[20] In a speech to the local Chamber of Commerce, Oland called for better transportation links with New England, lower taxes, and a greater role for entrepreneurs: "Governments can help, but they can't do it all. And when they do, it usually doesn't work very well."[21] In 2004 and 2005, Derek spoke out against provincial government financial assistance to Molson (recently bought out by the brewing giant Coors), then building a brewery in Moncton.[22] In an interview in 2007, Derek and Andrew expressed concern over recent price hikes by the provincial liquor commission and increases to business taxes and individual income taxes. They were also troubled by a hike in power rates by NB Power, the publicly owned provincial energy utility.[23]

Derek Oland, who served on the board of Nova Scotia Power (once a public utility, privatized in 1992), became a fairly visible and consistent promoter of regional business elites. In 1998, during the graduation address at UNB, he spoke of his family's long history of entrepreneurship. He also cited the "courage, expertise and imagination" of other regional business dynasties such as the Irvings, McCains, and Sobeys.[24] In 2008, as executive chairman of Moosehead, Derek supported a controversial proposal whereby the City of Saint John would have sold, at fair-market value, a former industrial site on the waterfront to Irving Oil. Irving then would have sold the land to the Saint John Port Authority in return for permission to construct a multi-purpose building on Long Wharf, a general-cargo wharf that had been expanded and maintained at taxpayer expense for decades. The complex was never built and the former industrial site sits empty to this day.

In the fall of 2007, Andrew, president of Moosehead Quebec, was informed by his father that he would be taking over as president of Moosehead Breweries in the spring of 2008. This was just after

Andrew, as part of a business working group promoting workforce expansion, had campaigned in public for the closure of the Saint John campus of UNB, which his grandfather P. W. had laboured so hard to create and expand. In its place would be an ill-defined polytech to educate people in the skilled trades. Oland was interviewed on CBC radio, and his comments on access to post-secondary education for youth in Saint John were regarded by many as shockingly elitist. The polytech plan was shelved after fierce community opposition.[25]

Richard (Dick) Oland, two years younger than Derek, joined the family firm in the mid-1960s, eventually becoming vice-president of operations.[26] Born in 1941, Richard attended Rothesay's private school for boys, but in Grade 10 was shipped to distant Kingston, Ontario, as a boarding student at Regiopolis College. This appears to have been motivated by disciplinary as opposed to academic considerations. Founded in the early nineteenth century, Regiopolis was a Roman Catholic boys school run by the Jesuits. The students slept in a common dorm room in bunk beds. The regime was strict and a former roommate later recalled that "Rick" was bitter about being sent to the institution. After high school, Oland attended the University of New Brunswick where he graduated with a BA in 1966. In 2016, Constance (Connell) Oland recalled that when she started dating her future husband at age sixteen, she realized that "his personality was different." She claimed that Richard was later diagnosed with Asperger syndrome by a clinical-psychologist friend. His personality issues supposedly became more difficult after he parted ways with Moosehead in the early 1980s, when, in her words, "he started a trucking company basically from scratch." Despite this, the couple's social life was described as "good" and included skiing and boating trips, vacations, and get-togethers with their children and grandchildren. In a letter to the court, Constance explained that she had attempted to raise her children "in a loving manner" with structure, reason, and a sense of self. She implied that these qualities had been lacking in her late husband's upbringing.[27] As the public would learn following his murder, Oland could be the guy without a filter. In one infamous episode, he acted badly at his own daughter's wedding, verbally abusing his son who was master of ceremonies.

In *Last Canadian Beer* by Harvey Sawler, Derek explains that both he and Richard had wanted to become president of Moosehead: "I mean that's it. It's natural in any company. You've got competition for the top job."[28] In the early 1980s, P. W. Oland decided that Derek was best suited to taking over the family business. This decision followed a bit of brinksmanship by Derek, who resigned from the company and was preparing to relocate with his family to New Zealand. The father ended up appointing him executive vice-president. A decade after parting ways with the family business, Richard diplomatically explained that he had been "looking for opportunities," and "Moosehead was just a career option like any other." Some speculated that sibling rivalry was the major factor.[29] Constance told police in 2011 that the split had occurred because her husband could not "get along with his brother."[30] In one interview, Derek remembered "a little bit of bitterness" over this arrangement.[31] Starting in 1996, following the death of their father, Derek's relationship with his brother was often tense.

A court case in 1998 revealed that although Richard was no longer part of Moosehead operations, he was not totally divorced from the privately held company. By this time, Moosehead was operating on the plan dictated by P. W. At the February 1998 meeting of Sevenacres Holdings Limited, the brewery's parent company, it was explained that because of poor sales in the United States in the period 1996–98 the shareholders (Derek, Jane, and Richard) would receive no dividends. The sole director of Sevenacares Holdings, which also owned Alpine Holdings Limited, the Premium Beer Company Inc., Atlantic Grand Prix Inc., the Molson Moosehead Partnership, 39994023 Canada Limited, Alpine Breweries Limited, and the Mooseheads hockey team in Halifax, was Derek Oland. Derek, with 61.1 percent of the shares in the holding company, was the sole director of Moosehead. His sister, Jane Toward, a resident of Montreal, controlled 25.7 percent and Richard was left with 13.2 percent. Richard took the company to court in 1998 to force it to provide consolidated financial statements. At the February meeting, he allegedly stated that he and his sister should have a greater part in running the company and that Derek, as controlling shareholder and chief executive officer, should not be the sole director of the board. Notes taken at the meeting suggest that Ms. Toward shared some of Richard's concerns and that there was a disagreement over how the company should be audited. In the end, the matter was settled out of court, with Derek promising to provide the requested documents to his siblings.[32] More trouble followed, and Richard went to court again. In 2007, Derek, in a process his father called "pruning the tree," bought out his siblings' shares and became sole owner of Moosehead.[33] The buyout gave Richard considerable capital to invest or with which to enjoy life. Indeed, there are suggestions that much or most of his considerable wealth was not self-generated but inherited from his father.

Richard was associated with other business ventures before and after leaving Moosehead, such as the Saint John Shipbuilding and Drydock Co. He was a director for a number of companies, including Ganong Brothers, Eastern Provincial Railways, and Newfoundland Capital Corporation. But for most of the 1980s and 1990s, his main business activity was trucking. It turned out that Richard only partly left the family business. He not only controlled a minority interest in Moosehead until 2007, but he also relied on the company now run by his brother for a major share of his trucking business, Brookville Transport.[34] Exactly who started the company is not clear. Interviewed in 1992, P. W. explained: "The two boys couldn't agree. The younger one wanted to be president and he hadn't the experience. But he's in the trucking business now. And he's doing all right."[35]

During the 1990s, Brookville Transport prospered and its operations extended into the United States, giving many drivers a start in the business.[36] In 1992, Richard was interviewed in the *Financial Post* on the subject of the possible abandonment of Canadian Pacific rail lines east of Sherbrooke, Quebec. McCain Foods Limited, the Port of Saint John, and various business organizations feared the impact of the loss of the rail link with Quebec and Ontario, but Oland hoped the trucking industry would fill the void.[37] His real problem was that major manufacturers such as the Irvings (forestry and petroleum products) and the McCains (frozen food) preferred to ship their products on their own trucks. Yet by 1994, Oland was CEO of the

Brookville group of companies that included Brookville Transport, which had annual sales of $60 million and whose business was growing yearly. That year, he made an unsuccessful bid to purchase Highland Transport from Canadian Pacific.

By 1997, Brookville's annual sales were $100 million and the company was dealing with more than five hundred trucks. According to one report, Brookville was at that time one the top ten trucking firms in Canada. Not everyone was a fan. Many inhabitants of the Saint John residential neighbourhood where the business was located resented heavy truck traffic and lived in fear of accidents. Financial problems developed and that year Brookville Transport was placed under court protection from creditors until it was sold to Contrans Corporation and its subsidiary Brookville Carriers. In August 1997, the new owner dismissed more than 170 drivers. Another casualty of the transition was Oland's former employee Robert McFadden, who later sued the new owner. According to one press account, "When one of his former companies, Brookville Transport, declared bank-ruptcy, he [Oland] never repaid the money he owed the mechanics."[38] At the time of its bankruptcy, Brookville relied heavily on its major client, the Repap Paper Mill in the Miramichi. Hauling for Moosehead accounted for only a third of the business, not enough to keep the company stable. This was a risky situation as North America's pulp and paper industry was in trouble by the 1990s.

In the Saint John area, Richard was best known to the broader public not for his business activities but his community work. As chair of the 1985 Canada Summer Games organizing committee, he was commonly credited with making that event a success. The games coincided with and contributed to a renewed sense of optimism in Saint John, which was hit hard by the recession of the early 1980s. They also happily coincided with the opening of Market Square, an atrium-enclosed collection of restaurants, bars, and boutiques fronted by a late-Victorian brick facade, meant to inject new life and vibrancy into the city's declining central business district. As part of planning for the games, a new aquatic centre was built across the street from Market Square and existing sports fields and facilities were upgraded. By most measures, the 1985 games was a success.

Four years of planning went into the event, which relied on more than five-thousand volunteers and involved three-thousand, one-hundred amateur athletes. It was supposedly Oland who helped convince key funders that a new track and field stadium should be built on the campus of the University of New Brunswick Saint John. When that $3.2-million facility opened, Oland hosted two federal cabinet ministers, three Members of Parliament, the premier, a MLA, and a number of Canadian Olympians. The Summer Games even bequeathed a $2.6-million surplus, which was converted into a grant program to support young athletes. As of 2002, the fund was worth $5 million. Oland remained on the board of the foundation and except during economic downturns, it doled out an average of $200,000 a year to athletes and sports organizations across Canada.[39]

Richard Oland was also president of the board of the New Brunswick Museum during a controversial era, 1991—98. The major development during this period was moving the exhibit space of the museum, which had been established in the 1930s on Douglas Avenue in an older residential neighbourhood of Saint John, to the Market Square complex, which was struggling financially. In 1996, a visiting Prince Philip opened the new three-storey, sixty-thousand-square-foot exhibition centre fronted by a storefront facade inside the mall's atrium. Richard was praised as the man who saved the museum, yet his time as president was not without controversy. The deal to move the exhibit space downtown was negotiated in secret, despite the fact that the museum was owned by the province and its board appointed by the provincial government. The City of Saint John, which was worried about the financial viability of Market Square, agreed to subsidize the museum for $300,000 a year for fifteen years. After the new exhibit space's launch, the museum's administration turned into a public-relations nightmare. The new executive director was embroiled in a series of disputes with staff and a number of the most vocal were laid off.[40] Although the executive director, who resigned and was given another provincial government job in 1999, was a divisive figure, some critics ultimately blamed board president Richard Oland and a provincial deputy minister for the mess. Despite this, Oland received the Order of Canada for his community efforts.[41]

Like his father before him, Richard Oland continued to be appointed to boards and committees and to receive public accolades. When awarded an honourary degree by the University of New Brunswick Saint John in 2002, he was serving on the boards of the Saint John Development Corporation and the Waterfront Development Committee. In 2006, he was presented with the Saint John YMCA-YWCA Red Triangle Award for public service. His contributions to the Canada Games and the New Brunswick Museum were cited.[42] Another important volunteer effort of Oland's was the project to build a new Roman Catholic church in his home parish of Rothesay. The Olands were an anomaly in past decades, when so much of Saint John's elite was Protestant and these distinctions mattered. Historically, the Catholics of the Saint John area, most of them Irish, felt discriminated against economically and socially. Saint John did not elect its first Catholic mayor until 1967. Traditionally, there were so few Catholics living in Rothesay and adjacent communities that Catholic children attended the public schools. The Olands were Catholics with money and could afford to place their children in private schools. Richard, who grew up next to the original smaller church, would be buried out of the new Our Lady of Perpetual Help Church that his family helped to build. Just before he was murdered in 2011, Oland met with the Bishop of Saint John to discuss another major fundraising project: the refurbishment of the Roman Catholic cathedral in Saint John.

Oland enhanced his reputation as a maverick by speaking out on some of the negative aspects of the provincial economy's domination by a handful of wealthy families, notably the Irvings. Apparently, he was forgetting his own family's quasi-monopoly on beer sales in New Brunswick, the direct result of provincial alcohol-control policies. He actually took the Irvings to an administrative tribunal over unfair pricing in the trucking business and won, a rarity in New Brunswick. Irving business practices were sometimes controversial, despite their continued explanation that they employed large numbers of New Brunswickers and invested in the province's communities. When legendary tycoon K. C. Irving died in his Bermuda tax haven in 1992, Oland sounded like a left-wing muckraker in denouncing

Irving's negative impact on the province. Four years later, when the Southam chain of newspapers was portraying the Irving empire as being at a crossroads, Oland argued that corporate concentration retarded New Brunswick's economic development.[43] It was one thing for union leaders, environmentalists, and left-wing politicians to become Irving-bashers, but almost unheard of for members of the business community or mainstream politicians to publicly criticize the Irving empire. The reasons behind this were fear and self-interest. Yet Oland's independent stand did not seem to hurt his stature as a business leader. He served for two terms, for example, on Enterprise Saint John, a publicly funded economic development organization dominated by business interests that constantly attempts to improve the area's economy and public image.[44]

The other sector where Oland clashed with the Irvings was energy, specifically natural gas, which in the 1990s was being promoted as the clean, cheap fuel of the future. In 1998, he joined with industrialist Harrison McCain and a number of other New Brunswick investors to form Gas New Brunswick, a bid to secure natural-gas distribution rights in the upper St. John River valley and north shore of the province. Two-thirds of the entity was owned by the powerful Consumers Gas Energy Limited of Ontario. At this time, Saint John boosters, in typical exaggerated fashion, were claiming the cheaper energy, in the form of offshore Nova Scotia natural gas, was the economic salvation of not only the city but the entire province. The provincial government was insistent that New Brunswick share in the benefits of a pipeline that would export cleaner energy from Nova Scotia to New England. Irving interests were also hoping to gain access to Sable Island natural gas that would be passing through the province via the Maritimes and Northeast Pipeline (M&NEP) and signed an agreement with Westcoast Energy Inc. to build a branch line. The Gas New Brunswick consortium promised to build pipelines, without aid from the provincial government, to service industrial and residential customers in the northern areas of the province. Oland was one of two investors from Saint John.[45]

The battle over the distribution of natural gas once again had Oland speaking out against monopoly and the suffocating power of the Irving interests. He warned a legislative committee in 1998 that giving a monopoly in energy to either the Irvings or NB Power would hurt consumers and require more government regulation in the name of public interest.[46] Kenneth Irving, whose partnership with Westcoast Energy Inc. was called Maritimes NRG, wanted to grow Irving Oil as an energy provider. His cousin Jim, who ran the empire's forestry operations, wanted something more specific: the right to bypass any distribution fees and buy gas directly from Maritimes and Northeast for the J. D. Irving pulp mill in Saint John and a planned gas-powered generating plant. J. D. Irving had told a legislative committee that large industrial customers including NB Power would consume more than 80 percent of available gas. Oland and his fellow investors were no doubt disappointed when the mayor and common council of Saint John narrowly voted to endorse the Irving proposal as they saw it as most beneficial for the area's struggling economy.[47]

By September 1999, investors faced a challenge in the need to raise considerably more capital to maintain their share in the renamed consortium, Enbridge Gas New Brunswick— named after the Calgary parent company Enbridge Inc.—or be bought out.[48] SaskEnergy Inc. and Co-op Atlantic were also interested in controlling gas distribution. Irving eventually lost its Vancouver partner. Enbridge ended up winning the distribution rights for natural gas in the province by default. A year earlier, the government had promised single end-use customers, such as the Irving Oil refinery, the right to purchase gas directly from M&NEP, bypassing the middleman that would otherwise control distribution. A report on the province's energy situation in 2010 revealed that although Enbridge had invested $400 million in New Brunswick, it had signed up only ten-thousand customers and was losing money.[49] As McCain had predicted, permitting the Irvings to opt out of the Enbridge distribution system contributed to the gas company's debt load and had the effect of driving up rates for natural gas, and discouraging small and mid-sized customers from signing up.[50]

Richard, although from a privileged background, appeared to be a man's man in that he loved to work with his hands, use tools, and fix things. He liked to work hard, and play hard. He wore suits made in Italy and shopped at Harry Rosen in Toronto. Some described his business style as aggressive and his personality as abrasive. Others have suggested that, when applied to community projects, his forceful personality ensured results. His son's July 7, 2011, interview with the police revealed that at Wood Gundy, there was a dedicated telephone to handle Oland's investment instructions, and if the phone was not answered after three rings, there would be hell to pay. An associate described him as "a very capable guy…but there would be a few people, after he got through with them, with footmarks on their backs.[51] The playing hard manifested in competitive sailing, salmon fishing, and downhill skiing. Some academics might attribute these costly sporting activities to the elite's need to display conspicuous consumption in order to differentiate themselves from the middle and working classes. But for outgoing personalities such as Richard Oland, the competition of sport may have been the flip side of a hard-driving business style. Just prior to his death, he took part in a salmon-fishing trip with New Brunswick businessman David Ganong and long-time friend A. W. (Bill) McMackin of Rothesay.

In recent years, Oland's real passion was competitive yacht racing where, according to his mistress, he could win and have "a great accomplishment." Oland began sailing out of the Rothesay Yacht Club as a boy and over the years gained experience on increasingly larger craft. Like many wealthy families in Rothesay and Saint John, the Olands enjoyed sailing on the scenic Kennebecasis and St. John Rivers and socializing at the Rothesay Yacht Club and the Royal Kennebecasis Yacht Club (RKYC). In 2008, Dennis, who as a boy had spent many hours at the Rothesay Yacht Club, reminisced about the family boat *Aloma II*, which had been built in Sydney, Nova Scotia, in 1910. For many years, the craft was based out of the RKYC and used for Moosehead office parties and brewery promotion events. *Aloma II* was destroyed by fire at St. Petersburg, Florida, in 2008, prompting Dennis Oland's nostalgic essay, which described his father as happy and relaxed when on the water: "With my father as captain, you could always count on a big adventure for every trip and he never let us down."[52]

In the years prior to his death, Oland was well known in competitive sailing circles as owner of *Vela Veloce* ("sail fast"). The beautiful blue-hulled vessel was designed by Reichal Pugh and built by Davie Norris Boatbuilding of New Zealand with a lightweight carbon-fibre composite hull. It is classified as a Southern Cross 52 and is capable of reaching a speed of twenty-five knots. The yacht draws 3.5 metres of water, is equipped with a fifty-six-horsepower engine, sports comfortable berths, a galley, and an enclosed head. The sale price was $695,000 USD. It requires a minimum crew of six but usually raced with fifteen. The high-tech sails were manufactured by Quantum of Spain. Competitive sailing at this level is an expensive hobby as a racing yacht, in addition to being constructed and maintained, must be crewed. Oland, who served as skipper, used a mixture of talented amateurs and professionals in races. In 2009, he entered into a race from Auckland to Tauranga, New Zealand, which the *Vela Veloce* crew won. After arriving in the Atlantic, it placed fifth in the Annapolis, Maryland, to Newport, Rhode Island, race. In July 2009, it was the first Canadian vessel to complete the annual Marblehead, Massachusetts, to Halifax match and the fifth overall. A few days later, Saint John residents watched *Vela Veloce* pass under the bridges at Reversing Falls, the mouth of the St. John River. The crew used a three-thousand-pound counterweight so that the sailboat would lean to one side, allowing its 34.6-metre mast to pass under the bridges.

In 2010, Oland entered *Vela Veloce* in the Royal Ocean Racing Club (RORC) Caribbean 600. Under Captain Scott Innes-Jones, the vessel placed second in the race and won the CSA division. That year, the boat won best overall performance at the Rolex US-IRC national championship at Newport. In 2011, Dick was awarded the Canadian Yachting Association's Gerry Roufs Award at Toronto for achievement in international offshore racing. In January 2011, his boat, under the direction of Richard Clarke and Stuart Bannatyne, did well at the IRC competition at Key West, Florida. The following month it placed fourth in the RORC Caribbean 600.[53] Early in 2011, the yacht triumphed at the Key West Race Week, where a victorious Richard was described as exhibiting a "Cheshire cat grin." In this regatta, professionals, Clarke at the helm and Bannatyne in charge of tactics, were key.[54]

Comments posted on *Seahorse* magazine's website in the wake of Richard Oland's death suggest that in the yachting world, as opposed to the business world and within his family, Richard was considered a nice guy. As he explained to a reporter in 2010: "My role in this whole thing has really been putting together the right team, making sure you've got the right players in each position."[55] *Vela Veloce* was for sale at the time of Oland's death, with an asking price of $850,000. He was working on securing a newer and faster yacht from Spain, a project that consumed some of the work day of his two employees.[56]

Oland's mistress of several years, Diana Sedlacek, is the daughter of John and Lina (Arsenault) Virgin of Saint John. According to the city directory, in the 1960s and 1970s American-born John was a welder at Saint John Drydock and Shipyard, an Irving-owned enterprise on Courtenay Bay east of uptown Saint John. The Virgin family lived at 17 Flecknell Avenue, a quiet cul-de-sac in a modest neighbourhood close to the Saint John campus of the New Brunswick Community College. John was also an old-time fiddler and played with various country-music groups. Diana grew up with two sisters and two brothers. Facebook posts from 2011 onwards list her favourite activities as downhill skiing, gardening, cooking, and kitchen design. She also followed the Southern Ocean Racing Council (an interest of Richard Oland's), posted in early 2011 on *Vela Veloce*, and made references to a trip to Spain that she took in May with her married lover. In Saint John, Diana worked as an interior designer and a real estate agent, including at the firm associated with Lesley Oland, Dennis's ex-wife. In his 2011 police interview, Dennis alleged that his sister had found Viagra in the family home: "My parents have not had sex in a long time, so there is no need for the Viagra." Given that his father was away from home for much of the year on sailing and other trips, Dennis speculated that Richard was involved with Sedlacek or possibly other women.[57]

At the time of Oland's murder, Diana lived on scenic Darlings Island east of Saint John with her husband, Jiri, a retired business executive. Much less parochial that the typical New Brunswick businessman, Jiri had been a corporate executive for Bata Shoes, founded in what is now the Czech Republic, in the 1890s. As part of first a

European and then global expansion, a branch of the firm, which also became involved in other sectors, located to Ontario in the 1930s. Sedlacek joined Bata in England in the 1950s where he worked with Thomas J. Bata, who later moved to Canada. The global headquarters for Bata Shoes was located in Toronto in 1964. By the 1980s, when the company was at its peak in Canada, it was a major retailer with more than two hundred stores. It also owned a chain of running-shoes outlets known as Athletes Word (later purchased by Canadian Tire). In 1989, with the end of the Cold War, Jiri, as director of corporate planning, spoke to the media on the company's planned return to Czechoslovakia, where its operations had been nationalized by the Communist government in the late 1940s. That year, he and another Bata executive met Václav Havel, the first president of democratic Czechoslovakia after the Cold War. A 1991 story on Bata's triumphant return to Czechoslovakia described Jiri as a retired executive who had been working "closely with Mr. Bata on the Czechoslovak project," which involved not only investing in the former homeland but also advising on the privatization of the government-owned manufacturing and retail sectors.[58] Both Bata and Athletes World are no longer part of the Canadian retail scene, but the company retains a global manufacturing and retail presence. Jiri met his wife, Diana, who was more than two decades his junior, in Toronto. The couple moved from Ontario, where their son, Jeremy, was born in the late 1980s, to New Brunswick, Diana's native province, after he retired.[59] Jeremy graduated from Rothesay Netherwood School in 2005, and in 2011 from the Moncton Flight College. Since then, he has worked as a commercial pilot in British Columbia and Nova Scotia.

Richard's only son, Dennis, was born in 1968. Two decades later, he was the object of media attention as a result of an accident that took place when he was hauling a trailer from Rothesay to Ottawa, carrying his father's horse Apocalypse. The twenty-year-old swerved to avoid an animal and the vehicle left the road and ended up in the ditch. Dennis, who was on his way to Ottawa's Capital Classic, was not injured, but his father's $25,000 racehorse had to be put down (given what was later revealed about Richard's temperament, this probably did not go over well at home).[60] According to his mother,

Dennis's first job was delivering newspapers. He bought a small motorcycle with his earnings and became interested in working on engines. Tinkering was a passion he shared with his father and through the years they repaired "boat motors, cars, stoves, and washing machines." As a child, he enjoyed boating, summer camp, and horseback riding; like his father, he had a practical bent and on top of being able to fix motors, he could also maintain canoes and boats.[61] He continued these pursuits with his own children in later years. As a teenager, Dennis worked at a YMCA/YWCA summer camp as a canoeing instructor and as a canoeing director at Camp Glenburn, an idyllic spot on the Kingston Peninsula. At age eighteen he was temporarily director of the camp. The family was outdoorsy, with all of them skiing, sailing, and snowmobiling, and all but Constance riding horses. The family took an annual ski trip that Dennis joined when he was working in Toronto. In 1995, Richard and Dennis competed against one another in the Marblehead, Massachusetts, to Halifax sailing race. In a letter to the court in 2016, Constance told the judge that her son "volunteered in the community" as an adult, especially with the YMCA. At age thirty, he was chair of the board of the Maritime division of the Canadian Automobile Association. Constance claimed that he was very active with Enterprise Saint John (a local regional economic development agency that is a cheerleader for the business community) and was set to become its chair "when his marriage came to an end."[62]

The hand of history can sit heavily on any family, but more so with business dynasties. Like his father, Dennis became fascinated with genealogy. His insistence on retaining his grandfather's house, despite his financial difficulties, may have been motivated by more than a desire to keep up with the Joneses. It was within walking distance of the house on Almon Lane where he had been raised. His parents's residence had been the home his grandmother Mary grew up in, constructed for her father, Saint John insurance executive Henry Walter Frink, during the First World War. Mary had attended Netherwood School, which began the tradition of private schooling in Rothesay for the Olands. In the 1950s, Dennis's aunt Jane graduated from Netherwood and Derek and Richard from the boys' school, Rothesay Collegiate School (RCS). P. W.'s house, where Richard grew up, near the Rothesay Common, was in the heart of the older, exclusive area of the town, and had associations with the Pony Club (to which the Oland children belonged, and the goal of which was to give riding lessons to young people of the community), started by Mary in the 1950s. In subsequent years, the two private schools were merged to create Rothesay Netherwood School (RNS). The principal of RNS is called the "head" and the school has "prefects," uniforms, and a faux English-public-school tone. These schools market themselves as academically superior to the public schools. Dennis and at least one of his sisters, Lisa, attended RNS or one of its earlier manifestations. Unlike Lisa, who graduated in 1984, Dennis finished Grade 12 at a public high school like his sister Jacqueline. Dennis went to public school, presumably in Rothesay, until Grade 8 when he switched to RNS. In 2016, his mother explained that because of his hearing loss (45 percent since birth) Dennis needed to be in a school with small class sizes. For Grade 11, he was sent to Bishop's College School in Sherbrooke, Quebec, "where he was a cadet officer and head of a unit," and participated in sports. As with his father's temporary exile to Kingston in the 1950s, this appears to have been a decision made by the parents, not the son. As he missed his family, he decided (or was allowed) to return to New Brunswick for his senior year, where he graduated from Saint John High School in 1986.

Peter Newman in *The Canadian Establishment* argues that much of Canada's economic and political elite traditionally has been educated in several dozen private schools, many of them with a snobbish British public school veneer, and that the purpose was not education so much as indoctrination and networking. This system perpetuates interlocking networks of old boys and old girls trained in the basic doctrine that "privilege exists and must be exercised."[63] Yet in Richard Oland's household, growing up privileged was not without its stresses, largely because of the personality and expectations (not to mention the tight-fistedness) of the patriarch. After his conviction, Dennis told a probation officer that as a child he was "provided with all of life's necessities" but expected to perform chores; his mother was nurturing and supportive, but his father was "old school." According to Dennis's 2016 pre-sentence report, his mother said that Dennis would not communicate with Richard "for weeks at a time."[64]

In 1990, Dennis completed his BA as the University of New Brunswick and then moved to Halifax where he did a term at Dalhousie University. Later, he went to work selling water-treatment systems. In Halifax, he married Lesley Phinney of Truro, Nova Scotia, a graduate of Dalhousie University, in 1995. After this, he moved to Toronto and began working in the mailroom of RBC Dominion Securities, advancing to stockbroker's assistant. In 2015, he told a court that his father helped him secure the entry-level job. After he returned to Rothesay, he was employed by Richardson Greenshields as an investment adviser. He purchased his grandfather's house in the late 1990s. He and his wife separated in 2005 and were divorced in 2006. Dennis later explained to a probation officer that his "wife was tired of being married to someone who was often way from home." Following the divorce, Lesley worked in real estate and moved to Renforth, an area along the Kennebecasis River that is now part of the town of Rothesay. Her Re/Max site describes her as "a mover and shaker." Under the terms of the divorce, Dennis was obligated to pay $4,300 a month in alimony and child support. Circa 2009, he began working at CIBC Wood Gundy as an investment adviser. Although the bulk of his father's investments were handled by experts in Toronto, a portion of Richard's capital (which increased after he was bought out by his brother) was invested through his son (who at trial downplayed Richard's investment abilities).

Either before or after his divorce, Dennis met Lisa (Andrik) Ferguson who also was divorced and had a son. They had two other things else in common: Lisa and her friend Mary Beth Watt had purchased a twenty-five-foot C & C sailboat, *Loki*, before she met Dennis, and she was a member of RKYC (as was Richard Oland). Andrik was the daughter of a Hungarian immigrant who died in Edmundston, New Brunswick, in 2003. That same year, Dennis was the official agent for a local Progressive Conservative (PC) candidate in an election. Lisa has worked as an aide for Saint John Conservative MP Rodney Weston, and in 2010 was campaign manager for provincial

PC candidate Dorothy Shephard. According to a friend, Lisa and Dennis were married in a small outdoor ceremony on Dennis's property in 2009, under the auspices of the Two Rivers Pastoral Charge of the United Church of Canada.

Dennis and Lesley Oland had acquired 58 Gondola Point Road from his grandfather's estate in the late 1990s. In 2009, following his divorce, Dennis became sole owner of the ancestral home, largely because of his father's financial assistance. Typically, this aid was not altogether altruistic, as Dennis agreed to sign over two parcels of land (from the former Philip Oland estate), totalling twelve acres, to Kingshurst Estates Ltd. This gave Richard control of a valuable parcel of land in the heart of Rothesay located between the property of lawyer Bill Teed and of Jim Irving (son of J. K. Irving), head of J. D. Irving, the forestry arm of the Irving empire. In 2011, Irving, according to a report in the *Globe and Mail*, was building a 6,100-square-foot mansion in this secluded area. Google Maps indicates that Irving's heavily wooded property is accessible via Gondola Point Road. There are rumours that in 2011 Richard was seeking real-estate advice on how to maximize the value of the newly acquired land.[65]

Classic family business empires are not built by patriarchs who are soft or fair with their children. Richard's assistance to Dennis has been described as a loan, an advance on his inheritance, even an informal mortgage, but it forced Dennis to pay monthly interest to his father and turn over part of his land. There were other conditions, which many would find intrusive or humiliating. As would be suggested through the murder investigation, despite Richard's intervention, his son's financial situation was far from certain. He did not have a regular, predictable income; as a financial adviser, he was paid fees and commissions on stock trades. In addition to acquiring a new wife and stepson, Dennis shared custody of his own three children and that placed burdens on his time and resources. As of early 2016, their ages were as follows: stepson, Andru, twenty-two; Emily, nineteen; Hannah, seventeen; Henry, fifteen. In 2010, Dennis and Lisa took out a collateral mortgage for $75,000. In March 2011, just over three months prior to Richard Oland's death, a second collateral mortgage was placed on the property, for

$163,000. In the case of a default, the CIBC, and not Richard Oland, now had a legal claim against the grandfather's home.[66] Dennis's financial situation in 2011, combined with his father's personality and lifestyle and the strained father-son relationship, would conspire to produce dramatic consequences.

NOTES: CHAPTER 2

1. Gordon Pitts, "Derek Oland: Raising a glass to 50 years with the family brewery," *Globe and Mail*, Sept, 7, 2012.
2. Canadian Press, "Moosehead president says Canadian beer industry disappearing," *Cape Breton Post*, May 14, 2007; "Moosehead to lay off 70 workers in New Brunswick," CTV News, Oct. 2, 2014.
3. Paul Brent, "Band of Brothers," *CPA Magazine*, March 3, 2014.
4. Bruce Livesey, "What have the Irvings done to New Brunswick?" *National Observer*, June 6, 2016, http://http://www.nationalobserver.com/2016/06/06/news/what-have-irvings-done-new-brunswick.
5. Fredericton *Daily Gleaner*, Oct. 24, 1914.
6. Saint John *Standard*, June 15, 1918.
7. Saint John *Globe*, Dec. 12, 1917.
8. Gord McLaughlin, "Life in a Dynasty." *The Financial Post*, Aug, 1, 1992, 31.
9. "Same Increase in Beer Prices Just Coincidence, Says Brewer," *Globe and Mail*, Oct. 28, 1959, 29.
10. McLaughlin, "Life in a Dynasty."
11. Sawler, *Last Canadian Beer*, 59.
12. McLaughlin, "Life in a Dynasty."
13. *Ibid.*
14. *Ibid.*
15. Sawler, *Last Canadian Beer*, 39–40.
16. McLaughlin, "Life in a Dynasty."
17. *Ibid.*
18. *Ibid.*
19. Michael Tutton, "Brewing Brotherhood," *Telegraph-Journal*, Dec. 28, 1999.
20. David Stonehouse, "Moosehead buys Niagara microbrewery; Saint John company gains ground in Ontario," *Telegraph-Journal*, June 22, 2004.

21. *Ibid.*
22. Mac Trueman, "Brewery Ups Ante," *Telegraph-Journal,* Nov. 18, 2005, A1, A8.
23. Rod Allen, "Brewers concerned about rising costs," *Telegraph-Journal,* April 25, 2007, B1.
24. Sawler, *Last Canadian Beer,* 100.
25. Sawler, *Last Canadian Beer,* 6; Canadian Press (CP), "Moosehead beer stays in family," *Red Deer Advocate,* Feb. 15, 2008, B7.
26. n. a. "Three to be honoured at UNBSJ convocation May 24," *Telegraph-Journal,* May 14, 2002.
27. Constance Oland to Justice John Walsh, Jan. 16, 2016.
28. Sawler, *Last Canadian Beer,* 58.
29. McLaughlin, "Life in a Dynasty."
30. Jennifer Pritchett and April Cunningham, "Nightmare for Dennis, family says," *Telegraph-Journal,* Nov. 14, 2013, A1.
31. Gord McLaughlin. "Life in a Dynasty."
32. David Young, "Brewery woes led brother to court," *Telegraph-Journal,* Aug, 27, 1998.
33. Sawler, *Last Canadian Beer,* 145.
34. Brent, "Band of Brothers."
35. McLaughlin, "Life in a Dynasty."
36. Deborah Jones, "McCain foresees higher costs," *The Financial Post,* Nov. 19, 1992, 5.
37. *Ibid.*
38. Meagan Campbell, "The murder trial that took New Brunswick by storm," *Maclean's,* c. December 30, 2015.
39. Bob Klager, "Saint John Games generated money and goodwill," *Telegraph-Journal,* Jan. 26, 2002; Nathan White, "Economic downturn hits Games Foundation," *Telegraph-Journal,* June 25, 2009, B10.
40. David Young, "Fear and Loathing at the New Brunswick Museum," *Telegraph-Journal,* July 10, 1998.
41. Stuart Allen Smith, "Museum board, director must go," *Telegraph-Journal,* July 18, 1998.
42. Maggie Estey-Smith, "Businessman honoured for volunteer service: YMCA-YWCA salutes Richard Oland," *Telegraph-Journal,* May 17, 2006, B1–2.

43. Bertrand Marotte, "Irvings at crossroads: Maritime market not enough, tough global market is next step," *Calgary Herald*, June 30, 1996, D12.

44. John Fogan, "Irving replies to 'bashers'," *Evening Times–Globe*, May 4, 1990, C1.

45. Richardson, "Battle lines drawn over natural gas," *Telegraph-Journal*, March 11, 1998; "New Brunswickers invest in natural gas consortium," *Daily Gleaner*, March 11, 1998.

46. David Young, "Beware energy monopoly-Oland," *Telegraph-Journal*, Sept. 3, 1998.

47. David Young, "City Backs Irving Bid," *Telegraph-Journal*, Sept. 15, 1998; "A squandered vote on natural gas," *Telegraph-Journal*, Sept. 16, 1998.

48. Alan White, "Local investors in Gas NB can pocket twice the cash," *Telegraph-Journal*, Sept. 8, 1999.

49. Rebecca Penty, "The making of a franchise," *Telegraph-Journal*, Oct. 19, 2010, B1.

50. Poitras, *Irving vs. Irving*, 158–62.

51. Nicholas Köhler, "Murder and a maritime dynasty," Macleans.ca, July 28, 2011, http://www.macleans.ca/news/canada/murder-and-a-maritime-dynasty/.

52. "Burchell's Yacht—The *Aloma*," *Cape Breton News*, posted Aug. 10, 2010; CP, "Dennis Oland Recalls Good Old Days," Moncton *Time and Transcript*, Nov. 13, 2013, C1.

53. Lonay Habib, "RORC Caribbean 600–A Race Comes of Age," Antiguanice.com. March 8, 2011.

54. "Key West 2011 presented by Nautica," *Sailing World*, http://www.sailingworld.com/racing/key-west-2011-friday-video.

55. Jon MacNeil, "It all comes down to managing well: local businessman wins prestigious American regatta by 13/100ths of a second," *Telegraph-Journal*, Aug. 3, 2010, C1.

56. Donna Paxton, "Vela Veloce claims title, *The Daily Sail*, July 24, 2010, http://www.thedailysail.com/inshore/10/56138/new-york-yacht-club-race-week-report.

57. Interview of Dennis Oland, July 7, 2011, http://atlantic.ctvnews.ca/video?clipId=732471.

58. Harvey Enchin, "Foot loose, Czech free," *The Globe and Mail,*
    May 9, 1991. B6.
59. Paul Koring, "Czechoslovakia hopeful return of Bata is first
    step to economic vitality," *Globe and Mail,* Dec. 14, 1989, A2;
    Harvey Enchin, "Footloose, Czech free"; "Backward Glances: A
    Conversation with Former Bata Executive Jiri Sedlacek," *Bata
    World News,* Feb. 24, 2014. The Sedlaceks appear to have lived at
    160 Meadow Drive on Darlings Island, New Brunswick.
60. "Brockville: horse dead after accident," *Ottawa Citizen,* July 5,
    1988, E2.
61. CP, "Cops search son's home in Oland slaying," Halifax
    Chronicle-Herald, July 15, 2011, A1.
62. Constance Oland to Justice John Walsh, Jan. 16, 2016.
63. *The Canadian Establishment: Volume One: The Old Order* (Toronto:
    McClelland and Stewart, 1975), 490.
64. Constance Oland to Justice John Walsh, Jan. 16, 2016; Pre-
    Sentence Report for the Court of Queen's Bench, *R v. Dennis
    James Oland,* prepared by Jim Peters, Feb. 2, 2016.
65. Transfer, Land Titles Act, S.N.B, 1981, c.L-1.1, s. 21, Dennis
    James Oland to Kingshurst Estates Ltd., 2010-01-06,
    Registration number 28230879; Gordon Pitts, "Warship
    contract burnishes Irving legacy," *Globe and Mail,* Oct. 20, 2011.
66. Collateral mortgage, Land Titles Act, S.N.B, 1981, c.L-1.1,
    s. 21, Dennis James Oland and Lisa Ferguson, 2011-03-29,
    Registration number 29936474.

CHAPTER 3

THE FIRST WEEK

July 8–14, 2011

T he headline of New Brunswick's *Telegraph-Journal* for July 8, 2011, was "Dick Oland Dead." It was accompanied by a colour photo of SJPF officers and two employees of Brenan's Funeral Home pushing the victim's remains, shielded from prying eyes by a body bag and cover, on a stretcher for transport to the morgue at the Saint John Regional Hospital. While the Oland family prepared for the funeral, politicians, business leaders, and friends expressed their shock and sadness. Within a few days, judging by documents called an "information to obtain" (ITO) which were filed with the provincial court, the police had formulated their basic theory of the case. Despite this, the evidence was almost entirely circumstantial and it would be more than two years before an arrest would be made. This delay was, in hindsight, perfectly reasonable, as one of the top tips for homicide investigators is to not give in to media and political pressure and rush an investigation. In the meantime the SJPF, under Chief Bill Reid, was under tremendous media and public scrutiny.[1]

The last time a member of a prominent local family had been the victim of a major crime was back in 1982 when John E. "Jack" Irving, third son of renowned industrialist K. C. Irving, had been kidnapped from his residence. Jack, fifty years old, was in charge of the steel fabrication, construction, and engineering components of the Irving group of companies. During his career, he also owned newspapers in Fredericton and Moncton. As noted by Jacques Poitras in *Irving vs. Irving,* Jack had spearheaded the effort to cover the Maritimes with Irving gas stations. He was appointed vice-president of Irving Oil in 1972 after his father moved his assets out of Canada to avoid federal and provincial taxes and relocated to Bermuda.

In May 1982, Jack was with his wife, Suzanne, when Stephen Gerald Childs, a young, unemployed security guard, entered their residence with an imitation pistol. Childs wanted to abduct Suzanne, but Jack volunteered to be taken in her place. Irving was gagged and bound, placed in a van, and driven to another location. Over the next few hours, the kidnapper, who was seeking a $600,000 ransom to open up a health club, placed several calls to the Irving residence from pay phones. After installing a tap on the Irving phone, the police traced a call to the uptown area, resulting in the arrest of the kidnapper. Jack was returned unharmed, and Childs pleaded guilty and was sentenced to more than a dozen years in prison. Despite the happy outcome, the experience supposedly adversely affected the victim, who became a less dominant player in the family business empire. Jack passed away in 2010.[2]

In criminal matters, lack of information feeds public gossip, and the Oland case became the subject of countless coffee-shop, barroom and kitchen-table conversations. Saint John is technically a city of sixty-five thousand, but in many ways it feels like a small town where many people know and are related to one another and like to know each other's business. Everyone from taxi drivers to members of university boards of governors had an opinion or theory about Richard Oland's death. In the days and months that followed the discovery of the crime, rumours continued to swirl about the motive, the guilty party, and the cause of death. The case was unique not only because of the social status of the victim, but also because of that of the possible suspect. The elite was in the spotlight and, in a sense, on trial in the court of public opinion. In June 2011, for example, the National Post reported that when traffic was tied up on Saint John's Harbour Bridge, a rumour spread that Dennis had jumped to his death from the structure.[3] Other rumours included that the killer was an irate investor, someone to whom Richard owed money, or a hit man, possibly working for the Russian mafia. The eventual revelation of Oland's affair spurred talk of womanizing and the theory that the culprit was a jealous husband. Although outside reporters were frustrated by the unwillingness of political and business leaders to be interviewed about the story, the murder and ongoing investigation attracted the attention of national media. *Globe and Mail* reporter Josh O'Kane, for example, wrote that Oland had spent the decade prior to his murder enjoying life and "winding down."[4]

Public figures issued statements and friends of the family posted messages of sympathy and praise for the victim. John Ainsworth, owner of Printing Plus and Richard's landlord, remembered "exhilarating conversations" and Oland's "zest and vitality."[5] Pat Darrah, the retired head of the Saint John Construction Association who would deliver Oland's eulogy, refused to be interviewed by the *National Post*, stating: "Everyone's having a difficult time given the circumstances."[6] Don Cullinan, a lawyer whose office was in the building next to Oland's, viewed the death as "a real shame." The head of Enterprise Saint John, described as a family friend, spoke about Oland's business acumen and devotion to promoting Saint John.[7] Businessman Clark Sancton, a frequent lunch companion of the victim at the Union Club, called Richard "intense and brilliant." Members of the Rothesay Yacht Club, where Oland was well known, also felt sadness and shock. Bruce Tennant recalled how Richard and his future wife, Connie, used to sail to his camp on nearby Long Island in the Kennebecasis River.[8] Saint John common councillor Bill Farren, a former Moosehead employee, stated: "You don't usually see this happening to classy people. You usually see it happening to guys like me. There's a lot of attention because of that, I think."[9]

The public naturally speculated about a motive for the killing. In crime movies and television shows such as *Forensic Files*, the usual suspects in the deaths of a prominent businessperson include business partners, rivals, and former associates, or anyone who bore a grudge against the victim. Crime novels and television dramas often point to economic motives such as insurance payouts when wealthy individuals are murdered, but criminology literature indicates that homicides can stem from relatively trivial disputes, a situation made worse by the presence of alcohol or weapons. According to veteran defence lawyer David Lutz, the typical murder in New Brunswick involves one or more of three factors: alcohol, drug debts, or sexual jealousy.[10] In the period 2010–14, none of the seven other murder or manslaughter cases in Saint John (one of which went to trial with a finding of not guilty, another of which was changed from manslaughter to criminal negligence causing death) was unrelated to drugs, personal disputes, or domestic violence. In keeping with standard procedure in these types of cases, the SJPF remained guarded in terms of information released to the public. Initially, it announced that the death was "suspicious" but that the crime was isolated; in other words, the public had nothing to fear from the uncaught killer or killers. On July 11, 2011, Chief Reid confirmed both that the death was a homicide and the victim probably knew his attacker. The announcement that residents had nothing to fear from the killer "alleviated a lot of concern," according to Mayor Ivan Court. Spokespersons for the Saint John Board of Trade and Fusion, a business networking group, confirmed that uptown business types were not worried about their personal safety. Oland's family remained silent and nothing was said about a reward.[11]

Soon after the discovery of Oland's body, the word on the street was that the murder weapon was an axe. If the victim had been bludgeoned or stabbed to death, this fit the national pattern, with firearms typically being responsible for only a third of homicides.[12] If the killer had brought a weapon to the office, this was a sign of premeditation and, presuming an arrest could be made, a case of first-degree murder. If the assailant had picked up a hatchet or hammer on-site, this suggested a crime of passion, possibly the result of a verbal altercation that escalated out of control. Given Oland's reportedly difficult personality, anything was possible. There was no arrest, reward posted, or statement from investigators or the family asking for the public's assistance. In fact, the SJPF had more or less advised the public that it had identified the suspect. The understanding was that Richard had opened his door to someone he knew and trusted, which seemed to rule out robbery as a motive. A crime-scene analyst would have noticed that the office appeared to present a "disorganized" scene, suggesting sudden rage and a struggle. An organized scene, in contrast, indicates premeditation and that the assailant maintained control over themselves and the victim.[13]

During this early stage of the investigation, the MCU, which was headed by Sergeant David Brooker, held daily briefings to compare notes and assign new tasks. For example, security-camera footage was acquired from several businesses in Rothesay and Saint John. One wonders what impact the Oland investigation had on a unit that normally has several hundred files in one year. The lead investigator, who was called in from vacation, was veteran Constable Rick Russell.

On July 7, the SJPF had conducted a canvass (a search for witnesses, a weapon, and security cameras) of the neighbourhood centred on 52 Canterbury Street. The canine unit searched the rectangular area bounded by Canterbury (west), Princess (south), Germain (east), and Grannan Street (north), as well as the back alley and the lot to the south where the victim's BMW had been parked. The canvass extended further into the South end. This activity would continue the following day, with a renewed "article search." The canine unit also was deployed. One problem with many security cameras in the neighbourhood was that they pointed at the door areas of businesses, not at the street. No potential murder weapon was found inside the building or in the immediate neighbourhood.

At a crime scene, the position of the victim's body, the cause of death, the location and nature of wounds, the condition of the clothing, the type of weapon (if left behind), and the pattern of the victim's blood are all important clues. Arriving back at the scene, Sgt. Smith took more than one-hundred photos of blood spatter. On the floor near the area where the victim's head had rested, blood was caked so thickly that it looked like a rug. Smith was not an expert on spatter, but his preliminary work would greatly help the RCMP bloodstain expert who would travel from Nova Scotia. Smith found no signs of forced entry and no blood outside of the inner office—for example, on doors or in the stairwell. He checked the second-floor bathroom where he found used paper towel in the waste can that would be tested for blood. Attempts to collect fingerprints from the office were stymied by the existence of too many overlapping prints. Smith later testified that processing the back-exit door was on his to-do list, but by the time he returned from the hospital someone (who had to be a police officer) had opened it and there was no point in testing for prints or blood (this would emerge as a major issue at trial). The building owner advised the police to search the pit under the elevator in the basement and under a grate covering a culvert in the back alley.

It appears that the police did not even photograph the back door until 2015, four years after the crime. In addition to the issue of the door, there was some definite sloppiness to the SJPF's handling of the crime scene. Part of the problem was that Smith was the only forensic-identification officer on duty that day. Police investigations are increasingly under greater scrutiny in terms of crime-scene continuity and the chain of evidence, meaning the need to professionally collect, document, secure, and track the use of exhibits such as photographs, blood swabs, and fingerprints. Although the SJPF had various systems, including a computerized database, for tracking evidence, during the early investigation it appeared to fail in terms of basic, low-tech investigation work. As noted earlier, someone opened the rear door before it could be checked, officers used the second-floor bathroom before it could be processed, and there were probably too many officers accessing the actual Far End Corporation office, especially before the body was removed. This is an important detail because blood, even stains not visible to the eye, can adhere to objects such as door handles.[14] Although officers are supposed to keep notebooks and write up "narratives" of events on their shifts, at the preliminary inquiry and trial no one could remember who had opened the door. And unlike cops in television shows, it is not clear that SJPF members even thought to wear disposable gloves when at the scene (for example when they returned to the Far End office on July 9 for another search).[15]

An important part of Smith's work was swabbing the scene for blood, a substance that was in plentiful supply, although then dried. Just prior to 7:00 P.M. as Smith was still processing the scene, two RCMP tech-crime specialists arrived from J Division in Fredericton. Payman Hakimian, a civilian with almost twenty years' experience with the RCMP, had carried out dozens of investigations into economic crimes and was an expert on seizing, copying, and analyzing digital evidence with software. He was accompanied by Sergeant Pierre Bourguignon, officer in charge of the Integrated Tech Crime Unit in Fredericton. The men waited for Smith to complete his tasks and as they entered the crime scene they donned protective booties before beginning their work. Starting at 9:00 P.M., they photographed, documented, and seized a dozen devices from the office, including computer CPUs, digital cameras, an iPad, and an external storage drive. To avoid active computers from updating files and programs when powered down, they simply pulled out their power cords. The seized items were loaded into the unit's vehicle and taken back to Fredericton, where "forensic duplicates" were made of each hard drive and its files. Hakimian's task was not to analyse the content of various data files (this was left to the SJPF) but he was interested in any computer activity that could help establish a timeline for Richard Oland on July 6. The key device was the main computer at the desk where Richard had been killed. Crime-scene photos indicated a white Apple connector cord plugged into that unit. One of the key findings would be the exact time that the victim had last used his computer to "sync," or backup, his iPhone 4 on the day of the murder.

The next day, July 8, was an important stage in the investigation as the forensic examination of the victim's body and the autopsy were conducted. The provincial Coroner Act mandates that in cases of deaths suspected to be caused by violence, accident, negligence, or misconduct, or in cases of sudden or unexpected death, the coroner must be notified. The body of the victim is under the custody of the coroner until after the autopsy is performed, usually within a day or two of the discovery of a body. Prior to the autopsy, Sergeant Smith and Constable David MacDonald conducted an examination of the body that lasted several hours. This involved using a CrimeScope forensic light source, taking digital photographs, taping the clothing of the victim for hair and fibres, swabbing the hands, checking between the fingers for loose hairs (possibly grabbed during a struggle with the attacker), and clipping the fingernails in case biological matter deposited underneath could reveal the DNA of an unknown person. Smith and MacDonald, assisted by morgue attendant Kirk Sweezey, found thirty-one hairs or fibres on the body, including two hairs in the victim's hands. After the initial exam was completed, the clothing, including a bloodstained shirt, was seized and bagged as was the victim's Rolex. Before the actual autopsy, the body was washed down, and x-rays were taken to determine if any foreign objects, such as knife blades or bullets, were in the victim. In addition, a penile swab was collected, and blood, urine, and vitreous fluid were extracted. The purpose of the blood, extracted from the femoral artery, was to allow a crime lab to establish a DNA profile of the victim. Vitreous fluid, which is found within the eyeball, is a standard forensic pathology substance for testing for the presence of alcohol, drugs, or toxic substances.

The head was shaved, and then each injury was photographed, numbered, measured, and documented. Smith noted forty wounds to the head and six sharp-force injuries to the victim's hands. There were also a minor bruise on Oland's chest and small cuts in the bridge of his nose and chin. Sharp incise wounds, no doubt defensive in nature, were found on both hands and the right wrist. There was one abrasion on the neck and five round contusions or impressions, 2.5 to 3 centimetres in diameter, on the head: three near the left ear and two near the right. The circular impressions revealed a cross-hatch pattern. No evidence was presented at the trial as to the sequence of blows. There was major trauma on the back of the victim's head, but most of the damage was on the left side (the side facing up when he died). Given the broken fingers and cuts to his hands, it is likely that Oland initially had faced his attacker before being overwhelmed. Then he was hit one or more times with either a blunt or sharp-edged weapon before he went to the floor. There, in the words of one witness at the trial, he was slaughtered. There were more than thirty sharp, incised wounds to the scalp and skull.[16]

Pathologist Dr. Ather Naseemuddin, assisted by Sweezey, began the autopsy at 4:30 P.M. It was not completed until close to midnight. Dr. Naseemuddin, who obtained his MD in India and trained as a pathologist in the United States, was fairly new to the job. Unlike in television shows, the pathologist did not speak into a recorder but was assisted by the police officers who made notes. The pathologist noted that the victim was a generally healthy man (his only medication had been the anti-anxiety drug Paxil). In preparing his report, Naseemuddin reviewed photos taken at the crime scene and the radiologic examinations of the head, neck, chest, and hands. The x-rays revealed fractures on both sides of the skull and of finger bones on both hands. The toxicology tests indicated a low level of ethyl alcohol in the blood (23 milligrams per decilitre), which suggested "alcohol consumption several hours prior to death." The pathologist also catalogued the wounds and retracted the scalp to measure and document the true extent of the injuries. The cross-hatched pattern of the five blunt-force wounds on the head were new to him. Many of the cutting or chopping blows overlapped, so that on the left posterior there was a generally traumatized area almost as big a cellphone. The examination of the skull revealed fourteen fractures, some penetrating into the brain area. Compounded with the fact that there had been brain matter on the floor at the scene, these fractures confirmed the obvious: the attacker had focused most of their rage on Oland when he was on the ground. One further fracture was detected: the orbital plate around one eye. This may have been caused when the victim fell to the floor. Naseemuddin concluded that death had resulted from "multiple sharp and blunt force injuries to the head."[17] His report did not offer any opinions on the type of weapon or weapons involved, the height or "handedness" of the attacker, or the time of death. The final stages of an autopsy are not for the faint of heart. After examining and measuring the wounds, the doctor usually opens up the chest cavity and examines that state of and weighs each organ, and then opens up the skull and removes and examines the brain. The organs are then replaced and the body sewn up in preparation for embalming and other procedures at the funeral home. The victim was embalmed and prepared for his funeral by funeral director Sharlene MacDonald, who had helped remove his body from his office.

After he returned to the police station later that evening, Smith, using a forensic light and a Hemastix blood-screening test, examined the logbook that Dennis had picked up during his visit to 52 Canterbury Street. This item appears to have been voluntarily surrendered by its owner, Jack Connell, who later demanded it back. (Without having the full disclosure for this case, some of the evidence details are difficult to track.) The book was a log for a family camp on Long Island in the Kennebecasis River that extended back to the early 1900s, and one of its past entries made reference to a younger "Dick" Oland. If blood and DNA (particularly that of the victim) could be discovered on this article, it would be highly damning to the victim's son, who had dropped it off to his mother's house early on July 7. The logbook would be examined in more detail by Const. MacDonald in December.

On July 8, police supervised the first of two underwater searches at Renforth Wharf, a popular park and swimming spot located between the Renforth Boat Club and the Kennebecasis Rowing Club. This is where Dennis had told police he stopped after visiting his father on the evening of the sixth. Officers also checked the area around the nearby Bill McGuire community centre and the shoreline of the river. The rowing club in the area was presumably where the Oland children did their kayaking. A week later, a search was carried out of the woods near a ball field to the west of the park. The river currents near the wharf are weak and the water is not very deep, so presumably an object deposited there would have been discovered. The search was conducted by five divers from All-Sea Atlantic, who used special cameras that revealed debris on the riverbed. (As part of disclosure, defence counsel were given video footage that was four hours long). Nothing of forensic value was found. The distance from the wharf to Dennis's home is 4.6 kilometres. The author examined the area in 2016 and the wharf projects roughly 20 metres into the Kennebecasis River. The distance from the centre of the water-side edge of the paved parking lot, where two witnesses were parked on July 6, is 30 metres or more. The witnesses saw a man, who was wearing a sports jacket and carrying a bag, walk to the end of the wharf and briefly sit down on the edge facing upriver towards Rothesay. This meant that his back would have been at an angle from anyone in the parking lot. Although the witnesses did not see any objects deposited into the river, given the distance and the angle, it would have been difficult, if not impossible, to determine from the parking lot if the individual held anything in his hands. (Oland's account of his stop at the wharf, another curious detail in the case, will be discussed in a subsequent chapter.)

Following his police interrogation and the news of his father's passing, Dennis Oland must have been under considerable stress. In addition to dealing with the news of the crime, he had to help prepare the funeral.[18] It was either an innocent coincidence that created bad optics, or an incriminating example of post-offence behaviour, but on July 8, ten hours after Dennis left the police station, someone dropped off dry cleaning and laundry to VIP Dry Cleaners in Rothesay under the name of Lisa Oland. The order included two sports jackets, a pair of pants, and sixteen shirts. The business, close to the Oland home, is situated in the heart of the Rothesay commercial strip and operated by a Korean-Canadian couple who use environmentally friendly dry cleaning methods. The previous evening Dennis had been told he was a suspect in his father's death and that the SJPF would be applying for search warrants, so he had to expect his behaviour would be monitored. He did not appear to know that he was under surveillance. One of the items dropped off for dry cleaning that morning was a brown Hugo Boss jacket. During his interview the night before, Dennis told Const. Davidson that he had worn a navy blazer on the sixth. Yet eyewitness testimony and security-camera footage suggested that Dennis sported a brown jacket on the day he visited his father. The defence would maintain that the clothing was dropped off by Lisa in preparation for Dennis's attendance at funeral-home visitations for his father on July 10 and 11, followed by the funeral on July 12. There was no evidence as to who actually dropped off and picked up the clothing the next day. The police, although supposedly having a tail on their suspect at the time, appear to have been unaware of the trip to the dry-cleaning establishment until July 14. On Saturday, July 9, after someone had already picked up the order, Lisa dropped by to pay and there was testimony at trial that Dennis waited for her in the car. What they took home, a freshly dry cleaned Hugo Boss jacket, would be the most contentious piece of physical evidence in the entire case.

One text on crime-scene investigation argues that jurors "expect physical evidence in a trial."[19] With the Oland case, physical evidence such as DNA was the only sure route to laying a charge. In the days that followed the discovery of the body, the SJPF gathered and collated evidence and statements in order to apply for a series of search warrants. A layperson might object to the fact that Dennis Oland, if guilty, had several days after his interrogation to dispose of evidence, but search-warrant applications have to list reasonable grounds and stand up to judicial review. According to defence lawyer David Lutz, this is "just the way it works." In many cases, the documents to obtain a warrant are completed by police officers and are not vetted by Crown attorneys.[20] The police also continued to talk to people, such as some of the musicians who occasionally used the third floor of 52 Canterbury for practice. There had been no musical activity on the evening of July 6.

On July 9, Smith was back at the scene, looking for a weapon, documents, and other items. He collected a number of blood swabs, marking the spots with stickers and photographing them. The goal here was to develop a DNA profile of the assailant or assailants, in case they had been injured during the attack, and determine if there were any other victims. He also took measurements and made a sketch of the crime scene. At some point, Maureen Adamson visited the office to advise investigators about possible missing items. She listed Oland's iPhone 4, the logbook, and a will as items she believed had been in the victim's office at the time of his murder. Other information gathered that day included her husband's statement to Const. Copeland about the man seen outside the Far End office at approximately 5:30 P.M. on July 6. John Dickinson, who lived in a third-floor apartment at 56 Canterbury Street, next to Printing Plus, told police that he had not heard any unusual noises on the evening of July 6. Const. Breen reviewed security-camera footage from Brunswick House on July 6, which appeared to show Dennis exiting the building wearing a brown jacket and carrying books, and footage from other cameras, which depicted a silver VW Golf driving east on King Street and south on Canterbury. Constable Sean Rocca tracked down a cellphone at the victim's residence but determined that it was not the missing iPhone 4.

On July 9, an affidavit was filed with the Court of Queen's Bench, requesting a judge to grant a production order to Rogers Communications for documentation of incoming and outgoing calls for three numbers (one supposedly belonging to Richard and the others to Dennis) as well as cell-tower data for July 6 and 7. The seven-page document, which laid out the grounds for the judge (in this case Justice William Grant), reflected the state of the early investigation. It recalled the discovery of the victim's body and the statements of Shaw and Ainsworth as to the noises they heard on the evening of the sixth. The document also repeated elements of Constance Oland's statement, especially about the victim's reliance on his cellphone and text messaging. She also recounted that Dennis had spoken to her brother about picking up the logbook from her husband's office and that she found it in her back hallway early on the morning of the seventh. The affidavit continued with elements of Diana Sedlacek's statement that recounted her manner of communicating with the victim and her attempts to text and phone him on the evening of the sixth. Adamson and McFadden confirmed Richard's cellphone number and that the device was not present in his office. Dennis was mentioned as the last known person to see his father alive. On this basis, Const. Stacy Humphrey argued that the victim's cellphone "will provide information and possible timelines surrounding his death."[21]

In recent years, cellphones have become key evidence in homicide and other criminal investigations. In most homicides in the United States, one of the three previous calls on a victim's cellphone is either to or from the killer.[22] Cell-tower data has also been employed to locate suspects in areas where victims' bodies have been found. One of the great mysteries of the Oland case is why the victim's iPhone 4 was taken. There was no point in removing it in order to hide evidence of text messages or calls, because these are available to investigators from service providers if the proper legal channels are followed. Had the victim been trying to call 911? Was the phone grabbed in the heat of the moment? Did the killer take it with the hope of sending text messages in the name of the victim in order to buy time and avoid detection? The RCMP tech-crime experts would soon discover that the iPhone had been backed up on Oland's computer just after 4:30 P.M. on July 6, meaning that it had been in the office late on the afternoon on the day of the murder. The logical inference was that it had left with the killer or killers.

Following a request from the SJPF, on July 9, Rogers Communications attempted a "forced registration" to check on the status of the missing phone as of that day. In this test, the service provider sends a message to try to track a phone from the nearest cell tower. The response was "roaming error" (a term that would be discussed during the trial). On July 10, the department was sent data from Rogers Communications that indicated the last outgoing signal from Richard's phone was at noon on July 6, and that the last incoming signal pinged off a cell tower not in Saint John, but in Rothesay at 6:44 P.M. This was hugely significant for the developing theory of the case as it suggested the victim's iPhone was in the same part of Rothesay as Dennis Oland at a specific time on the evening of the murder. On July 11 and 12, Sergeant David Brooker spoke to a Rogers analyst about the meaning of the technical term "absent subscriber": it refers to a cellphone that is turned off, out of the coverage area, or destroyed.

On July 11, RCMP Sergeant Brian Wentzell, a bloodstain analyst from Nova Scotia, arrived at the scene to photograph, document, and analyse blood-spatter evidence in order to develop theories about the attack. His work extended into the twelfth. Working with Smith, he documented hundreds of spatter stains and made his own sketch of the scene. Spatter is created by blood leaving the victim's body during and after a blunt- or sharp-force attack, or when blood flies off a knife, stick, or other weapon. Low- and medium-velocity impacts are created by fists, knives, hammers, and other weapons; gunshots are associated with high-velocity impacts. When the head and neck are struck with blunt or sharp-force objects, blood is forced out of the victim's body at medium velocity and can land on walls, floors, ceilings, furniture, and the attacker. Cast-off spatter is created with the upward and downward motion of weapons that come into contact with the body. Experts can determine the trajectory of blood spatter by the shape of the stains. The size and patterns of stains are determined by the force of impact. The scene surrounding Richard Oland's body showed evidence of medium-velocity spatter. Photographs of the scene indicated hundreds of small spatters, but they were not necessarily all individual stains: when a blood droplet hits a surface like a wall or a floor, it can produce satellite spatter.

One sample was detected nine feet from the body, which suggested the ferocity of the attack. On or near the victim's chair alone (which had rolled a few feet away from his desk) were dozens of small stains. Wentzell detected no evidence of a post-attack cleanup at the scene, and neither he nor Smith discovered a trail of blood or footwear impressions leading out of the room. Wentzell would also examine the red grocery bag seized from the suspect's car. In an application for a search warrant, both Smith and Wentzell opined that an attacker would have been covered with significant blood spatter.[23]

On July 12, Const. Breen advised Const. Humphrey that Diana Sedlacek had agreed to voluntarily provide some type of information or evidence (possibly phone records or a polygraph test) to the SJPF. In one or more of her interviews, Diana had stressed that her lover did not have a high opinion of his son's work ethic. That same day, Constable Bruce Weston spoke to John Travis, Oland's supervisor at CIBC Wood Gundy, and was told that Dennis was not earning his usual income and had asked his employer for assistance.[24]

The public accolades following Oland's death contrasted with Lisa (Oland) Bustin's chilling statement to police that her father could have had "anyone for an enemy."[25] The Irving-owned *Telegraph-Journal* praised Richard Oland as "a powerful force for community development," a hardworking man with "a no-nonsense approach to forging consensus." He was credited with helping "move Rothesay and Saint John forward" and helping to promote "civic pride"[26] Ironically, this influential publication, never known to exercise restraint when lionizing wealthy New Brunswickers, became one of the more aggressive media outlets in using the courts to unseal documents relating to the Oland investigation. In this quest, the Irving interests were usually joined by the Canadian Broadcasting Corporation. The *Telegraph-Journal* published a lengthy obituary of Richard, which noted, amongst other things, his passion of skiing and riding horses.

Saint John is a mid-sized city with a stagnant population and an uncertain economic future. Few people move there and most of the young people leave. Its political culture is largely based on desperation.

For much of the twentieth century it was viewed from the outside as a brash, drab, and polluted industrial centre and port city, dominated by aggressive entrepreneurs such as K. C. Irving. Because of economic weakness and limited opportunity, it has attracted few immigrants, making it one of the least diversified metropolitan areas in Canada. Although the rate of poverty has declined by 20 percent in recent years, it remains frustratingly high (19 percent in 2010).[27] Saint John's social and economic problems are legion, and have attracted a wide assortment of government initiatives and volunteer activities. It also has an influential and vocal business community. This group reflects an historic sense of entitlement, a distrust of government, and faith in common-sense solutions to problems.

To the east of Saint John, where demands for municipal services are outpacing its tax base, are the prosperous suburban towns of Rothesay and Quispamsis. Here live the well-educated and well-paid blue- and white-collar workers, managers, and business owners, who work in and, in a sense, profit from the city of Saint John. These family centred enclaves are peaceful and prosperous to the point of being boring. Rothesay is the oldest and most prestigious of these outlying communities; its historic associations, which have changed in recent years, were British, Anglican, and conservative. As noted in a previous chapter, an iconic institution for Rothesay is the elite Rothesay Netherwood School, a private institution where the annual fee for day students is $20,000, almost the total average annual family income for residents of Saint John. The Rothesay elite enjoys fashionable homes, private schooling, travel, upscale recreational activities such as tennis and boating, and is able to send its children to elite universities. In 2011, the town was home to much of the Oland family and it was where Richard would be buried six days after his murder.

That Richard Oland was not a typical victim of homicide in New Brunswick was evident not only in media coverage and commentary, but in statements by public officials. Then premier David Alward of New Brunswick issued a sympathetic message but so did Darrell Dexter, then New Democratic Party premier of Nova Scotia.[28] New Brunswick's Lieutenant Governor Graydon Nicholas told reporters he felt honoured to attend Oland's funeral: "I think it's important that in

as public a way as we can, not only myself but other officials in government, we be here to give not only our condolences but to be present
with the family.... This man accomplished a lot. He did a lot of good
for New Brunswick, and when you stop and think of the legacy that
he left behind for athletes, that itself is amazing."[29] Oland had been
a director of Ganong Brothers for almost three decades. According
to company president David Ganong, his friend "was enjoying life
these last few years." Ganong had gone fishing with Oland in the past,
including the trip to the Miramichi just before the murder, and was
stunned by the news. He told a reporter that Oland loved fishing, but
in recent years sailboat racing had become his real interest.[30]

Like that of his father, P. W., in the 1990s, Richard's funeral
mass at Our Lady of Perpetual Help Church in Rothesay was a meeting of the provincial elite. Four priests and two monsignors were at
the altar, and scriptural passages were read by niece Victoria Laskey
(daughter of Jane Toward) and Dennis Oland. Pallbearers included
nephew Patrick Oland, Alistair and Hugh Toward (presumably sons
of Richard's sister Jane), Kim MacKay, Charles Saunders, and Scott
Laskey. There are few accounts of people being visibly upset at the
funeral, yet many online condolences offered positive comments
about the deceased that attested to his zest for living. One of the
song's played (possibly a favourite of the victim) was the ultimate
narcissist anthem, "My Way," made famous by Frank Sinatra.[31]

Attendees were filmed by the police "like a Montreal mob
funeral only this was the heart of the bluebloods," in the words of one
observer.[32] The point of this surveillance was to gather clues, which
indicates that despite their accusation of Dennis on the evening of the
seventh, investigators were attempting to collect more leads. Images
taken at the funeral were useful when the police interviewed Barbara
Murray and Douglas LeBlanc, who had been sitting in their vehicle at
the Renforth Wharf on the evening of July 6. They saw a man dressed
in a sports jacket and carrying a grocery bag acting "strangely" at
the wharf. The individual they identified from police images of the
funeral was Dennis Oland.[33]

Of course, the other aspect of a Mafia funeral is to ask the questions: who shows up, who does not, and why? The class politics of the

Maritime provinces are most starkly revealed at the funerals of the wealthy. In this case, dignitaries included the premier, the Lieutenant Governor, several MLAs, one Member of Parliament, two senators, and three mayors. Representatives of the business elite were also on hand, including J. K. Irving, one of the surviving sons of K. C. Irving, whose personal wealth, according to a 2015 *Forbes* magazine article, is $6.5 billion. (Irving and the deceased had clashed in the past when the former, testifying before a provincial regulatory board in 1989, had described Oland's trucking company as "damned lousy"[34] and accused Oland of resorting to bribes and even a having spy in the Irving organization to gain business from Irving customers.) No other Irvings were reported to be in attendance and none of the many Irving enterprises appear to have sent flowers or memorials.

In the interview room a few days earlier, Dennis had told Const. Davidson that his father, because of his difficult personality, had a hard time keeping friends. Yet Pat Darrah, former head of the Saint John Construction Association, considered himself a close friend of the victim. In his eulogy, he explained that he was overcome with emotion at the "tragedy and senseless act," and that Richard was "a dear friend and a wonderful, wonderful community person, and we're going to miss him tremendously." He described "Team Oland" as "a wonderful family."[35] Following the service, attendees were invited to a reception at the house on Almon Lane where Richard had lived with his wife for decades. Richard was buried in the small parish cemetery in Rothesay, located in what is now the unattractive commercial-strip section of the town, wedged between a Sobeys supermarket and a Canadian Tire store and across the street from fast-food joints. Unlike the larger more accessible Roman Catholic cemeteries in Saint John, it is surrounded by a chain-link fence and a locked gate.

A photo by *Telegraph-Journal* photographer Kâté Braydon, later featured in the *National Post*, depicted a tearful Lisa, Dennis's wife, leaving Our Lady of Perpetual Help Church, accompanied by Dennis who appears to be smiling. Perhaps, in this moment of stress, he was recalling a happy memory of his father. Many would consider the photo to be damning evidence; others would say there is no proper way to act at a funeral, especially for that of a family member who has been murdered. But most people at funerals have not been warned by police that they are suspects in the killing of the deceased. The image did not appear in the media, however, until almost two years later.[36]

After the funeral, Justice William McCarroll granted a search warrant for the residence and vehicle of Dennis Oland. In a document filed for the application, Const. Stacy Humphrey wrote: "I believe that Dennis Oland is responsible for the death of Richard Oland." On July 14, Constable Sean Rocca requested that Dennis attend the police station for a meeting. Oland, accompanied by lawyer Gary Miller, went to the City Hall headquarters at 10 A.M. where they met with Rocca and Constable Greg Oram. It is assumed Oland was informed about the search that was to unfold that morning. Oland and Miller then drove to the Olands' residence in Rothesay where the police were executing the warrant. Bill Teed also appeared to be present. Fifty-eight Gondola Point Road had huge symbolic and emotional significance for the Olands and their friends and associates. It had been the home of P. W. who, with his wife, had founded the Rothesay Pony Club to teach children how to ride. After his death in 1996, P. W. Oland's body had been laid out not at a funeral home but in his own home.

A large number of SJPF officers were on-site that day, divided into inside and outside search teams. Although the warrant covered a period of four days, the search spanned nine hours; the scene was released to Teed at 8:00 P.M. The *Toronto Star* reported that the murder weapon was an axe and members of the public assumed that this was the chief object of the search.[37] A search plan was developed and officers were organized into two-person teams with all activity recorded on paper. All items seized were photographed and documented. Miller handed over his client's BlackBerry; the search also netted three desktop computers and a large number of documents. Oland's VW Golf was towed away at 12:15 P.M. The search of the extensive grounds and outbuildings appears to have been thorough, with officers operating from a grid plan. Constable Michael Horgan and his police dog searched the grounds, including the road, a barn, a woodpile, and a compost area. (The horse barn was searched without the dog.) Each room of the house was searched, the basement and attic were explored, and even the lint from the clothes drier was collected. Constables Stephen Davidson and Jay Henderson checked the sun room, living room, dining room, pantry, and kitchen on the ground floor. The master bedroom received special attention and some of the items seized here included a duvet, a pillow, and even toilet paper. The officers seized several articles of men's clothing and several pairs of men's footwear from a closet, including a brown sports jacket that still had a dry-cleaning tag inside the collar. Nearby was a receipt for the dry-cleaning order that matched the tag. The search netted a total of fifty-seven items, but the Hugo Boss jacket would prove the most important, and controversial. Without it, there would have been no trial of Dennis Oland for second-degree murder. Const. MacDonald, acting as the "seizing officer," would later testify that he was annoyed that none other than the lead investigator, Rick Russell, touched the jacket with an ungloved hand before it could be properly secured. It was rolled up and then folded into a small paper bag (an act that would be criticized at trial) for transport to the forensics section of the SJPF.[38]

Sleepy Rothesay, where kids playing road hockey is considered public disorder, was shocked by the police operation. A long-time neighbour, who explained that the Olands were "nice people," commented on the police operation: "It's just dreadful that they're so secretive about what's what....I'm sure if they would come out with some information, it would be much better for everybody."[39] The police continued to refuse to publicly identify a suspect but the search sent a strong message to the public. The day following the search a private security van was blocking the entrance to 58 Gondola Point Road, where a sign read "Private: Friends Open."

At 5:45 P.M. that day, Sgt. Smith began a detailed examination of the impounded VW Golf. Between July 14 and 16, this task absorbed at least fifteen hours of his time. Smith employed the CrimeScope, the Blue Star chemical-reagent test, the Hemastix presumptive test for blood, and the LMG chemical-reagent test on the interior of the vehicle, which, by its cluttered nature, indicated no evidence of a cleanup. A total of eleven swabs were collected in case they revealed blood or DNA evidence. In the rear hatch of the VW, Smith found a red, reusable Our Compliments bag, presumably the same bag William Adamson had seen outside of the Far End Corporation on July 6. At trial, Dennis would describe this bag as his "man purse" and admit to having carried it into his father's office on his visit. It contained maps, a book, documents, a cellphone charger, and a plastic bag. Swabs were taken from the inside and outside of the bag in case it had contained a weapon. Other items found in the trunk and tested were a sail cover and a lawn mower blade. (The SJPF did not realize at this time that these items had been purchased the morning after the murder).

That the SJPF officially viewed Dennis Oland as the suspect in his father's murder would be confirmed in the media only in May 2013, but the implications of the search of his residence and vehicle were fairly obvious. On the surface, Dennis appeared to be an unlikely candidate for murder. But the theory of the Crown, once a charge had been laid, was that "Anyone is capable of doing bad things."[40] In contrast, Dennis Oland's family, as well as friends and associates, remained steadfast from day one in their belief that Richard's killer had escaped justice. This would create a somewhat unique situation, in that those who believed Dennis was indeed guilty either did not attend the judicial proceedings or kept a low profile. Things were different in the more anonymous word of social media. In 2013, for example, after the arrest of Dennis, "Kennebecasis Bay Sailor" who earlier had posted on the Sailing Anarchy website about how Richard had "grabbed him off a wharf" as a boy thirty years earlier for a run on his E22 (Etchells) sailboat, made the following comment: "Good to see an arrest finally. Even the wealthy deserve justice."[41] But in contrast to many assault and homicide prosecutions, there would be no evidence of warring parties in the public gallery or corridor at court. This point was driven home to the author one day in a break in the proceedings, when a spectator turned to ask: "Excuse me, can I ask you a question? Who is here for the victim?"

NOTES: CHAPTER 3

1. April Cunningham, "Police chief remained confident during investigation," *Times & Transcript*, Nov. 14, 2013, B4.

2. Jacques Poitras, *Irving vs. Irving: Canada's Feuding Billionaires and the Stories They Won't Tell* (Toronto: Viking, 2014): 61, 65, 72; Sandra Martin, "Jack Irving, 78, Businessman, Philanthropist," *Globe and Mail*, July 14, 2010; Kim MacRael, "Kidnappings for ransom rare, but dangerous,'" *Globe and Mail*, July 18, 2011.

3. Tamsin McMahon, "Mystery brewing around Dick Oland's murder," *National Post*, July 24, 2011.

4. Josh O'Kane, "Killing brings Oland's name into spotlight after a decade of winding down," *Globe and Mail*, July 19, 2011. See also, Köhler, Nicholas Köhler, "Murder and a maritime dynasty," Macleans.ca, July 28, 2011, http://www.macleans.ca/news/canada/murder-and-a-maritime-dynasty/; Bruce Livesey, "Company Province, Provincial Company," *Report on Business*, Feb. 26, 2016.

5. ["Richard Henry Oland,"] Brenan's Funeral Home webpage, July 2011.

6. McMahon, "Mystery brewing around Dick Oland's murder."

7. Geoff Bird and Sabrina Doyle, "Oland remembered as consummate businessman," *Telegraph-Journal*, July 9, 2011, B1.

8. Mark Iype and Natalie Stechyson, "'Death shocks friends, Dick Oland,'" *Telegraph-Journal*, July 8, 2011, A1.

9. Eric Andrew-Gee, "Murder in the family: Business Dynasties Are Torn Apart by Money and Rivalry All the Time: Dick and Dennis Oland were in a league of their own," *Report on Business Magazine*, April 1, 2016.

10. Interview with David Lutz, March 8, 2016.

11. Josh O'Kane, "Oland investigation puts Saint John in eerie calm," *Globe and Mail*, July 21, 2011.

12. Tina Hotton Mahony, "Homicide in Canada 2010," *Juristat*, 2011, Statistics Canada: http://www.statcan.gc.ca/pub/85-002-x/2011001/article/11561-eng.pdf

13. Curt R. Bartol and Anne M. Bartol, *Criminal Behaviour: A Popular Approach*, 9th edition (Toronto: Prentice Hall, 2011), 292.

14. Cause No. SJCR-2-2015, In The Court of Queen's Bench of New Brunswick Trial Division Judicial District of Saint John between: Her Majesty the Queen Applicant and Dennis James Oland Respondent Jury Instruction (Final) Delivered by: The Honourable Mr. Justice John J. Walsh at: Saint John, NB Crown Counsel: P. J. Veniot Q.C., Patrick Wilbur, and Derek Weaver, Defence Counsel: Gary A. Miller Q.C., Alan D. Gold, and James R. McConnell, 43. (Hereafter, Jury Instructions (Final).

15. Testimony of Staff Sergeant David Brooker, Oct. 28, 2015.

16. Testimony of Sergeant Mark Smith, Oct. 7, 2015.

17. *R. v. Dennis James Oland*, Final Post-Mortem Report, Richard Oland, July 8, 2011, Exhibit P-59.

18. Val Streeter to Justice Jack Walsh, Jan. 8, 2016.

19. Barry A. J. Fisher, *Techniques of Crime Scene Investigation*, Seventh Edition (New York: CRC Press, 2003), 4.

20. Interview with David Lutz, March 8, 2016.

21. Affidavit, Court of Queen's Bench, Constable Stacy Humphrey, July 9, 2011.

22. Police Executive Research Forum, *Future Trends in Policing* (Washington: PERF, 2014), 3.

23. Chris Morris, "Forensic expert details examination of victim's body at Oland murder scene," *Daily Gleaner*, Oct. 3, 2015, A3.

24. Testimony, Oland trial, Nov. 5, 2015.

25. Chris Morris, "Inside the Oland investigation," *Daily Gleaner*, Sept. 14, 2013, A3; "Oland trial heads into tenth week," *Daily Gleaner*, Nov. 16, 2015, A3.

26. "Dick Oland 1941–2011," *Telegraph-Journal*, July 13, 2011, A8.

27. Vibrant Communities Saint John and the Saint John Human Development Council, *A Poverty Outline for Saint John, NB*, August 2014.

28. CP, "New Brunswick Business Community Shocked by Oland's death," CTV News, July 8, 2011.

29. CBC, "N.B. businessman Oland's funeral draws hundreds," CBC News New Brunswick, July 12, 2011.
30. O'Kane, "Killing brings Oland's name into spotlight."
31. Eric Andrew-Gee, "Murder in the family."
32. Julian Sher, "The inscrutable murder of a magnate," *Globe and Mail*, Oct. 15, 2011.
33. *R v. Dennis James Oland*, Agreed up statement of fact, Exhibit P102, Oct. 29, 2015, C1.
34. Robert Jones, "Irvings lose truck licensing bid," *Globe and Mail*, Oct. 25, 1989, B1.
35. Natalie Stechyson, "Death called tragic, senseless; Hundreds turn out to mourn businessman and community leader Richard Oland at service in Rothesay," *Telegraph-Journal*, July 13, 2011.
36. Kâté Braydon, "Capturing a Moment," *Telegraph-Journal*, Jan. 1, 2014, C1.
37. CP, "Cops search son's home in Oland Slaying," Halifax *Chronicle-Herald*, July 15, 2011, A1.
38. Chris Morris, "Forensics officer concerned about washroom near Oland murder scene," *Telegraph-Journal*, Oct. 7, 2015, A1, A4.
39. McMahon, "Mystery brewing around Dick Oland's murder."
40. *R. v. Dennis James Oland*, Opening address, P. J. Veniot, Oland trial, Sept 16, 2015.
41. "Justice delayed or denied?" Sailing Anarchy website, https://sailinganarchy.com/tag/dick-oland/, posted on November 18, 2013.

CHAPTER 4

THE EARLY INVESTIGATION

July 15, 2011–December 2012

F ollowing Richard Oland's murder, the lack of an arrest, and the search of Dennis's home and vehicle, the Oland family naturally valued their privacy. The *National Post* of July 24, 2011, reported that the family was not responding to media requests and had hired private security to watch both the home on Gondola Point Road and Richard and Constance's secluded residence on Almon Lane. It was revealed during the preliminary inquiry of 2014 that at least one private investigator was working on behalf of the family soon after the murder. One rare family comment came from Dennis's mother-in-law, Esther Andrik: "It's been very hard on them, very hard....They're getting a lot of calls. It's depressing not knowing what and how." Andrik cautioned the public not to rush to judgment and explained the intense media interest in terms of the family's prominence. She described Dennis as "a really nice person" and his whole family as "very nice people."[1]

Over the next eighteen months, the investigation proceeded slowly, largely because of the SJPF's need to assure Crown attorneys that there was sufficient evidence to lay a charge. Without having insider knowledge, it is impossible to know if the police chief and the MCU were also worried about the legal resources that the suspect and his family could bring to bear once a charge was laid. The MCU usually responded to one hundred "dead on arrivals" each year but in the case of homicides, victims and suspects were usually poor or working class and often criminally involved. The SJPF was probably unprepared for the detailed and thorough push back of Oland's legal team.[2] In a largely circumstantial-evidence case, it was important to test, and in some cases re-test, seized items for forensic purposes.

As was later revealed, the investigation also sought the advice of outside organizations and individuals. In the fall of 2011, with the retirement of Const. Rick Russell, Const. Davidson, who had joined the MCU just before the discovery of Oland's body, became lead investigator in the case. Although a twelve-year veteran of the SJPF who had served five years with the RCMP Proceeds of Crime unit, Davidson's relative lack of experience with homicide investigations would be exploited by the defence during the preliminary inquiry and trial. The other notable development in this period was an unprecedented legal battle by media outlets to unseal affidavits and other documents pertaining to search warrants. Both the Crown and the yet-to-be-charged (or publicly named) suspect contested these applications, for different reasons.

The class dynamics of the investigation continued to be apparent. Former mayor Norm McFarlane (also a former PC MLA and cabinet minister) was supportive of the police but seemed to suggest that in Saint John, not all families are created equally: "They can't have a mistake with something like this. With a family like the Olands they've got to be absolutely sure."[3] The SJPF continued to be pressured by the media, politicians, and the public to make an arrest or at least show major progress with the investigation. Yet a departmental spokesperson explained that it was standard to not reveal too much about homicide investigations until there was an arrest.[4] One common councillor expressed his frustration in the fall of 2011: "There comes a time when, for me as a citizen and as a councillor, I will have to ask: what have you got and why don't you have what you're supposed to have?"[5] Witnesses such as Robert McFadden, Oland's accountant and sailing partner, refused to discuss any details of the crime with the media because they had been advised so by the police. Constable Glen Hayward explained: "The type of weapon would be hold-back information we would never release....That's something that would only be known by the culprit."[6]

Attacks on the SJPF by *Telegraph-Journal* editorials and supportive politicians appeared to be part of the publication's broader assault on the public sector. The chief and the police union defended the reputation of the force, and even the New Brunswick Police Association stood by the investigation, explaining that forensic-lab testing took time and that Crown prosecutors had to vet any charges. In a July 2012 news conference, the association accused the *Telegraph-Journal* of practising "yellow journalism." Citizens, by the time of the Oland murder, were already conditioned by negative reporting and comments by local elected officials on the costs of the police service and police pensions. In 2014, when in contract negotiations with the police union, the Saint John Common Council took the bizarre step of voting to explore the logistics and costs of replacing the municipal force with the RCMP. Mayor Mel Norton (who was a member of the police commission), purporting to speak on behalf of taxpayers, defended the decision, even though RCMP policy limits municipal policing contracts to communities under fifteen thousand. Norton would continue to take potshots at the police service in 2015.[7]

The Saint John Police Force (SJPF), founded in 1849, is one of the oldest in Canada and reports to a police commission. The chief during the Oland investigation was career officer Bill Reid, originally from Cape Breton. Although the Fraser Institute, a conservative think tank, has criticized the department as being one of the costliest (based on population) in Canada, under both Reid and new chief John Bates, who assumed command in the fall of 2015, the SJPF has been involved in some innovative areas. In 2012, for example, it ranked among the top forces in the nation in terms of clearance rates (an internal police measure of solving crimes) particularly for assaults and robberies. As with any city, the daily concerns of the SJPF are traffic, drugs, alcohol, the homeless, and the sex trade. The city's overall reported crime rates (with the exception of assault and sexual assault) are low by national standards and the rate for the Saint John Census Metropolitan Area fell by 19 percent from 2007 to 2012.[8] Given the high concentration of poverty in the city's several priority neighbourhoods, the department faces challenges that are more severe than in other parts of the province. It partners with other agencies such as the Kennebecasis Regional Police Force (formerly the Rothesay Regional Police), the RCMP, and the Canadian Border Services Agency. Social agencies, health-care professionals, academics, and activists were impressed with Reid's progressive attitudes towards intravenous drug users, those affected by HIV, and vulnerable sex-trade workers. Professor Mary Ann Campbell of UNB Saint John attributes the high clearance rates to the department's embrace of "crime mapping," studying crime and public hot spots, and deploying resources accordingly. Like other police services, the SJPF is confident that new technology can make crime prevention and detection more efficient. But public safety, in the words of Chief Bates, "comes with a cost."[9]

According to the famous American lawyer Alan Dershowitz, who was involved in the O. J. Simpson case, "a mountain of evidence" is not always necessary to secure a conviction.[10] Yet, to convince a jury beyond a reasonable doubt in a case where there are no eyewitnesses or incriminating wiretaps, body-pack recordings, or jailhouse conversations, the police require compelling tangible evidence. And in the Oland investigation this was reflected by a flurry of activity in the summer of 2011, when the SJPF applied for and executed a series of search warrants and production orders, and began to send seized articles for forensic testing to the RCMP lab in Halifax. (Production orders, similar to search warrants, are judicial orders requiring a person or organization not under investigation to surrender documents or other information such as banking and phone records.)

In July 15, 2011, Justice Grant issued production orders for the call-detail records for Dennis Oland's cellphone and call data, cell-tower data, and GPS information for Diana Sedlacek's phone. On July 20, Justice McCarroll granted a search warrant and a general warrant for the sailboat *Loki* located at the RKYC in Millidgeville. During his July 7 interview, for some reason Dennis was not asked about his whereabouts that morning, but CIBC Wood Gundy staff told police he had been working on a boat and RKYC members confirmed seeing him there, acting normally. The sailboat and the waters around it were an obvious location for the disposal of evidence, including bloody clothing. For several hours on July 21, the SJPF, assisted by a diver, searched the vessel and surrounding waters and removed more than thirty items from the boat.[11] At the preliminary hearing held in 2014, a forensic-identity officer revealed that the items seized at the yacht club revealed no trace evidence linked to the murder.

As mentioned earlier, the rumour in the community in the days that followed was that the murder weapon had been a hammer, an axe, or a hatchet. The latter two are not commonly found in business offices, although the former is sometimes in a drawer or a tool box. Even before the 2014 preliminary inquiry, whose proceedings were under a publication ban, it was apparent that some within the SJPF had been speculating that the weapon was a drywall hammer or a roofer's hatchet. The former is a specialized tool designed for removing and installing drywall. The hammer edge is wide and flat, with a cross-hatch pattern (which appears to match the round, blunt-force injuries on the victim's head). This allows nails to be hammered without the drywall being damaged. The cross-hatched pattern also creates a round impression around the head of the nail that more easily holds drywall compound. With the availability of utility knives, the hatchet end, used for scoring wallboard, is not as useful, but it has a notch by which the hammer can act like a handle for carrying the board. Other possible candidates were a roofer's hammer or hatchet, a shingler's or lather's hammer or hatchet, or a rigger's axe. Depending on the model, each of these tools has a sharp hatchet end and a round or square hammer end with a cross-hatched surface. In the construction industry, most of these traditional tools have been replaced with nail guns, but they are still readily available for purchase in hardware stores and are useful for do-it-yourself carpenters.

In 2011, Tom Oland, a cousin of the victim, told a reporter that he had been interviewed by the SJPF, who asked if he possessed a drywall hammer. According to Oland, who presumably was not the only interviewee asked this question, "the only weapon they mentioned was a drywall hammer."[12] Dennis was not asked about tools or weapons during his five-hour police interview, probably because investigators as of July 6, 2011, had not had sufficient time to study the victim's wounds. It is possible that he was asked about a drywall hammer on the day of his arrest, but the transcript of that interview was used in court as an exhibit.

Although not generally known to the public at the time, one factor delaying the investigation was a bottleneck in sending and receiving exhibits for testing at the RCMP crime labs. In 2012, the allegedly tough-on-crime Harper government sought further budgetary reductions from the RCMP. That year, the RCMP announced that three of its six crime labs, including the Halifax lab that processed Oland investigation exhibits, would be shut down.[13] The SJPF had to discuss testing strategy in advance with lab consultants in Halifax or Ottawa, each request had to be approved from Ottawa, and then a limited number of items were forwarded at a time. Once those test results were completed, another batch of exhibits could be sent. Another cause for delay is when newer investigative techniques come on line and exhibits are returned for new testing. On July 21, 2011, the SJPF sent the swabs from Oland's fingernails and his blood sample from the hospital for DNA typing, and swabs from the inner door handle and the hatch release of Dennis Oland's VW Golf to the crime lab. A few days later, Justice McCarroll issued a production order for the victim's CIBC financial records. The SJPF began to analyse these records, which would form a key part of the prosecution's case, on August 11, 2011. On August 4, 2011, McCarroll granted a general warrant for the items seized at the Oland house. Around this time, the department issued a statement explaining that it was awaiting the results of forensic exhibits seized during the course of the investigation. On August 11, McCarroll issued a search warrant pertaining to Dennis Oland's computer at CIBC Wood Gundy. This would prove to be a controversial issue during pretrial hearings in 2015.

Given that no murder weapon was ever discovered, DNA would prove the only forensic evidence in the Oland case that could suggest a physical link between the suspect and the victim. Yet as would be seen, DNA evidence in itself is not automatic proof of guilt. One sign that investigators may have been worried about the DNA angle was an attempt by the SJPF to enlist advice or involvement from Dr. Henry Lee, the famous forensic scientist involved with the O. J. Simpson and JonBenet Ramsey cases. At the suggestion of Chief Reid, information on the case was mailed to Lee, presumably at his Institute of Forensic Science at New Haven University, but investigators did not receive a reply.

In the meantime, forensic officers worked on seized items. Constable Shawn Coughlan, for example, was tasked with reviewing the search history of the three computers seized from 58 Gondola Point Road. Browser histories often contain evidence of premeditation. During the Oland trial, the defence mentioned the Melanie Getson murder of 2010. Her estranged husband, Jason, had brutally stabbed her in a Saint John parking lot in view of witnesses. A search of his workplace computer revealed searches on a Canadian Tire website for hunting knives. Two days before the attack, Getson had purchased two knives from the retailer. Getson was charged with first-degree murder but pleaded guilty to second-degree. Both the Crown and the defence supported Justice Hugh McLellan's sentence of twenty years before parole eligibility.[14] The search histories of Oland's computers revealed nothing incriminating.

One month after the discovery of the crime, the media reported that the Oland family had engaged Gary Miller Q.C. of Fredericton, one of New Brunswick's top defence lawyers. Miller appears to have been on the case much earlier, and there is also evidence that a private investigator was involved. The former head of the NB Criminal Defence Lawyers Association was described by a veteran Saint John barrister as the leading defence lawyer in the province and "very up to date on the finer points of criminal law." Miller was critical of media reports speculating on how the victim was killed.[15] In court, he displays a superb knowledge of the law and a folksy charm that can easily lapse into a sarcastic intensity—this can be valuable in cross-examination. Over the years, Miller had been involved in a number of interesting cases, such as the defence of Premier Richard Hatfield in 1985 on a charge of possession of marijuana. In 1987, he defended an American, Anthony Romeo, accused of shooting New Brunswick Highway patrolman Manny Aucoin. Romeo had relied on a defence of insanity but was convicted of first-degree murder. Miller later helped argue an unsuccessful appeal of the conviction before the Supreme Court of Canada. Perhaps his best-known trial was the murder prosecution of Mi'kmaw leader Noah Augustine of the Metepenagiag First Nation. In 1999, Augustine, after consuming several drinks, took a handgun belonging to a friend to Bruce Barnaby's residence on Eel Ground Reserve. The purpose of the visit supposedly was to discuss Barnaby's alleged role in the death of a relative. Augustine testified that Barnaby, during an argument, tried to attack him with a knife, so he shot him in the stomach and head. He then fled to Florida with a friend. His 1999 trial for murder took place over a two-week period in Miramichi City. The jury, which accepted the self-defence argument, deliberated for only two hours before acquitting Augustine, who four years later was elected chief of Metepenagiag First Nation. Augustine, once regarded as one of Canada's up-and-coming aboriginal leaders, died in a highway accident in 2010.[16]

Although he would not appear in a Saint John court until November 2013, the other major member of Dennis Oland's defence team was Alan D. Gold, one of Canada's top criminal defence lawyers. Based in Toronto, he has practised law with Edward Greenspan and argued dozens of cases before the Supreme Court of Canada. Gold is in high demand as a speaker for conferences intended for defence lawyers, prosecutors, and judges, and has served as president of the Criminal Lawyers Association of Canada. A skilled practitioner, he is author of The Practitioner's Criminal Code (also known as the Gold Code), a standard annotated Criminal Code that is updated annually. In addition to many articles, Gold has written Expert Evidence in Criminal Law: The Scientific Approach, which promises to help counsel deal with "bogus experts and junk science" in the courtroom. In the 2009 edition, he claims that an explosion of often dubious expert-witness opinion has invaded the courts in recent years.[17]

Gold, whose command of the law is obvious, is not an uncontroversial figure. In 1992, journalist Michele Landsberg took issue with his remarks, at a Criminal Lawyers Association conference on sex-abuse trials, on how to counter the testimony of therapists in so-called "recovered memory" cases, where parents are allegedly falsely accused by their children. This discussion was in response to the controversial "recovered memory therapy" movement, where adults, often through psychotherapy, recall lost memories of being abused as children. Critics regarded these recovered memories as false memories. In some cases, this led to arrests and prosecutions, and the existence of this "syndrome" was rejected by the Canadian Psychiatric Association in the late 1990s. In 1998, Gold sent a letter to the federal Minister of Justice calling for an inquiry into recovered-memory convictions and the release of all prisoners involved.[18] In 1999, he criticized a decision by the Supreme Court of Canada as a "radical feminist judgment" that "turns (human sexuality) into a business-like formalistic affair where everything must be absolutely clear." The court had overturned a decision by the Alberta Court of Appeal that acquitted a man for sexually assaulting a seventeen-year-old girl. In this case, the Supreme Court of Canada rejected the defence of "implied consent." According to Gold, the decision supposedly puts "complainants on a pedestal" and absolves them of any responsibility when they are sexually assaulted.[19]

In 2003, his thirtieth year in practice, Gold was engaged by the Toronto Police Services Board to defend the Toronto Police Service, not in a court of law but the court of public opinion. In an extensive piece of investigative journalism, the *Toronto Star* had published a series of articles arguing that the police engaged in racial profiling. Its evidence were statistics on drug arrests in the period 1996–2002 and traffic stops that appeared to indicate differential treatment of blacks and whites. The Toronto Police Association was so incensed by the allegations that it filed a $2.7-billion lawsuit. At this time, the department was under controversial chief Julian Fantino. Gold and a sociology professor were hired to analyse and rebut, at a meeting of the Police Services Board, the statistical methodology on which the *Star* had based its conclusions. (In 2009, Chief Bill Blair would finally admit that racial profiling was a problem in Toronto).[20]

Gold has also been involved in organized-crime cases. In 1979, he represented Richard Sauvé, a Satan's Choice member and one of several men convicted in the murder of a fellow biker at a Port Hope, Ontario, bar. Other defence counsel in this controversial case included Eddie Greenspan, Clayton Ruby, and Brian Greenspan. Sauvé, convicted of first-degree murder, was one of six men to be sent to penitentiary.[21] In 2004, Gold defended two Ontario men in a Montreal organized-crime case. Former Hells Angels Walter Stadnick and Donald Stockford were accused of drug trafficking, conspiracy to commit murder, and membership in a criminal enterprise. At this time, Gold acknowledged "considerable negative press" associated with the case, largely because of the biker war in the past decade that had resulted in more than one-hundred-and-sixty murders, including of innocent bystanders, and twenty disappearances. Both of his clients were convicted and sent to penitentiary for twenty years. In 2007, Gold represented a Toronto motorcycle-shop owner arrested as part of a national sweep, known as Project Develop, against outlaw bikers. Although the raids netted drugs and guns, his client was on record as claiming that the Hells Angels were "motorcycle enthusiasts." That year Gold was also involved in representing Aniello Peluso, considered by the RCMP to be a leader of Toronto organized crime, in the context of a botched police sting operation that collapsed before charges were laid.[22] Just before becoming involved with Oland case, Gold represented Dale Sweeney, former heard of the Manitoba Hells Angels, who was sentenced to eleven years in penitentiary for heading up a cocaine-trafficking ring.[23]

One question in the Saint John area in 2011 and 2012 was why, given the lack of an arrest, the Oland family refused to offer a reward for information leading to the arrest of a suspect. As revealed recently, this was actually attempted behind the scenes. On September 27, 2011, lawyer Bill Teed, acting on behalf of Dennis Oland's sisters and mother, met with Chief Reid to discuss a reward to be provided by the family if the real killer were apprehended. The SJPF was tight-lipped on this issue, but according to an affidavit sworn by Dennis Oland on January 12, 2016, Reid refused on the grounds that "it would be unethical for the Saint John Police Department to accept it from my family" given that the police service believed he was the murderer.[24]

It was not generally known to the public until late 2012, when search warrant information was unsealed, that Richard Oland's businesses at 52 Canterbury Street continued to operate after his murder. Despite the earlier plan, there was no move to Brunswick Square. Robert McFadden took possession of the office after the police investigation had finished. A forensic cleaning company from Fredericton was hired to deal with the bloodstained floor (the victim's blood had seeped through three or four layers of flooring and was visible on the ceiling of Printing Plus). Apparently, the restoration job took several days and cost $40,000. This must have been difficult for the hard-working John Ainsworth, who, in addition to suffering the emotional trauma of losing an acquaintance he admired, had his business disrupted and associated with a notorious murder. While the office was being restored and painted, Maureen Adamson and McFadden operated out of the empty suite next door. They were joined occasionally by Dennis Oland, now president of Richard Oland's holding company and a director of the Far End Corporation and Kingshurst Estates, who used McFadden's former office. This appeared to be a part-time job. According to court testimony, Dennis earned $50,000 a year from the two companies.

On July 4, 2011, the building comprising 115-17 Germain Street, one street to the east of Canterbury and whose rear almost abutted the back of 52 Canterbury Street, was transferred from the British Bible Society to the Canadian Bible Society. The latter had operated a store at the location for decades, but in 2010 the outlet had closed. The transfer took place two days before Oland's murder. This building, as would be revealed in court (but not to the public) in 2014 and in court proceedings not under a media ban in 2015, had a connection, at least in theory, with the Oland murder, which will be discussed later in this book. The property was listed for sale on July 29, 2011 (if not earlier), for $299,900, and the sale was closed on November 30, 2011, for a price of $275,000. The new owner was the numbered company 660673 N.B. Inc., whose business address was Cox and Palmer: Bill Teed's firm. The president of the company was Lisa (Andrik) Oland and the secretary was Dennis Oland. Annual taxes on the property, which also included two apartments on the upper floors, were in the range of $6,000. At the time of his father's murder, Dennis had a negative cash flow. His main bank account was overdrawn by several hundred dollars, his credit card was well over the limit, and a recent payment on a line of credit had been rejected because of insufficient funds. After the murder, he lost his job as a financial adviser. How a couple that was in financial straits in July managed to acquire this property less than six months later is not clear (no mortgage is on file), but it is reasonable to infer than they received help from their family. Dennis's mother had access to the interest (and if necessary the capital) from a trust fund worth $36 million.

Negative publicity associated with the murder investigation caused Dennis to lose his job with CIBC Wood Gundy. For a person in financial straits and who owed his former wife more than $50,000 a year and his father's estate $20,000, this was not good news. Though he no doubt received a severance package as well as some compensation for the value of his investors' "book," rumoured to have been between $200,000 and 300,000. As later revealed in court, Dennis Oland and Robert McFadden benefitted on two levels from Richard Oland's death. Both were executors of the victim's estate, and based on its value, the executors' fees were roughly $1 million. The two men agreed to a split, with McFadden being paid $765,000 and Dennis more than $100,000. Secondly, the two were remunerated as trustees of Oland's estate.

Neither the media nor the jury for his 2015 murder trial were aware of another facet of Dennis Oland's life after the murder of his father. In the two years following July 6, 2011, Dennis, who was basically broke in early 2011, undertook more than a dozen trips outside of Canada, usually with his wife and other family members. The details were listed in a document later filed as part of a bail application. In October 2011, he and Lisa vacationed in Bermuda, followed by a trip to New York City in November with daughter Hannah. In March 2012, he flew to Houston, Texas, with Lisa to drive a truck (presumably a new purchase) back to New Brunswick. Then there was an automobile trip to Maine, New York, Connecticut, and Maryland between May 6 and 11. Later in May, Dennis travelled to Camden, Maine, to help bring a friend's boat back to Rothesay. In October, he was in Boston with Lisa and the following month he took daughter Emily to Florida. Between December 2012, and early January 2013, there was a trip to Orlando (home of Disney World) with children Henry and Hannah, two of their friends, and stepson Andru Ferguson. Between February 23 and March 8, 2013, Dennis and his family were part of a larger Oland family vacation to the Turks and Caicos in the Caribbean. A month later, Dennis flew to Washington, DC, drove to Oxford, Connecticut, "to look at a boat," then drove to New York City to meet family members, followed by the return trip to Rothesay. In April and May, he travelled twice to

Tufts University Veterinarian Hospital in Worcester, Massachusetts, with a sick pet dog. He made a third trip to Worcester in late October 2013, less than two weeks before his arrest.[25]

On July 12, 2013, Dennis flew to Baltimore, Maryland, to take possession of a boat that was sailed back to Rothesay. According to the 2015 membership roster of the Rothesay Yacht Club, which is located within walking distance of the two Oland residences, Dennis and Lisa Oland were the owners of the forty-two-foot Grand Banks motor yacht *Heritage*. This class of trawler yacht, built by American Marine Limited, has been on the market for more than three decades and comfortably sleeps several people. It is a solid and stable vessel with a diesel engine. According to listings on Yachtworld.com, the price for a used Heritage 42 can range from under $100,000 USD for a vessel built in the 1970s to more than $400,000 for a '90s model. Oland was able to enjoy this vessel in the summers of 2014 and 2015 after he was released on bail. At one point, he had the canvas coverings on the boat redone. *Heritage* was stored for the winter of 2016 at the Saint John Power Boat Club. Given that Oland knew he was the prime suspect in a murder investigation that was based in part on his uncertain income, debts, and lifestyle, these trips and the purchase of the yacht seem like poor choices.

Journalist Julian Sher did manage to interview Robert McFadden, whom he described as Richard's "accountant, sailing buddy and confidante," in 2011.[26] McFadden refused to elaborate on the scene of the crime the morning the body had been discovered and explained that the SJPF had advised witnesses to refrain from speaking to media as long as the investigation was underway. Writing three months after the murder, Sher described a "wall of silence" erected by the police and the Oland family. The lack of public updates on the case was creating "grumblings and frustration." Councillor Bill Farren was quoted as expressing this sentiment on behalf of the community. It is not known if Farren, a former member of the police commission and a veteran Moosehead employee, had ever commented on other ongoing investigations. Paul Zed, the former Liberal MP who had once been married to an Irving, commented: "It's a whodunit, but nobody really knows who the suspects are."[27]

Given its importance to the case, it is ironic that the SJPF was relatively slow to examine the Hugo Boss jacket that remained folded up and wrinkled in the box for weeks after its seizure. Const. MacDonald finally scrutinized the garment in November—four months after Oland's death—and then personally transported it to the RCMP Halifax crime lab on November 30. As defence counsel would argue in 2015, given the terms of the relevant search warrant, this was possibly a violation of the legal rights of Dennis Oland. Sgt. Wentzell examined the jacket starting on December 6, taking digital photographs which he then magnified by a factor of twenty. He had been asked to detect any stains on the garment and determine how they may have been deposited. Although other areas had been circled by MacDonald, Wentzell documented small bloodstains on the right outer and inside sleeve, the left inside sleeve, and the upper chest. The exhibit was sent back to the Halifax lab in 2012 and by this time several test areas had been cut out. Wentzell was unable to identify any further stains. He also examined the victim's blood-soaked shirt and his shoes, which had spatter on the tops. The lab reports on the items sent for RCMP testing in late 2011—the jacket, red grocery bag, other articles of Dennis Oland's clothing, and swabs from his BlackBerry—did not appear until March 2012, whereupon another series of exhibits, including blood swabs from the crime scene, were sent to Halifax.

One week before Christmas 2011, counsel for the CBC and *Telegraph-Journal*, employing the services of Nova Scotia media lawyer David Coles, applied to have a number of search warrants and ITOs released for publication. Judge Leslie Jackson decided to seal investigative details for a further six months on the grounds that the investigation was still active and that the release of the information would breach the privacy of individuals. The hearing revealed that one unnamed witness was refusing to co-operate with the police. The public also learned that the lead investigator in the case had retired. The sealed court documents contained details on what the SJPF had been looking for when they executed search warrants in Saint John and Rothesay months earlier. Gary Miller, acting on behalf of Dennis Oland (who had not yet been named publicly as a suspect) requested that Jackson release the documents to his client so that he could assess the grounds for the searches. Bill Teed represented Lisa Oland and Mary Beth Watt at the in-camera hearing.[28]

A graduate of the UNB law school, Teed had been in practice since 1978 and made a Queen's Counsel in 1989. His area of expertise is corporate law, specifically in commercial and property leasing, but also banking, finance and securities, and corporate restructuring. Indicative of the sometimes closed world of the Saint John area (and especially the corporate world), Teed not only lives in Rothesay, he is actually a neighbour of Dennis Oland. He shares another apparent connection with the Oland clan: support for the PCs. In the summer of 2014, when the Oland preliminary inquiry was underway, he nominated the incumbent MLA in Rothesay, Ted Flemming, as the PC candidate for the Rothesay riding. He is also of the class of lawyers and businesspeople that end up being elected or appointed to various public boards and agencies such as Enterprise Saint John, another reality for the Saint John elite.

In December, following Judge Jackson's decision to seal all documents and search warrants for six months, Chief Reid issued a statement explaining that his officers were still working on a "complex" case, the type that did not get "settled in an hour on a TV show." Reid continued: "It's in the community, people talk about it, it's got national attention and at the end of the day, while you can appreciate everyone's curiosity, while you can appreciate most people want this to be solved, time and patience are the most important thing here." As St. Thomas University criminology professor Michael Boudreau noted, Reid's press conference, held within days of the start of the investigation, was somewhat unusual, but other observers explained that centralized control of statements to the media was becoming the new normal for Canada's police services.[29]

Dennis and Lisa Oland, whose financial situation appeared to have improved, were involved in other transactions in the new year. In February of 2012, 660673 N.B. Inc. secured a collateral mortgage on the Germain Street property for $182,000.[30] In April 2012, Dennis and Lisa acquired a $462,000 collateral mortgage on their

Rothesay residence. On May 1, 2012, the couple's 2010 collateral mortgage for $75,000 was discharged, meaning it was paid off. Three weeks later, the $163,000 collateral mortgage from 2011 was also discharged. As of June 2016, the April 2012 mortgage had not been discharged and the degree to which it had been paid down is not a matter for the public record.[31] Later in 2012, Lisa opened a vintage-clothing consignment shop in their new property, which is located on a picturesque section of Germain Street, a gentrified streetscape in the Trinity Royal heritage zone. The shop, Exchange on Germain, features designer wear and by May of 2012 had more than 1,200 Facebook likes. Somewhat ironically, it is located one street away from where her father-in-law was bludgeoned to death. According to a 2013 story in *Maclean's*, Dennis, who no longer seemed to have a job, was involved in his wife's new business, appearing at a Heritage Preservation Board meeting to discuss the building's exterior. The story noted that Dennis's aunt Jane Toward, sister of the murder victim, posted a positive comment on Exchange on Germain's Facebook page. One Facebook photo, dated April 14, 2014, showed a smiling Dennis standing at the counter during a fashion show featuring young models.[32]

As would be revealed at the preliminary inquiry (but not to the public) in 2014, and at the subsequent trial, the investigation continued in 2012 with further forensic testing of swabs and other exhibits and a series of field tests by the SJPF to track with which cell towers an iPhone 4 would connect based on the location of the caller. There were also DNA samples to obtain. When the bathroom sink in the lobby of the Far End office had finally been tested in July 2011, there was a presumptive positive result, which was confirmed as blood by follow-up testing. Could this be the blood of the killer? Investigators would not complete this task until 2015, but they set out to surreptitiously collect samples from a number of people other than Dennis Oland. One was Richard's right-hand man, Robert McFadden, who, for whatever reason, refused to provide a voluntary DNA sample. In December 2012, in a scene out of a movie, he was tracked to the East Side Mario's restaurant in Saint John where an undercover officer, sitting at a table a few feet away, acquired a cast-off drinking straw. (In the *Stillman* case in 1997, the Supreme Court of Canada ruled that the seizure of cast-off evidence such as straws, cigarette butts, drinking glasses, and Kleenex tissues is entirely lawful in the case of persons not in custody.[33])

In June of 2012, as the anniversary of the crime approached, Chief Reid gave an interview where he spoke of the case as "long" and "complicated" and explained that the investigation was waiting for the results of forensic tests. He told the *Telegraph-Journal*, "We have to be absolutely right." Reid explained that investigators had identified a suspect who was known to the victim, but were still exploring leads and were aware of the problem of tunnel vision. The chief also explained that charges could only be laid after the Crown prosecutor's office gave its approval. He declined to comment on whether the case turned on one single piece of evidence and disagreed with any suggestions that the prominence of the victim or his family had forced the department to treat the investigation differently.[34]

In the summer of 2012, the Crown, the SJPF, and lawyers acting for Dennis Oland and others renewed their legal battle against the application by the CBC and the *Telegraph-Journal* to have the court unseal search-warrant information in the name of public transparency. The Supreme Court of Canada in 1982 had ruled that once a warrant had been executed and the evidence in it obtained, it became a public document. Sections of the *Criminal Code*, however, still gave judges some discretion to prevent the publication of suspects' names until after they had been arrested. The latter provision has been subjected to Charter of Rights challenges.[35] On June 15, Judge Jackson, who was the province's chief provincial court justice, ruled that search-warrant information would remain sealed until he made a determination on a request by the SJPF for a further six-month publication ban. On July 31, Jackson released to the media Const. Davidson's affidavit of June 7, 2012, but several ITOs, search warrants, and lists of seized items, were not unsealed. In the document, the lead investigator claimed that the SJPF wanted to test 243 of 378 seized items but to date fewer than 50 had been forensically examined. The police had interviewed sixty people to date, but Davidson's affidavit argued that further publicity might discourage other potential witnesses from contacting them. Testimony by Davidson the following month indicated that unlike the police chief, the lead investigator did not believe an arrest was imminent.[36]

On July 31, the Crown agreed to permit the release of some of the documentation in connection with several warrants, including those relating to 58 Gondola Point Road, the sailboat *Loki*, an unidentified automobile, and the CIBC on King Street, Saint John (the victim's primary bank). The Crown and lawyers for the Oland family objected to the publication of items seized as evidence, anything that could identify certain individuals interviewed by police, and those who allegedly were with Oland on the day of his death (including a person with whom he had a meeting). On August 16, Jackson released a series of documents, heavily redacted, that made no mention of a weapon, a cause of death, or a suspect, which the Crown still considered "hallmark" evidence. Yet, the unsealed documents did reveal, for the first time, that the SJPF believed it was investigating a murder (as opposed to homicide) and that the crime had been committed on July 6, 2011.[37] Prior to Jackson's next release of documents, Gary Miller, on behalf of Dennis Oland, and Bill Teed, acting for the Oland estate and other members of the family, requested that they be given the opportunity to examine the documents first in order to safeguard the interests of their clients. The SJPF continued to oppose the unsealing of any details that could compromise its investigation.

In late September, the judge issued a written decision announcing that he would be unsealing more search-warrant documentation. One-hundred pages of documents released the first week of October revealed, without directly naming the suspect, many of the stages of the investigation. They indicated that immediately after the murder, police believed there was a financial motive. The name of the suspect was redacted in the release, but the unnamed person allegedly owed the dead man half a million dollars. The unsealed material also indicated that DNA evidence and security-camera footage was important to the investigation. There was reference to a video interview of the last known person to see the victim alive, a description of the clothing he had worn, and an account of his activities on the evening after his meeting with the victim.

Items seized in the investigation, such as clothing and a red shopping bag, were listed. The release also revealed that John Ainsworth and Anthony Shaw, working in Printing Plus, told investigators they heard pounding and thumping noises from the second storey on the evening of the murder. The supporting documents revealed details of Richard Oland's last day alive, that there were tensions within the family, and that he had a mistress. They confirmed that Far End Corporation was still in business under McFadden, but made no mention of the involvement of Dennis Oland. One reporter argued that fifteen months after Oland's murder's case, the murder was "unsolved," but from the SJPF's point of view, that was not quite true. Despite the formal publication ban on much of the warrant information, other details leaked out on social media such as Twitter. In late October, lawyer David Coles revealed that he would be making further submissions on behalf of the media for the release of the names redacted in the documents.[38]

Justice Jackson's rulings on the Oland warrants broke new ground in terms of New Brunswick legal history, according to an interview the judge gave after his retirement.[39] With the release of the warrant information, newspaper columnist Kurt Peacock, who coincidentally owned a rental property next to 52 Canterbury Street and had been there briefly on the evening of July 6, 2011, to collect rent, wrote that "the pressure to obtain justice for this crime will likely be greater than ever."[40] The state of the investigation by late 2012 raised three basic questions: Was Dennis Oland the suspect in his father's murder? Would an arrest ever be made? And if so, would the accused, in light of the mounting publicity, receive a fair trial? The police were also on trial, both for the Oland matter and their failure to make an arrest in the death of twenty-two-year-old Selena Perry, a psychiatric patient who wandered off her ward in February 2012 and was found dead in another part of the Saint John Regional Hospital. In addition, Matt Foley, president of the Bacchus motorcycle club (or gang, according to its critics), had shot dead a young man on the street in broad daylight and eighteen-year-old A. J. Dennison had been fatally stabbed while taking part in a home invasion on the city's West side in early November.

The *Telegraph-Journal* published an over-the-top editorial that concluded the SJPF had a "poor recent record of solving murders," and that the public was actually alarmed by "killers who remain at large."[41] (By way of comparison, Nova Scotia Crime Stoppers lists fourteen unsolved murders for Halifax since 2010.)

NOTES: CHAPTER 4

1. Tamsin McMahon, "Mystery brewing around Dick Oland's murder." *National Post*, July 24, 2011.
2. Mike Landry, "Police tried to get DNA from Moosehead boss, jury told," *Telegraph-Journal*, Oct. 29, 2015, A1-2.
3. McMahon, "Mystery brewing around Dick Oland's murder."
4. *Ibid.*
5. Julian Sher, "The inscrutable murder of a magnate." *Globe and Mail*, Oct. 15, 2011.
6. *Ibid.*
7. CBC, "Police call the *Telegraph-Journal* a 'yellow rag,'" CBC News New Brunswick, July 24, 2012; "RCMP likely not interested in Saint John contract," CBC News New Brunswick, Jan. 14, 2014; Karissa Donkin, "Saint John police to implement some recommendations from MacNeil report," *Telegraph-Journal*, Feb. 11, 2015, B5; Kelsey Pye, "Police commission wants to take a new, more positive direction," *Telegraph-Journal*, April 3, 2015, B1.
8. Craig Babstock, "Crime statistics don't tell full story," Moncton *Times & Transcript*, Feb. 8, 2014, A1; Statistics Canada, Police-reported crime statistics, 2012, http://www.statcan.gc.ca/pub/85-002-x/2013001/article/11854/tbl/tbl03-eng.htm.
9. Interview with Chief John Bates, March 11, 2016; Interview with Mary Ann Campbell, March 14, 2016.
10. Alan M. Dershowitz, *Reasonable Doubts: The Criminal Justice System and the O. J. Simpson Case* (New York: Touchstone, 1996), 17.
11. Josh O'Kane, "Oland investigation puts Saint John in eerie calm," *Globe and Mail*, July 21, 2011.
12. Robert Jones, "RCMP forensic delays not a problem, says Toews," CBC News New Brunswick, Aug. 21, 2012.
13. NBQB 051, Sentencing, *R v. Jason Alderich Getson*, Jan. 4, 2011.
14. Tamsin McMahon, "Son of murdered Saint John businessman hires top defence lawyer," *Financial Post*, Aug. 8, 2011.
15. Chris Morris. "Acquittal appealed Augustine may face another trial," *The Daily Gleaner*, May 22, 1999.

16. Jennifer Pritchard, "Oland Toronto lawyer 'well suited' for case," *Telegraph-Journal*, Nov. 20, 2013, A1.

17. Editorial, *Globe and Mail*, April 15, 1998; Michele Lansberg, "False Memory Label Invented by Lobby Group," *Toronto Star*, Nov. 13, 1993.

18. Clare Hoy, "A feminist highjacking of justice," *Toronto Star*, March 3, 1999.

19. John Honreich, "Star's statistical analysis hold up to scrutiny," *Toronto Star*, March 1, 2003; Greg Marquis, *The Vigilant Eye: Policing Canada from 1967 to 9/11* (Halifax: Fernwood, 2016), 219.

20. Mick Lowe, *Conspiracy of Brothers: A True Story of Murder, Bikers and the Law* (Toronto: Seal Books, 1989).

21. Betty Powell and Peter Edwards, "Angels in Court," *Toronto Star*, April 6, 2007; Tony Van Alphen, "108

22. How the RCMP botched a sting," *Toronto Star*, Dec. 23, 2007.

23. Dean Pritchard, "Former Manitoba Hell's Angels leader Dale Sweeney sentenced to 11 years in prison," *Winnipeg Sun*, April 29, 2013.

24. Affidavit of Dennis James Oland, January 12, 2016.

25. *Ibid.*

26. Sher, "The inscrutable murder of a magnate."

27. *Ibid.*

28. Jennifer Pritchett, "Sealed Oland search warrants contested," *Telegraph-Journal*, Dec. 16, 2011, A1.

29. April Cunningham, "Richard Oland murder remains shrouded in mystery six months later," *National Post*, Dec. 30, 2011.

30. Collateral mortgage, Land Titles Act, S.N.B., 1981, c.L-1.1, s. 26, 660673 N.B. Inc., 2012-02-27, Registration number 31197495.

31. Collateral mortgage, Land Titles Act, S.N.B., 1981, c.L-1.1, s. 26, Dennis James Oland and Lisa Andrik Oland, Registration number 31360879. (30) Discharge of mortgage, Land Titles Act, S.N.B., 1981, c.L-1.1, s. 26, Dennis James Oland, 2012-05-01, Registration number 31412787; Discharge of mortgage, Land Titles Act, S.N.B., 1981, c.L-1.1, s. 26, Dennis James Oland, 2012-05-23, Registration number 31494314.

32. Nicholas Köhler, "Murder and a maritime dynasty," Macleans. ca, July 28, 2011, http://www.macleans.ca/news/canada/ murder-and-a-maritime-dynasty/; Tamsin McMahon, "After years of gossip and rumours, Oland charges may finally lead to answers," *Maclean's*, Nov. 12, 2012.

33. *R v. Stillman* [1997] 1 SCR 607.

34. April Cunningham, "'We have to get it right' Probe Richard Oland homicide investigation is 'long and arduous' to ensure case is airtight: police chief," *Telegraph-Journal*, June 30, 2012, A1; CBC New Brunswick News, Aug. 16, 2012.

35. Dean Jobb, "Lifting the seal of search warrants," J Source: The Canadian Journalism Project, Oct. 22, 2006, http://www.j-source.ca/article/lifting-lid-search-warrants.

36. Affidavit, Constable Stephen Davidson, June 7, 2011, Provincial Court of New Brunswick.

37. Bobbi-Jean MacKinnon, "Richard Oland murdered, search warrants reveal," CBC New Brunswick News. Aug. 16, 2012.

38. April Cunningham, "Inside the Oland case; Crime Documents reveal police push for forensic evidence in the murder of prominent Saint John businessman," *Telegraph-Journal*, Oct. 8, 2012, A1; Chris Morris, "Forensics critical in Oland probe," *Telegraph-Journal*, Oct. 10, 2012, A1; April Cunningham, "Chief the face of Oland probe," *Telegraph-Journal*, Oct. 11, 2012, A1.

39. Jennifer Pritchett, "Chief provincial court judge retires following a 43-year career in law," *Telegraph-Journal*, Jan. 6, 2014, A3.

40. Kurt Peacock, "A Quiet Night on Canterbury Street," *Telegraph-Journal*, Oct. 6, 2012, A10.

41. Editorial, *Telegraph-Journal*, Dec. 7, 2012, A10.

CHAPTER 5

A PERSON OF INTEREST

January 2013–December 2014

I n early January 2013, Chief Bill Reid promised that an arrest would be made for Richard Oland's murder before the end of the year. He expressed confidence in his police service and stressed that prosecutors had asked investigators to tie "up loose ends" by speaking to more witnesses and waiting for "scientific reports." Although homicide in Canada is exceedingly rare, representing under 1 percent of all violent crime, media coverage and commentary was still pressuring the SJPF. The final decision on laying a charge was not the purview of the police. Lead prosecutor John Henheffer had no comment on the Oland matter but did explain the policy of vetting and providing feedback on criminal investigations. One reason that New Brunswick has one of the highest conviction rates in Canada for adult defendants (77 percent in 2011–12) is its policy of pre-charge screening (where experienced Crown prosecutors examine the evidence in each case and make a recommendation as to whether or not it should proceed to court on the basis of their sense of a successful outcome.)[1]

The SJPF continued to explain that its lack of press conferences and disclosures was standard procedure designed to ensure a successful investigation. In the community, people speculated it was the wealth and power of the family potentially involved or the inconclusive nature of the evidence that was delaying an arrest. Media scrutiny no doubt gave the case special urgency, which was not necessarily helpful for the investigation. As John Grisham's gripping non-fiction study *The Innocent Man: Murder and Injustice in a Small Town* suggests, police and prosecutors under demands to solve difficult murder investigations can produce costly mistakes.[2]

In 2016, Val Streeter, a boyhood friend of Dennis, described the period between the crime and the arrest as "a waiting game…a slow form of water torture" for a man whose main concern supposedly was protecting his family. Dennis was a "wonderful caring father" who was involved with his kids. The stress in the family, beginning in 2011, was directly affecting his children, who had also lost their grandfather.[3] In March 2013, Diana Sedlacek, who had relocated to Victoria, BC, posted the following on Facebook: "Living true to myself from my heart—2 years of breaking away—emerging into a world of possibilities." None of her ensuing posts ever referred to the Oland tragedy.

By the end of 2011, the SJPF had received only two laboratory reports from the RCMP Forensic Services Laboratory in Halifax, with nothing linking Dennis to the crime. Things began to change in 2012 when the lab, using the Profiler Plus technique, began to examine DNA deposits on Dennis Oland's seized clothing. A March 1, 2012, report indicated there was a strong statistical probability of Richard Oland's DNA being present in two spots on his son's Hugo Boss jacket. Tests of the red grocery bag, the BlackBerry, and other articles of Dennis's clothing such as shoes, a dress shirt, brown pants, and a pair of blue shorts, revealed nothing of forensic value. A report dated June 26, 2012, noted three more areas on the jacket that matched the DNA profile of the victim, but with a lower rate of probability. This report also confirmed that the blood swabs from the crime scene matched the DNA of Richard Oland and no "second bleeder." The only exception within the Far End Corporation office was a stain on a banker's box. This produced a profile labelled Male # 2, which belonged to either Robert or his son Galen McFadden. Galen's profile (Male #3) also matched a swab taken from the bathroom sink. The younger McFadden gave a voluntary DNA sample in June 2013. The October 24, 2013, report covered more of the blood samples from the Far End Corporation office as well as swabs from the victim's knuckles and palms. These revealed nothing of forensic interest. The exception was material from a swab of the sink and paper towel from the bathroom later determined to be a match with the DNA of Galen McFadden, who had been ruled out as a suspect. His profile was also found on the mouse of a computer the SJPF labelled P-11. The last two lab reports of 2012 suggested that another spot on the brown Hugo Boss jacket (on the outside back near the bottom) matched the DNA of Richard Oland. Testing of a cigarette butt supposedly seized as cast-off evidence from Dennis Oland provided no match, which suggested that the police had watched the wrong man.[4] In May, 2013, under the authority of a court order, Constable David MacDonald obtained a buccal sample (cheek swab) from Dennis Oland.[5]

Although the RCMP lab had detected that the victim's DNA was on the suspect's jacket (which allegedly he had worn on the day of the murder and which was then dry cleaned the following morning), the Crown, which approves all charges in New Brunswick, was being cautious. In November of 2012, it advised the SJPF that the investigation required more information and that certain exhibits needed additional testing before prosecutors were comfortable with proceeding. As would be revealed during the trial, the acquisition and testing of exhibits continued well after the arrest and even after the completion of the preliminary inquiry.[6]

Some insights into aspects of the investigation would only became part of the public record in 2015 (and in 2016, when the publication ban was lifted on the preliminary inquiry). At one point, the SJPF sought advice from police in British Columbia on how to manage the investigation. For example, in March 2012, Sgt. Brooker emailed Vancouver Police Department Inspector Les Yeo on the topic of investigation strategies such as employing wiretaps and undercover officers, and there was mention of a planned conference call. During the preliminary inquiry, the lead investigator was asked by Miller about any planned operations based on listening to phone conversations, monitoring text messages, and tracking credit-card use. Davidson's answer suggested that such an operation may have been considered but had not been put into effect, possibly because of the cost.[7]

Early in 2013, Const. Coughlan was tasked with obtaining a cast-off DNA sample from Scott Laskey, a pallbearer at the victim's funeral who was married to his niece Victoria Toward. Although a patrol officer, Coughlan had assisted with searches at the crime scene and at the wharf. Working alone, Coughlan monitored the subject, but attempts to acquire a sample on January 7, 8, and 14 failed. With the assistance of other officers, he managed to retrieve a cigarette used by Scott Laskey on January, 17, 2013, at Place 400 in the city's North end. In December 2012, he had followed Robert McFadden for more than a week until he finally retrieved cast-off evidence. In October 2013, the officer was tasked with monitoring Dennis Oland's routine for a week.[8]

In 2013, investigators continued, without any success, to try to track down the unidentified young Middle Eastern gentleman who had showed up at Printing Plus looking for help with a fax (and who was captured on security camera parking his car). The SJPF had contacted the Pacific Language Institute in Vancouver looking for former student Bander Jemel Khalifa. The RCMP was also involved at some level. In January 2013, a landlord in Saint John identified the individual as a UNB Saint John student who had lived in Millidgeville. This took the investigation to UNB Saint John and Saint John College (the university's language training institute). It appeared that Khalifa, who was never contacted, had returned to Saudi Arabia.

As noted in the previous chapter, in 2012 lead investigator Davidson had made over two-hundred test calls from an iPhone 4 from nearly two dozen locations around Saint John and Rothesay. In January 2013, there was another series of field tests, in this case to determine the driving time between Saint John and Rothesay. Taking different routes and encountering varied traffic conditions, Davidson made more than a dozen test drives from Canterbury Street to Renforth Wharf and Gondola Point Road. On average, the drive to the wharf took fifteen minutes and the trip from the wharf to Oland's home five minutes. Another interesting revelation from the preliminary inquiry was that sometime in 2013 the Crown had consulted with the respected veteran Moncton defence lawyer Scott Fowler to get an independent assessment of the case. This appears to be a highly unusual move in a murder prosecution in New Brunswick.[9]

Prior to an arrest being made, three more lab reports arrived. An April 13 report, based on tests of a dress shirt seized from Dennis Oland's bedroom and areas of the red shopping bag, revealed nothing incriminating. DNA profiles, for comparison purposes, had been established for William Adamson, husband of the victim's secretary, Robert McFadden, and Scott Laskey. In June came another lab report. The buccal sample from Dennis Oland matched the profile Male # 1 (found on a pillow from the master bedroom). This report also listed more results (negative) of tests on a pair of pants and shorts belonging to Dennis and of a section on the Hugo Boss jacket labelled Al, the inside left cuff. This yielded a mix sample with the minor component having a not overly strong match with Richard Oland. The final report of 2013, produced in late August, confirmed Galen as the donor of profiles in the sink, on the paper towel, and the computer mouse.[10]

The murder scene led to another legal matter in 2013, a small-claims case over who would pay for the cost of the cleanup. In order to deal with the presence of blood and other biological material, workers wore Hazmat suits. In April, Global News, which published photos of the repairs, reported that Far End Corporation had gone to court over the matter. The details were not divulged but it is probable that Far End (meaning Robert McFadden and Dennis Oland) was in dispute either with its own insurance company or that of building owner John Ainsworth. In the end, the matter was settled out of court.[11]

In April, Judge Henrik Tonning had ordered that the sealed materials for the remaining search warrants be released to the counsel of Dennis Oland, Lisa Oland, Mary Beth Watt, and the estate of Richard Oland as well as the CBC and the *Telegraph-Journal*. None of the information could be published in the interim, but the various parties could not agree on which details should be redacted. On May 17, based on an earlier ruling by Justice Grant, a new set of released documents confirmed what public gossip had long speculated: Dennis Oland was the suspect in his father's murder. The documents claimed that he had been "on the edge" financially in 2011. The police had seized more than fifty items from the suspect's home, examined his computer, and reviewed video surveillance at his place of work. Judge Jackson refused to release any "hallmark" evidence that would be known only to the perpetrator of the crime. This included information relating to the crime scene and the condition of the victim's body.[12]

In September, Jackson authorized the release, for publication, of documentation stating that Constance Oland did not believe her son capable of physically harming his father. This was not search-warrant information, but the transcripts of the July 2012 hearings where both Crown and Oland family lawyers had opposed the release of warrant-related information. David Coles, on behalf of media outlets, had reminded the court that case law dictates the police are obliged to release warrant information after the fact. John Henheffer had opposed the release on behalf of the Crown, citing the need to insulate the investigation. Bill Teed had criticized the "frenzied media" for potentially damaging the privacy of his clients, the Oland family. Miller, acting for Dennis Oland, now identified to the public as a suspect, spoke of a "poison climate" created for his client. A police investigator had argued that all warrant-related information should remain sealed and that "innocent third-party witnesses" deserved to have their privacy protected.[13]

An affidavit released to the media in September 2013 suggested that Richard and his son had a strained relationship. Richard's widow, Constance, had described the victim as having "a very strong and controlling personality," being "verbally and emotionally abusive," and that all of her children had been affected."[14] Daughter Jacqueline Walsh had opined that her father "was the type of guy that some people got along with, and some people did not" and "could be very difficult to deal with at times.[15] It was revealed that research on family history was one of the few positive points of contact between Dennis and his father. The document explained "it was the one thing they could have a conversation about and not fight." Dennis explained that as the only son he "took most of the pressure" from Richard. The report recounted that the son claimed he had sought to avoid arguments with his father. The police considered Dennis the last known person to have encountered the victim before his death, when they met at the Far End Corporation office late on the afternoon of July 6, supposedly to discuss family history.[16]

In October 2013, there was a final release of documents. Some hallmark evidence was still redacted (such as the times of Dennis's visits to the office) but Jackson unsealed all DNA test results.

These contained the dramatic allegation that DNA in bloodstains on a sports jacket seized from Dennis's residence matched that of the victim. The unsealed documents also indicated that the victim's cellphone was a key piece of evidence, but did not confirm if it was in the possession of the police. Another item police wanted kept under wraps was the grocery bag owned by the suspect. The released materials revealed that investigators contested Dennis's claim that he had worn a blue blazer when he visited his father on the day of the murder. The release also confirmed that the SJPF had security-video footage, at least one eyewitness, and proof that some of Oland's clothing had been dropped off at a dry cleaner in Rothesay. The transcript indicated that the police were not thrilled about the role of private investigators (possibly engaged by Miller), who allegedly had been contacting witnesses after they had spoken to the police. Davidson had told the court that witnesses "weren't co-operative because they were approached by private investigators." In his October 4 decision to release the 2012 hearing transcript, Judge Jackson noted that Miller had asked for all mention of private investigators to be removed from any unsealed documents as the public might make "unreasonable inferences" about his client.[17]

Another interesting revelation was witness Barbara Murray's statement about seeing a person who resembled Dennis "behaving strangely" at Renforth Wharf on the evening before the crime was discovered. Walking quickly, he allegedly had picked something off the ground and then gone to the wharf's end where he appeared to remove an object from a red bag, wrap it around whatever he had picked up, place it back in the bag, and then leave. Murray had told police: "I knew it wasn't right....There was a purpose to what he was doing, a real purpose." The October release also revealed that Dennis had told police he had stopped at the wharf in case his kids where swimming there. The documents indicated that in July 2011 divers checked the waters near the wharf for something that "would not have been in the water for a long period of time" but found nothing helpful to the investigation.[18]

Following the October revelations, the two media outlets ceased their legal efforts to have more details from search warrants released.

Their quest had added a new chapter to New Brunswick legal history. The media had been reporting that the chief motive in the crime, as identified in police documents, was financial. If Dennis was indeed the last person to see his father alive, this was potentially damaging evidence. As any number of true-crime television documentaries remind us, homicide investigators look for three factors when narrowing their list of suspects: motive, opportunity, and method. On the surface, Dennis matched at least two items on the checklist. He stood to gain financially from his father's death and had an antagonistic relationship with the victim, and he was the last known person to see his father alive. The blood evidence, if reliable, may have covered the method category, but investigators would have preferred to find the murder weapon and more trace evidence. UNB law professor Nicole O'Byrne explained that although the evidence in the Oland case by this point appeared to be largely circumstantial, this was not necessarily a weakness for a prosecutor.[19]

In a move that may have tempted fate, on November 9, Dennis changed the profile picture on his Facebook page to a bearded Harrison Ford in the 1993 movie *The Fugitive*, inspired by the 1960s television series about a doctor wrongfully convicted of killing his wife.[20] On November 10, Chief Reid told a radio station that a suspect would be apprehended before year's end. That same day, Dennis was arrested, according to the *Globe and Mail*, "near his tony Rothesay, N.B. home."[21] The arrest was far less exotic, taking place at the King's II Carwash, a self-service operation located in the Rothesay commercial strip across the street from Richard Oland's grave. The suspect supposedly was "very emotional" during the arrest. Grainy surveillance video indicated that Oland had just started washing a green SUV when a marked SJPF car, along with two unmarked vehicles, arrived and blocked his exit. Officers put Dennis's hands behind his back, placed him in handcuffs, and escorted him to one of their vehicles. A few minutes later, a Rothesay Regional Police Force cruiser showed up. The *Telegraph-Journal*, which obtained a copy of the video from the operator of the car wash, revealed that officers searched the front and back of the SUV and appeared to find nothing significant. After the search was completed, one of the officers drove the vehicle out of the car-wash bay.[22] The police chief later explained that Crown prosecutors had signed off on a murder charge three weeks earlier. Oland, according to Reid, "was brought in to have a conversation." The nature of that interview was not revealed at the preliminary inquiry or trial but is no doubt buried in a mountain of disclosure evidence. What the public did not know at this point was that the day after the murder in 2011, Dennis had been subjected to a five-hour interrogation.[23]

On Wednesday, November 12, presiding judge Marco Cloutier read the charge: Dennis was formally charged at the Saint John Law Courts with second-degree murder. The now prisoner, described as unshaven and "wearing a scruffy grey sweatshirt," did not speak in court. The Criminal Code of Canada defines second-degree murder as all other murder other than first-degree (meaning all murder not planned in advance). Typically these are "heat-of-the-moment" crimes but the Crown still has to prove the intent to kill.[24] In the ensuing months, there was occasional speculation that Oland may have been offered a deal if he plead guilty to a charge of manslaughter; there is no evidence of this. Fighting a charge of second-degree murder, according to Professor O'Byrne, is "a roll of the dice," as a guilty verdict results in a mandatory ten years in prison before parole eligibility. In an interview with the author, O'Byrne spoke of a scenario where an individual charged with killing a family member as the result of an argument would be advised by a legal-aid lawyer to accept a deal. A manslaughter conviction can result in more than ten years in prison, but a person with a clean record and positive character references could plausibly be sentenced to five years, and be subjected to early release after three.[25]

Members of Oland's family, including his wife, mother, and uncle Derek, were present when Dennis was brought to court. So were several reporters. Bill Teed sat with the family and Gary Miller represented Dennis. It is rare to see well-dressed middle-class people, a significant number of reporters, and private defence lawyers in a criminal proceeding in Saint John (or anywhere else in Canada). Neither the lawyers nor members of the family spoke directly to the media, but the family did issue written statements that week expressing their unquestioning support for Dennis, claiming that he was innocent, and vowing to trust "the judicial process." Their official statement read: "We believe our nephew and cousin Dennis is, in fact, innocent, and we will support him and his family members through the course of whatever legal actions unfold." A statement issued and signed by his mother, wife, and sisters explained: "We know Dennis is innocent. We are devastated that this nightmare for Dennis and for all of us is going to continue."[26] The statement also called on the SJPF "to turn their attention to figure out who is really responsible for Dick's death."[27]

At a news conference held a few hours prior to the court appearance, Chief Reid confirmed that the victim had died as a result of repeated blows from an object that Reid could not or would not identify. The department had been under criticism for not making a timely arrest; Reid reminded the media that in New Brunswick, police services require the approval of the Crown before proceeding with charges.[28] He also stressed the importance of forensic evidence for the case and its complex nature: "We got a little piece of evidence and that would direct us in an area. We built a case from nothing, essentially." Reid credited his "members" with doing "a fantastic job." He added that "for some reason the media was under a time constraint and we weren't." The lack of eyewitnesses meant that the case was "process driven on the forensic side."[29] Reid probably had to indulge in some gloating to protect the morale of his officers. But while it is true, as Alan Dershowitz has written, that most people charged with a crime are guilty, the prosecution in the Oland case, as things turned out, had reasons to be less optimistic.

Oland would spend a total of nine days in custody, most of them at the provincial correctional facility at Black River Road in East Saint John. Remand prisoners are usually placed with the general population but it is rumoured Oland was housed in a safer "trustee" unit. The suspects sent to this facility are generally poorly educated, low-income, mentally ill individuals charged with or guilty of probation violations, assault, drug offences, or impaired driving. Many if not most of the prisoners in the provincial system are awaiting bail, court, and sentencing appearances. Oland's bail hearing on November 18 was overseen by Justice Hugh McLellan of the Court of Queen's Bench.

Unlike with older court facilities in the province, where prisoners are driven from provincial jails and loaded into back doors in full view of media cameras, the Saint John Law Courts, which had just opened in September, were connected by tunnel to an underground lockup in the adjacent headquarters of the SJPF, which had opened in August. Prisoners on remand, usually brought to court in handcuffs and ankle shackles, are afforded some privacy in transfers.

The big surprise this day was the appearance, as part of the defence team, of Alan Gold. The presence of one of Canada's leading defence attorneys at a bail hearing in New Brunswick was a news-worthy event but it also hinted at the resources the Oland family was prepared to marshal in defence of one of their own. In addition to Miller and Gold, Dennis Oland was supported by his family, Teed, and up to fifty friends and acquaintances. The hearing, like all aspects of the Oland matter, was open to the public, but the details, including the reason for Justice McLellan's decision, were subject to a publica-tion ban. The prisoner was released on $50,000 bail, with the sur-ety provided by his uncle Derek Oland. A number of lawyers felt this was an excessively low amount. Oland was required to surrender his passport, reside at his residence in Rothesay, and report to the police any travel outside the province. Many in the community wondered why a person charged with a vicious murder could be released while those prosecuted for lesser offences (such as First Nations men pro-testing shale gas exploration in Kent County) were remanded into custody. Part of the answer is that Dennis had no criminal record.[30] Although he had been arrested and was now released, Oland, as Miller explained, was not required to enter a plea until he was in front of a jury. And for that to happen, a provincial court judge had to rule that the case would proceed to trial. In the meantime, Dennis Oland was home for Christmas.

On January 22, 2014, Judge Andrew LeMesurier scheduled the preliminary inquiry in the Oland matter for six weeks starting in May. He advised Miller and John Henheffer to submit a list of wit-nesses and questions they planned to ask. Henheffer, the lead Crown attorney, who had been admitted to the bar in 1989, was assisted by Patrick Wilbur, admitted in 1992. They would be assisted by a junior counsel, Derek Weaver, who joined the bar in 2009. The preliminary inquiry is like a trial in that evidence is introduced, police, civilian, and expert witnesses examined and cross-examined, and then a judge has to make a decision, guided by legal precedent, on a basic question: has the Crown introduced sufficient evidence to allow a jury of reasonable people to return a verdict of guilty? If the answer is yes, then the case goes to trial.

Crown attorneys like a preliminary inquiry because often it leads to a plea bargain (a common occurrence in our justice system). There are also a number of reasons why the defence likes the preliminary inquiry. First, as a result of the Supreme Court of Canada's *Stinchcombe* ruling (1991), the Crown has to disclose every document, report, transcript, physical exhibit, photograph, video recording, and computer file, and even copies of police officers' notebooks, to the defence—even material it does not intend to introduce as exhibits. The defence is not obliged to disclose anything in advance. General disclosure as well as the introduction of specific Crown exhibits and witnesses during the actual inquiry stage allows the defence to test the evidence and poke holes in the other side's case. And both sides can compare witnesses' inquiry statements of witnesses with their statements at trial in order to undermine their credibility.[31] The Crown has full discretion as to the number of witnesses it can call; the accused has the option to testify but any of that testimony can be used against them at trial.[32]

In May 2014, almost three years after Richard's death, the *R. v. Dennis James Oland* preliminary inquiry began. Although an evidence ban was in place, members of the media were present from time to time. The Canadian Press, for example, had a note taker in the courtroom for most of the summer, even though none of the details of the proceedings could be reported in traditional or social media. That did not prevent court watchers from conveying information from court to friends and family by word of mouth. Although a preliminary inquiry is important for the reasons discussed earlier, it does not form the evidentiary base of any subsequent trial. Its details are usually under a publication ban, in order to ensure a fair trial. The Oland trial judge would instruct the jury in 2015: "The fact, purpose and result of the preliminary inquiry is not something you can consider in deciding [if the Crown proves its case beyond a reasonable doubt]."[33]

The presiding judge for the preliminary inquiry, which was interspersed with a number of *voir dire* hearings (pretrial hearings on evidence), was Judge Ronald LeBlanc of Bathurst, a former Crown attorney. The exercise, which began on May 12, 2014, would continue until December 12 and consume almost forty days. The transcript of the proceedings would run to more than five-thousand pages and the judge's written ruling in December more than fifty pages. The judge's options, under the *Criminal Code*, were to discharge the accused or place him on trial if there was sufficient evidence. The key issue is whether a "reasonable" jury "properly instructed" by a trial judge *could* find the accused guilty. This threshold is much lower than what is needed to secure a conviction. The inquiry is designed to avoid needless or frivolous prosecutions and, as noted earlier, is also a forum where the accused can learn about the Crown's case. LeBlanc's job was not to try the case, but to determine if the prosecution's evidence, if believed, could be used by a jury to infer guilt. The proceedings began with the Crown laying out its case, and then proceeded to testimony from and the cross-examination of police, civilian, and expert witnesses called by the Crown, such as the pathologist, Maureen Adamson, the RCMP tech-crime specialists, and former RCMP DNA expert Joy Kearsey.

A well-dressed Dennis Oland was present each day. Constance Oland, who had patiently waited for her son at the police station on July 7, 2011, was the most faithful attendee other than Bill Teed, who presumably was being paid to sit with the family each day. Mrs. Oland is a small woman with short hair and glasses and obviously has a strong bond with her only son. The courtrooms in the new Law Courts complex are high-tech, with large video-monitor screens for the spectators and computer screens for the judge and lawyers. All testimony is video recorded and it is possible to project documents onto overhead screens. People in the witness box are able to mark on digital images such as maps and photographs and create new exhibits.

Microphones are positioned on the witness stand, the judge's bench, and at the tables where the lawyers sit. During the Oland hearings, a number of wireless headsets were available to help members of the public better hear the proceedings (these would be in short supply during the trial). Much of the evidence was in digital format, and its smooth flow was provided by Const. Rocca. BlackBerrys and laptops were put to good use by counsel.

On the second day, as journalist Chris Morris reported, when disturbing photographs of the crime scene were displayed on monitors in the courtroom, some of the family walked out and Dennis lowered his head.[34] But as the weeks proceeded, the atmosphere became fairly relaxed and the Olands and their supporters often socialized in the corridor during breaks, with coffee and treats brought in through the security checkpoint. One day, Pat Darrah, who had delivered the victim's eulogy, came to court and embraced Dennis in a show of support. This was highly symbolic of much of the Saint John business and political elite's response to the unfolding case. At times, family and friends made small talk and even cracked jokes, which may have struck some observers as a bit odd given the circumstances. Lisa, the defendant's wife, was often present and photographed by reporters outside the Law Courts. A petite woman with blonde hair, she sometimes held hands with Dennis as they walked to and from the building. Aside from taking pictures, the media was quite respectful of the family both within the courtroom and on the street outside, an approach it would continue during the trial.

For court watchers who were not legally trained, the evidence presented by the Crown, although circumstantial, initially appeared strong. Given problems of scheduling, the flow of the proceedings was somewhat choppy. And the defence subjected many of the witnesses to vigorous cross-examination, to the point where many observers felt that the Crown would have an uphill battle. At times, Miller or Gold became a bit intense but lead Crown Henheffer maintained a low-key, matter-of-fact tone. Given that there was no jury in the room, the sometimes flamboyant tactics of the defence were a bit puzzling. The defence strategy appeared to be putting the SJPF on trial by raising doubts about its professionalism and technical capabilities. Gold certainly displayed his mastery of cross-examining on forensic/scientific testimony. There was an inordinate amount of questioning about how the body of the victim was removed from the crime scene, which appeared to suggest that Gold and Miller, if the matter did proceed to trial, would possibly suggest that too many people came into contact with Oland's blood/DNA. The defence also honed in on the mystery of the building's back door and even introduced a video that it had produced to suggest an alternate escape route for the "real killer."[35]

On November 25, 2014, Henheffer used one hour to make his closing arguments, discussing motive, opportunity, and means. In his written decision (discussed below), Judge LeBlanc summed up the Crown's case as follows: (1) Dennis had opportunity to kill his father; (2) the manner of death and state of the crime scene indicated a crime of passion; (3) the DNA evidence on the jacket was incriminating and the reasonable inference was that it was derived from the victim's blood; (4) the accused had lied to the police about the jacket; (5) the taking of the jacket for dry cleaning ten hours after the completion of Oland's interrogation was potentially incriminating; (6) all text, cellphone, telephone and computer activity by the victim terminated after the arrival of his son at 52 Canterbury Street.[36]

According to journalist Julia Wright, once the preliminary inquiry had ended, Dennis supposedly celebrated with friends at a November 26 concert at Harbour Station by American rocker Bon Seger: "While Bob and the Silver Bullet Band revisited classics like *Against the Wind*, [Dennis] and his buds conspicuously rocked out—to some eyes, an odd way to cap off 37 days of court proceedings determining he'd be tried for murder. As Dennis and friends stood up in their seats, working on their night moves, saucy fellow Seger fans surreptitiously snapped pics of the local celebrity in their midst, stealth-texting photos with captions like 'OMG look who it is!'" In hindsight, Wright wrote of the special irony of Oland enjoying himself at Saint John's biggest hockey arena and concert venue given its later connection to the case.[37]

On December 12, LeBlanc made his ruling. He began by reviewing the arguments of the two sides. His summary of the arguments of the defence was: (1) the crime-of-passion theory did not limit potential attackers to the accused; (2) there was no evidence of a financial motive or of planning on behalf of Dennis; (3) Anthony Shaw and John Ainsworth had not heard any quarrelling or shouting; (4) the Crown had failed to prove ill will between Dennis and Richard, and the two appeared to be getting along well on July 6, 2011; (5) the prosecution had failed to establish the type of weapon used in the crime or whether the accused possessed such as weapon or weapons; (6) Dennis's behaviour after leaving the Far End Corporation was at odds with the conduct of a person who had just committed a brutal crime; (7) a guilty person would not keep the jacket after being told that the police would be obtaining search warrants and would not tell police about his visit to Renforth Wharf if that is where he had ditched the cellphone or murder weapon; (8) the forensic evidence was weak: there was no DNA of Dennis at the crime scene or on the victim's body and no transfer evidence on Dennis's shoes, shirt, pants, cellphone, car, or the red grocery bag; (9) there was no theory to explain why the accused would take the victim's iPhone; (10) when the cell provider pinged the phone three times on July 11, 2011, it registered as functioning but as outside the country (this is debatable, as explained elsewhere); (11) the timing of the noises heard by Shaw and Ainsworth do not match the time of Dennis's visits to his father's office.[38]

Significantly, LeBlanc wrote that the Crown had failed "to establish a reason for Dennis Oland to kill his father." The prosecution's theory that father and son had a confrontation that ended with an attack was not supported by any evidence. Indeed, this "speculative" theory of the Crown was undermined by positive evidence that the two men were enjoying a friendly conversation when last seen together. He also questioned if the pinging of the cell off the Rothesay cell tower was actual proof of the iPhone being in the area at 6:44 P.M. on July 6, 2011. He also pointed to questions raised by the evidence on "roaming error," suggesting that a jury could conclude that the victim's missing phone was not in Canada on July 9, 2011, when Dennis was. (As will be discussed later in this book, this was a possible misreading by the judge of a technical term in evidence.) [39]

The judge went in the other direction on DNA evidence, ruling that a jury could conclude that the DNA typing profiles were a match and a reasonable inference could be made that the DNA on the jacket was derived from blood. Records seized on September 10, 2012, from VIP Dry Cleaners confirmed that Lisa Oland was the customer under whose name clothing had been dropped off on July 8, 2011. Jin Hee Choi, co-owner of the operation, testified that Lisa paid for the items on Saturday, July 9, 2011, and that Dennis had waited for her in the car. The judge described the defence argument that the jacket was cleaned because of the upcoming funeral of Richard Oland to be "pure speculation" because there was no actual evidence behind the claim. LeBlanc clearly had problems with the arguments of the Crown about the significance of the dry-cleaning evidence, but his job was only to determine what a jury could infer. And on that basis, he stated that a jury could conclude that the purpose of having the jacket dry cleaned was to "destroy evidence." On the issue of the amount of blood spatter that could be expected on an attacker, LeBlanc noted that the important testimony of Sgt. Wentzell was "unchallenged." The judge opined that the lack of blood evidence on the logbook was not overly important and "there is no evidence it remained there during the entirety of Dennis Oland's visit."[40] Yet, the issue of blood also favoured the defence. Wentzell had admitted that if Dennis was the perpetrator, then one would expect to have found more blood evidence. LeBlanc also pointed out as "meaningful" the fact that a dress shirt Dennis claimed to have worn on his visit to his father's office, and which he appeared to be wearing in video-surveillance footage, contained no blood or DNA of the victim. Also, the crime scene had no evidence of a cleanup.[41]

In terms of the timeline for the evening of July 6, 2011, the judge described the evidence of Ainsworth and Shaw as a "serious setback" for the prosecution. Under cross-examination, Shaw stated that he thought he had heard the thumps from the Far End Corporation office at 8 P.M. Under re-examination by the Crown, he fixed the time as 7:30–8:00 P.M. Ainsworth testified that the pounding had been heard between 6 and 8 P.M. Despite strong cross-examination by Miller based on the fact that this differed from his initial police statement, Ainsworth refused to budge. The defence had contended that when Dennis was seen on security-camera footage on Canterbury Street at 6:12 P.M., he was not heading back to his father's office but walking to the drugstore in Brunswick Square. Changing his mind, he stopped at his car and prepared to go home. A video displayed in court had portrayed a man putting something in the rear hatch of a car, taking off his jacket, and then driving south along Canterbury. Yet at 6:21 P.M. the same silver vehicle appeared on Canterbury again, having driven up King Street past the decorative clock. The Crown contended that Oland had not in fact gone home, but returned to the area of his father's office.[42]

On December 12, 2014, Judge LeBlanc delivered his decision. The document, which remained under a publication ban until February 2016, cited a number of cases and took seventy-five minutes to read out in court. He described the prosecution as based "entirely on circumstantial evidence," yet this did not alter the test for committal. His role was not to assess the credibility of the Crown's evidence, but to examine each element of the prosecution's case. For example, it would be up to the "trier of fact" to assess the credibility of Const. Davidson who had testified that the back door had been locked when he examined it the day after the murder.[43] In his opinion, the evidence entered during the inquiry could allow a jury to conclude that the attacker had intended to kill the victim. LeBlanc found that motive behind the murder had not been "positively proven." Financial information gleaned from the testimony of Maureen Adamson and Robert McFadden failed to convince LeBlanc that the Crown had established a financial motive. The son's only direct benefit would be his fee for being made an executor and trustee for the victim's estate. The Crown's theory was that a financially desperate Dennis had gone to his father's office seeking further assistance.[44]

The Crown had argued that the 6:44 P.M. text that allegedly reached the victim's iPhone via the cellphone tower at 2524 Rothesay Road was incriminating, yet LeBlanc was less convinced. As noted above, he cited the cellphone "roaming error" evidence of July 9, 2011, as significant, as a jury could conclude that the missing cellphone was outside of Canada (when Dennis Oland was still in Rothesay). LeBlanc did note the significance of evidence that apparent computer activity ceased after Dennis arrived at the office and that the victim, who had backed up his iPhone as of 4:44 P.M. did not use it later in the day.[45]

The judge's views on the crucial July 7, 2011, interview of Dennis Oland were not flattering to the SJPF. According to investigators, Oland become a suspect because of inconsistencies in recalling where he parked and walked and because of his body language during the interview. As discussed in an earlier chapter, Davidson and especially Copeland had been pushing for a confession that evening. LeBlanc described their conclusion as "totally unjustified and indeed irrational" and was puzzled as to how an "unsubstantiated" hunch could be reasonable grounds for suspicion. In fact, Oland had been allowed to leave, as there were no grounds to detain him. Possibly speaking as a former prosecutor, LeBlanc was surprised that the police had failed to ask the suspect to voluntarily surrender the shoes and pants he admitted to having worn the previous day.[46]

Given the lack of other trace evidence, the Hugo Boss jacket was hugely important in LeBlanc's decision. Either Dennis Oland had lied about which jacket he had worn on July 6, 2011, or had been honestly mistaken. In the case of a preliminary inquiry, when more than one inference can be drawn from evidence, LeBlanc explained, the judge must favour the one supporting the prosecution. In other words, a jury could determine that Dennis has lied to cover up evidence. On the other hand, the handling of the jacket after it had been seized was far from perfect. Still, the DNA evidence from a number of locations on the jacket seemed compelling. An RCMP expert had testified, based on the legally accepted test of random-match probability, that DNA samples taken from cuttings from all six locations matched those of the victim. The sample from location AB (outside right sleeve) had a weaker DNA profile so it had been sent to a private lab, Maxxam Analytics, for retesting. The lab concluded that the victim "could not be excluded as the source of this DNA profile."[47]

The judge reminded counsel that absence of clear motive, according to case law, was not enough to prevent a court from committing a case to trial. Precedent also dictated that in cases based on circumstantial evidence, a preliminary-inquiry judge should not allow inferences and theories from the defence to "usurp the function of the jury." LeBlanc concluded that "certain unassailable facts," in combination with the rest of evidence, *could* allow a jury to find Dennis guilty of murdering his father. In other words: not mere speculation, but a conclusion based on reasonable inference. He focused on six key points in making his determination: (1) Dennis was the last person to see his father alive and was with him for some period of time; (2) the DNA typing profiles from the victim discovered on Dennis's jacket, which were reasonably inferred to come from Richard's blood, was "very probative evidence"; (3) a jury could conclude that the son lied to the police about which jacket he had worn the previous day; (4) a jury could also conclude that the dry cleaning had been an attempt to destroy forensic evidence; (5) the manner of death and the state of the crime scene could indicate a crime of passion; (6) the termination of all email, cellphone, phone, and computer activity by the victim after his son arrived at his office was potentially incriminating. On this basis, Judge LeBlanc committed Dennis Oland to stand trial for second-degree murder.[48]

As defence lawyer Gary Miller explained, the threshold for sending a case of this nature to trial was low. Yet he claimed to be surprised by the outcome: "I mean, I've been doing this 37 years and this is the first time I've ever contested a murder committal at a preliminary inquiry." Oland's family issued the following statement: "The question of who is really responsible for Dick's death haunts us. We despair at the time that has been lost and worry the perpetrator of this terrible crime may now never be found and brought to justice." One media report claimed that the family was "devastated" by the judge's decision, but the author was in the courtroom when the decision was read and detected little outward reaction to the news.[49]

It had been three years and four months since Richard Oland was butchered on the floor of his office. As the end of 2014 approached, Dennis Oland was still a free man, able to spend the Christmas holidays with his family and socialize with friends. His financial affairs were apparently in order and he and his wife, Lisa, were owners of a new business. In the fall of 2014, as the preliminary inquiry was drawing to a close, there was another development in the uptown area involving the Oland family. In October, Handworks Gallery, a venue for New Brunswick artists and craftspeople, suddenly closed. Shortly after this, the media reported that Lisa Oland, described as "a veteran retailer," and Leslie Oland, the wife of Dennis's cousin Andrew, head of Moosehead Breweries and an experienced operations manager, were re-opening the gallery as the new owners. In another example of the complex connections between the Olands and the community, Lisa became vice-president of the New Brunswick Crafts Council. Since 2011, Dennis had travelled outside of Canada, purchased a new yacht, and enjoyed boating and socializing in the summers on the Kennebecasis River with family and friends. Where would he be on December 25, 2015?

NOTES: CHAPTER 5

1. April Cunningham, "Cops tying up 'loose ends' in Oland case," *Telegraph-Journal*, Jan. 9, 2013, C1; Statistics Canada, Adult criminal court statistics in Canada, 2011/2012, http://www. statcan.gc.ca/pub/85-002-x/2013001/article/11804-eng.htm.

2. John Grisham, *An Innocent Man: Murder and Injustice in a Small Town*, New York: Doubleday, 2010. Kindle Edition.

3. Val Streeter to Justice John Walsh, Jan. 8, 2016.

4. *R. v. Dennis James Oland,* 2015-11-24, Oland Laboratory Test Results.

5. Testimony of David MacDonald, Nov. 2, 2015.

6. Stephen Kimber, "Spilled secrets: The Richard Oland murder mystery." *Atlantic Business*, Dec. 19, 2013.

7. *R. v. Dennis James Oland,* Preliminary inquiry, Sept. 3, 2014.

8. Testimony of Shawn Coughlan, Oct. 28, 2015.

9. Testimony of Stephen Davidson, Oct. 23, 2015.

10. *R. v. Dennis James Oland,* 2015-11-24 Oland Laboratory Test Results.

11. Paul McLaughlin, "Photos offer glimpse into office where Richard Oland was murdered," Global News, April 26, 2013, http://globalnews.ca/news/513633/photos-offer-glimpse-into-office-where-richard-oland-was-murdered/.

12. CP, "Son named as suspect in murder of New Brunswick businessman Richard Oland: court documents," *National Post*, May 17, 2013; Bobbi-Jean MacKinnon, "New evidence in Richard Oland murder, documents reveal," CBC News New Brunswick, July 26, 2013.

13. Bobbi-Jean MacKinnon, "'Enough is enough,' Oland lawyers argue," CBC News New Brunswick, Sept. 7, 2013.

14. Kevin Bissett, "Richard Oland, son would get into 'big fights,' document says," CTV Atlantic, Sept. 6, 2013.

15. Bobbi-Jean MacKinnon, "Documents shed new light on the Oland murder investigation," CBC News New Brunswick, Sept, 6, 2013.

16. Chris Morris, "Inside the Oland investigation," *Telegraph-Journal*, Sept. 14, 2013, A1

17. Saint John Police Force vs. The Canadian Broadcasting Corporation et. al, NBPC, Oct. 25, 2013.

18. MacKinnon, "Documents shed new light."

19. Chris Morris, "Complex case revealed in Oland documents," *Telegraph-Journal*, Oct. 28, 2013, A1.

20. The series was inspired by the real story of Dr. Sam Sheppard, an Ohio resident who was freed from prison through a second trial twelve years after being convicted of murdering his wife.

21. Jane Taber, "Dennis Oland charged with second-degree murder in father's death," *Globe and Mail*, Nov. 13, 2013.

22. Bruce Bartlett, "Murder suspect sent back to jail," *Telegraph-Journal*, April 15, 2014, C1.

23. April Cunningham, "Police chief remained confident during investigation," *Telegraph-Journal*, Nov. 14, 2013, B4. Parts of the news conference can be viewed online.

24. Taber, "Dennis Oland charged."

25. Interview with Nicole O'Byrne, March 9, 2016.

26. Taber, "Dennis Oland charged."

27. *Ibid.*; Chris Morris, "Olands burdened by dark turn in family saga," *Daily Gleaner*, Nov. 16, 2013, A9.

28. Taber, "Dennis Oland charged."

29. April Cunningham, "Police chief remained confident during investigation."

30. Jennifer Pritchard, "Oland hearing adjourned until year later," *Telegraph-Journal*, Nov. 30, 2013, C1.

31. Interview with Nicole O'Byrne, March 9, 2016.

32. Interview with David Lutz, March 8, 2016.

33. *R. v. Dennis James Oland*, proceedings, Nov. 2, 2015.

34. Chris Morris, "Oland preliminary hearing completes second day," *Telegraph-Journal*, May 15, 2014, C1.

35. These observations are based on the author's attendance at most of the preliminary inquiry.

36. *R. v. Dennis James Oland*, Province of New Brunswick Saint John provincial Court, *Her Majesty the Queen v. Dennis Oland*, Ruling

following a preliminary inquiry by the Honourable Ronald LeBlanc, judge of the Provincial Court, in Saint John, New Brunswick, Dec. 14, 2014.

37. Julia Wright, "Blood, Beer, and the Maritime Rumour Mill: The Dennis Oland Murder Trial," *Vice Canada*, Nov. 30, 2015.

38. Ruling following a preliminary inquiry by the Honourable Ronald LeBlanc.

39. *Ibid.*

40. *Ibid.*

41. *Ibid.*

42. *Ibid.*

43. *Ibid.*

44. *Ibid.*

45. *Ibid.*

46. *Ibid.*

47. *Ibid.*

48. *Ibid.*

49. CP, "Dennis Oland to stand trial on second-degree murder charge in father's death," *National Post*, Dec. 12, 2014.

CHAPTER 6

A DEFENCE COUNSEL'S DREAM?

March 1–October 1, 2015

The Oland trial was perhaps the most closely watched and extensively reported court contest in New Brunswick history. In part, this was due to the popularity of live tweeting from the courtroom, which had only been permitted in New Brunswick as of 2012. It would involve the largest jury call in the province's history, sit for sixty-five days over a period of nearly four months, and hear from dozens of witnesses, including nine expert witnesses. But before this, both the Crown and the defence requested a series of *voir dire* hearings to rule on the admissibility of evidence. The details of the hearings, and the judge's rulings, were under a publication ban until after the trial. The Crown wanted to enter new evidence relating to cellphones. The defence sought rulings on the legality of search warrants and their execution. As many legal observers had predicted, the defence attempted to have Dennis Oland's brown jacket and associated forensic evidence excluded from the trial, knowing full well, as the Crown admitted, that without this single piece of evidence the prosecution would collapse. The judge assigned to the trial was John (Jack) Walsh, who in the early 1990s had been one of the prosecutors of multiple murderer Allan Legere. Although not the senior Crown during that prosecution, he held the important job of presenting a new type of evidence, DNA, to the jury. Walsh had sparred with Legere's defence over the suggestion that there was "inbreeding" in the Miramichi region. Despite Walsh's down-home expressions, he is considered by colleagues to possess one the sharpest legal minds in the province.[1]

At the end of April 2015, Chief Reid retired after thirty-seven years with the SJPF. He continued to defend the handling of the Oland case, noting that every police service was criticized at some point, and described the prosecutors in the case as "very competent people." He admitted that lessons had been learned from the investigation and would be corrected in the future.[2] For several months (including during the first two months of the Oland trial) the acting chief was Deputy Chief Glen McCloskey. During this period, and for the duration of the trial and beyond, the department (and especially McCloskey) would be the subject of considerable controversy, all related to the Oland matter.

In the community, aside from the usual rumour mills and social media posts, things were fairly quiet as the media could not even report on the topics of the pretrial hearings that took place in the spring and summer of 2015. As would be revealed at trial, the investigation continued into that year, with Const. Coughlan being tasked with obtaining a cast-off DNA sample from Derek Oland, brother of the victim. In late May 2015, a lab report, based on the newer and more sensitive Identifier Plus process, confirmed that the DNA on locations AA, AC, and AO on the brown Hugo Boss jacket matched that of the victim. A few weeks later, the last report in the series provided a DNA profile of Derek, for comparative purposes, based on the cast-off sample.[3]

In early February, the two sides met in court for motions day, where they discussed with the judge scheduling and logistical issues such as the date when the transcripts of the preliminary inquiry would be completed as well as motions to be argued about evidence in advance of the trial. The size of the jury pool was also discussed, with Walsh speculating that at least fifteen hundred would have to be summoned.[4] He later consulted with Sheriff George Oram who advised an additional five hundred to a thousand. To date, the biggest jury call in the province had been two thousand (the Grand Manan Five case of 2006). The judge speculated that jury selection could be slowed down by "challenges for cause" by the two sides in the case. Walsh asked counsel for advice on the vetting questions to be put to potential jurors. One issue that was not settled on March 30 was where Oland would sit in court. Miller requested that he be permitted to sit at the rear table for the defence, with one of his lawyers.[5] In the end, Oland sat as his own table next to the prisoner's box, close to the defence tables.

The pretrial hearings, the topics and contents of which could not be reported in the media, began in May and would extend over the summer. Oland was present each day. The discussion was highly technical, with both sides producing briefs and making oral arguments. The defence made many negative comments about the SJPF, accusing it of conducting an investigation based on tunnel vision, drafting erroneous and misleading ITOs, and failing to legally execute search warrants. It was also quite disdainful of the Crown's arguments. Much was riding on these hearings, as they would determine exactly what evidence a jury would see. Judges at this level are always conscious of the chance of appeals down the road. Each major issue was addressed by Justice Walsh in a written decision that cited case law.

Between late March and early September, Walsh made several rulings on the admissibility of evidence, the details of which were made public after the trial. At a March 30, 2015, *voir dire*, the Crown requested the release of two items entered as exhibits at the preliminary inquiry: forensic DNA extracts from the jacket, for retesting by a more powerful typing method. The Crown also announced that it wanted the RCMP to test two other extracts from the jacket and a blood sample from the victim and a buccal (cheek) swab from the accused (the latter had been acquired via DNA warrant and had not been entered at the preliminary inquiry). The reason being, the RCMP in August 2014 began to employ Identifier Plus, a more exact and powerful DNA amplification kit. The defence argued that Section 605 of the *Criminal Code* required the prosecution to have a court authorize the testing of all six items.[6]

The defence argued that the post-seizure testing of the jacket violated the defendant's Charter rights as an unreasonable search and seizure. It had been seized under the warrant issued by Judge William McCarroll on July 13, 2011, which expired on November 2, 2011. The defence argued that, given that Justice Walsh would be ruling on a Charter challenge on the testing of the jacket, it was best to wait until that bigger issue was decided. Rather than delay proceedings, and recognizing the upcoming Charter challenge as well as another complex *voir dire*, Walsh decided to grant the Crown its request. The tests, he wrote, had the potential of "contributing reliably probative evidence bearing on a critical issue in the case, namely identity."[7]

In June, there were two important rulings: one that favoured the Crown and another that favoured the defence. The defence claimed that the ITO drafted to obtain judicial authorization to search Oland's residence, and search specifically for a brown jacket, had been flawed. Secondly, it repeated the argument that no warrant authorized sending the jacket outside of Saint John for forensic testing. Walsh agreed that sections of the ITO had been misleading and poorly worded, but defended the legal acumen of his provincial court colleague who had issued the warrant. In response to Gold's assertion that the Charter rights of the accused had been violated with the testing of the jacket, Walsh cited common law practice. He concluded that the "house warrant" was sufficient authority for allowing the testing of the jacket, despite the lapse of a "general warrant," and that Section 8 of the Charter had not been violated.[8] The second ruling was detrimental to the Crown and especially the SJPF. Under the cover of a warrant, the police had approached CIBC Wood Gundy for access to Oland's workplace computer files. At the time, investigators had not known that there were personal files on the business's "H" or public drive, which were forwarded to the SJPF in the fall of 2011. The Crown now wanted to enter new evidence: pay stubs and two letters from Dennis to his father in 2003. Walsh, pointing out that the material had been seized after the expiration of the warrant and violated the search and seizure provisions of the Charter of Rights, refused.[9]

On July 29, 2015, Walsh decided on another important question of evidence admissibility. In order to establish that both the victim's iPhone and the accused's BlackBerry were in Rothesay after 6:30 P.M. on July 6, the Crown sought to have call-detail records (CDRs) entered into evidence at trial. CDRs include the first and last cell towers with which a cellphone connects "for each outgoing or incoming call/text message." The coverage areas for the two devices

Richard Oland in a happy moment in February 2011, a few months before he was murdered, wearing his Royal Kennebecasis Yacht Club blazer.
Sail Canada

Fifty-two Canterbury Street. Printing Plus is shown in front-centre, and the entrance to the Far End Corporation is on the far left.
Kâté Braydon

52 CANTERBURY STREET, 2ND FLOOR

ADJACENT OFFICE

WASHROOM   ELEVATOR

EXIT TO ALLEYWAY

FAR END CORPORATION

ENTRANCE FROM STAIRS

Panoramic shot of the lobby outside Far End Corporation, including rear-exit door (left).
Court Office Photos

The victim's desk the day after the murder.
Court Office Photos

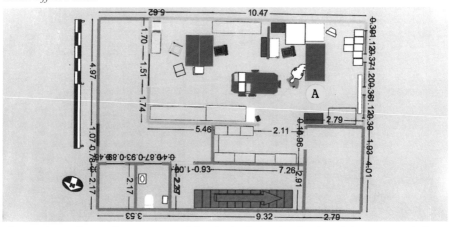

Floor plan of murder scene, with victim's body depicted in upper right.
Court Office Photos

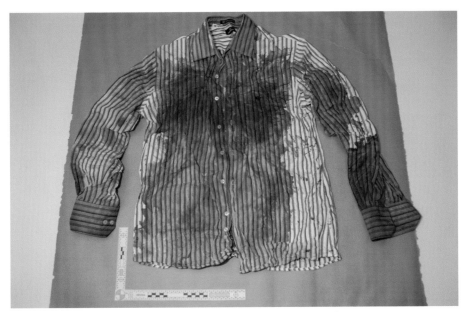

The victim's blood-soaked shirt, which was covered by a sweater.
Court Office Photos

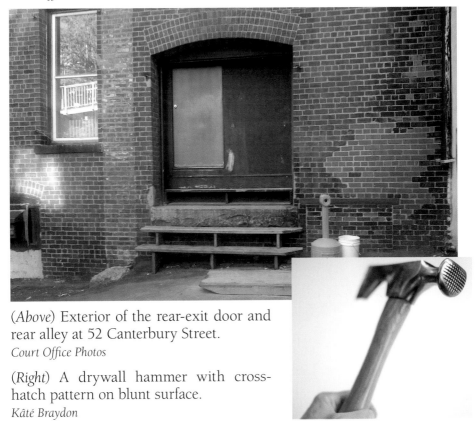

(*Above*) Exterior of the rear-exit door and rear alley at 52 Canterbury Street.
Court Office Photos

(*Right*) A drywall hammer with cross-hatch pattern on blunt surface.
Kâté Braydon

Dennis Oland approaching the Saint John Law Courts during the trial.
Kâté Braydon

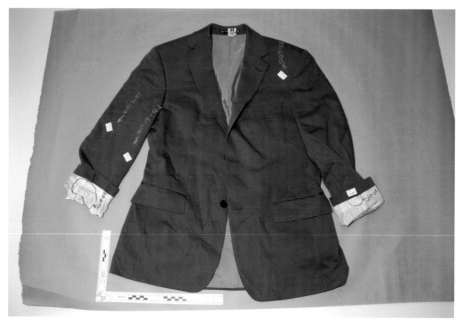

The trial's key exhibit: Dennis Oland's Hugo Boss sports coat.
Court Office Photos

The home of Dennis and Lisa Oland, 58 Gondola Point Road, Rothesay.
Kâté Braydon

Diana Sedlacek, left, leaving the Saint John Law Courts after testifying on Tuesday, November 10, 2015.
Canadian Press, photographer Andrew Vaughan

Defence lawyers (L–R) Garry Miller, QC, Alan Gold, James MConnell, and William (Bill) Teed, QC.

Kâté Braydon

Crown attorneys (L–R) Paul (P. J.) Veniot, QC, Derek Weaver, and Patrick Wilbur.

Kâté Braydon

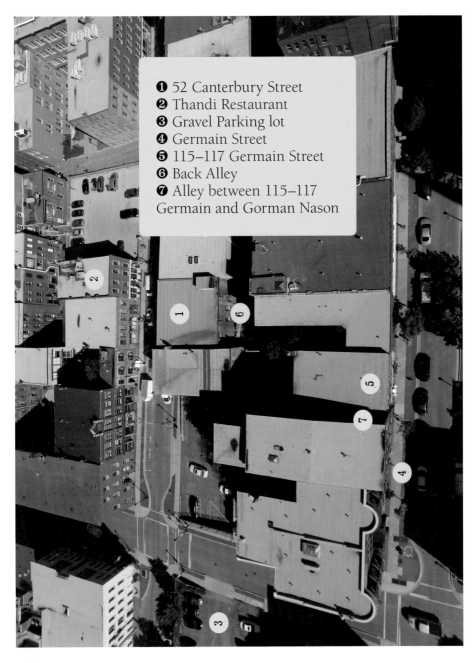

Overhead view of the area surrounding the crime scene, including the rear alley.

Jim Turnbull

Artist's rendering of the jury in Dennis Oland's murder trial.
Carol Taylor

Artist's rendering of Justice John (Jack) Walsh during Oland trial.
Carol Taylor

were determined by "propagation maps" of area cell towers, to be explained by radio-frequency engineers. This is a relatively new area of law; as Walsh noted in his decision, the provincial Court of Appeal had yet to rule on any cases relating to cellphone location. Following cross-examination of the deponents of supporting affidavits, the Crown withdrew its application in reference to the CDRs and the two sides proceeded with argument on the admissibility of the evidence of the engineers. The key issue was the significance of the 6:44 P.M. text from Diana Sedlacek to the victim's phone. The defence objected to the accuracy of the propagation maps and radio-frequency engineer Joseph Sadoun's ability to advise the court on the location of the iPhone based on a lone text message. It also argued that the location of the missing phone was not important, given there was no evidence that Richard Oland did not leave his office at some point before his death. The Crown's evidence, if admitted, could convince a jury either that the victim had been in the range of the Fairvale tower in Rothesay (which was eleven kilometres from Oland's office) and had not responded to Sedlacek's text, or that he was not in Rothesay at 6:44 P.M. but his phone was. The propagation maps depicted not exact coverage but a "predicted region" where each site would "offer the best service" according to Sadoun and were prepared by the use of software. The judge also had to rule on the admissibility of the cellphone field tests made by the SJPF in Rothesay and Saint John in 2012. In the end, he agreed to accept Sadoun as an expert witness, but limited what could be asked of him by the Crown. The cellphone field tests were also admitted.[10]

The fourth *voir dire* on evidence was held in August with a ruling of September 2, 2015. The issue was the admissibility of cellphone evidence, in particular cell-tower information, for the phones of Richard and Dennis Oland. The defence consented to the records of Diana Sedlacek but opposed admission of the other CDRs. In the wake of the third ruling, the defence was now opposing admission of its client's Telus records on the basis of the court's refusal to allow radio-frequency engineering reports on the locations of Dennis Oland's cellphone. For the judge the big issue was the admissibility of cell-tower information on the victim's phone as contained in the Rogers CDRs. During the preliminary inquiry, Rogers Communications investigator Sylvie Gill had explained that cell-tower information was collected for the purposes of billing and resolving customer complaints. The defence opposed the admission of cellphone-related evidence in electronic format, but Walsh ruled that they were business records recognized in law. The judge admitted the Rogers CDRs for the victim's phone but awaited further submissions on the Telus CDRs for the accused.[11]

The Crown obviously wanted a jury to see the Telus CDRs and propagation map for Dennis Oland's BlackBerry relative to his movements after he left uptown on July 6, 2011. Given that Oland's statement to the police as to his whereabouts would be admitted by consent, and there was evidence of his 6:12 P.M. text to his sister and the 6:36 P.M. call from his wife, the judge on September 10 ruled that the CDR records would be admitted minus the cell-tower information.[12] On the same day, he ruled on a defence bid to exclude a May 31, 2011, text message and two June 1, 2011, email exchanges between Dennis and Lisa, on the grounds of spousal privilege. This is the old common-law rule (no longer observed in England) that a person cannot be compelled to testify against a spouse. This information, seized from the defendant's cellphone and work computer, was useful for the Crown's theory of financial difficulty. Walsh noted that the *Criminal Code* protected direct evidence and wiretap intercepts, but that the trend was away from spousal privilege. This evidence was admitted.[13]

Based on pretrial discussions with counsel, it was eventually decided to issue a call for five-thousand jurors, the largest in Canadian history to that date. Despite this, the judge later expressed the fear that sheriff deputies might have to hit the streets and conscript prospective jurors on the spot. He saw the main challenges of finding a jury to be the expected length of the trial and the extensive pretrial media exposure. Prospective jurors are chosen at random from the provincial voters' list. In New Brunswick, they have to be at least nineteen years of age and under seventy. Lawyers and police officers and their spouses, clergy, veterinarians, doctors, dentists, firefighters, and those convicted of criminal offences are automatically excluded. Prospective jurors are mailed a summons from the sheriff and have only a few days to mail or deliver it back. Refusal to show up for jury selection is a serious offence and can result in a fine of up to $1,000. Jurors are paid $20 for a half day and double that for a full day for the first nine days. After that, the fee is doubled.

Over the years, Saint John's Harbour Station has hosted the Saint John Flames (a National Hockey League farm team) and performers such as Bob Dylan, Drake, David Copperfield, and Taylor Swift. On September 8, 2015, it served as a giant courtroom where Dennis Oland entered a plea and the jury-selection process began. Although nearly four-thousand people were granted exemptions by the sheriff, more than one thousand, some of them in wheelchairs, were present. They were drawn from Saint John and King's Counties, which combined contain only one-hundred-and-forty-thousand people of all ages. The defendant, standing on the floor of the arena, was formally arraigned in front of the large crowd. Using a microphone and speaking in court for the first time, Oland entered his plea: "Not guilty." Less than a year ago, he and his friends had enjoyed themselves at a rock concert in this very complex.

The prospective jurors were organized into eight groups, each assigned a time for showing up at the Saint John Law Courts. Before this, Justice Walsh explained the reasons why certain people may not be able to serve, such as knowing a party to the case. He asked people to be patient and explained that the jury was the corner-stone of democracy. On the following day, one-hundred-and-thirty prospective jurors were rejected by the judge, counsel, or two triers (members of the jury pool who assist with the vetting process). The reasons for the objections could not be revealed by the media. In the case of second-degree murder, each side has a number of peremptory challenges (where a juror can be rejected without a specific reason being stated). One veteran defence lawyer describes jury selection in Canada as more of an art than a science. In recent decades, the only information lawyers receive on the jury pool are names, addresses, and occupations. There is not much talking during this process, and a lawyer usually has a minute or less to challenge a prospective juror.

There is a provision to "challenge for cause" (when one of the two sides formally asks a judge to exclude a prospective juror based on a demonstrated lack of impartiality) but the incidence of this is extremely rare. Once a juror is accepted, they are sworn in.[14]

The jury was in place by September 10, 2015, a few days ahead of schedule. Twelve people were chosen and sworn in on the ninth and four more on the tenth. In the end, the jury consisted of nine men and seven women. Two were selected as spares given the length of the trial, the possibility of sickness, and other matters that might arise. Justice Walsh thanked everyone for their patience and especially Sheriff Oram and the court staff for running so smooth an operation. The people selected for this crucial civic duty faced not only a lengthy period away from their jobs, but also legal penalties if they deviated from the rules. They were compelled not to discuss the case, their deliberations, or the reasons behind their verdict. The penalty for divulging information is up to six months in jail and a fine of up to $5,000.[15] On top of this, as they may have sensed at the time, they were members of what would be the most scrutinized jury in New Brunswick history and would be exposed to graphic evidence that could induce psychological harm.[16]

On September 16, 2015, four years, two months, and two weeks after the murder of Richard Oland, the trial of Dennis Oland began. Despite the introduction of technology such as computers, interactive software, and wireless headphones for jurors and spectators, the modern courtroom retains many of the anachronisms of Canada's British legal system. Judges in provincial court wear robes and are addressed as "Your Honour." Walsh, as a judge of the Queen's Bench, was addressed as "My Lord." When a judge enters or leaves the room, counsel, witnesses, and spectators stand, and some even bow their heads. The jury is accorded the same respect. New Brunswick courts are traditional in another manner: photo and television cameras are banned.

Justice Walsh began by explaining to the jury its role and the rules of the court. Aside from reporters, family members and friends, and court watchers, there were few members of the public in attendance. One irritating logistical issue was the constant lack of wireless headphones that allow listeners (including jurors) to hear what is spoken by the judge, the lawyers, and witnesses. Walsh told the jury members that they would be the triers of fact and should avoid media coverage and third-party opinions, and maintain an open mind through the proceedings. "Crown counsel has the job of proving the charge," he explained, and defence does not have to prove anything. The key question in this case was: did Dennis cause Richard's death? He advised the jury that if, after hearing all the evidence, they did not believe the defendant was guilty beyond a reasonable doubt, he must be found not guilty. Even if they felt that Oland was "likely guilty," they would have acquit the defendant.

The judge warned members of the jury not to talk about the trial, evidence, or witnesses with anyone other than fellow jury members when deliberating and to avoid all radio, television, newspaper, and magazine reports of the case, and all social media messages and reports. This is a standard warning in jury trials, but in this case, with its heavy media coverage, the message was even more important. They also were not to speak about the trial to their families, neighbours, and friends. In an increasingly networked society, where even preschoolers have iPads, following these instructions would be a major test of will-power and judgment. Walsh also explained to the jury that nothing a lawyer says in court can be considered evidence.

There was no publication ban for the most part on evidence entered at trial, but the ban remained on the preliminary inquiry, Justice LeBlanc's written decision to send the matter to trial, and pre-trial rulings on evidence by Justice Walsh. In addition, when legal points were raised by any of the lawyers during the trial, the jury would be excluded and any discussion among the lawyers and judge of these points was under the ban. The much-anticipated trial began with intensive media coverage both inside and outside the court-room, with six cameras set up near the steps of the justice complex. Reporters from the CBC, the Canadian Press, Global, CTV, and the *Telegraph-Journal* were usually in attendance. From time to time the *National Post*, the *Globe and Mail*, and *Maclean's* also had journalists present. The outside media tried to interpret the trial—and Saint John—for a national audience, suggesting for example that the Oland family was "resented for its wealth" and that "virtually everyone in

Saint John has an Oland connection."[17] Christie Blatchford of the *National Post* wrote that the case "will be rich with scandalous detail about the rip-roaring dysfunction within one of this province's most famous families."[18] The CBC usually had two reporters in the courtroom, both posting tweets and other updates, plus a cameraperson outside (no photography or video recording is allowed within the court building). The print media, CTV, and Global reporters, and Laura Lyall, a reporter for local radio station CHSJ, had to do double duty, taking notes, posting online, and taking video and still photography as lawyers, witnesses, and Oland family members exited and entered the building, plus filing stories. The media was under the gun to file interesting and dramatic content, and the Oland matter, partly because of the prominence of the parties involved, the many unknowns, and the revelations of infidelity, did not disappoint. On the other hand, much of even a high-profile criminal trial is routine.[19]

Dennis Oland walked in and out of court a free man, always smartly dressed in a suit or jacket and tie. Small of stature and with boyish looks despite being in his forties, he continued the pattern of socializing and drinking coffee during breaks with the family members and friends who often formed the bulk of the spectators. And in bad weather, Oland, who would describe his sartorial tastes as old-fashioned, sometimes resembled a much older man, with a topcoat, cloth cap, and full-sized umbrella.

In early August, the media learned that Henheffer, for health reasons, had stepped down as lead prosecutor. He was replaced by Paul (P. J.) Veniot, formerly the senior Crown prosecutor for northern New Brunswick, who was brought back from retirement to head up the team. Admitted to the bar in 1981, he had been made a Queen's Counsel in 2006. In 2014, Veniot had been one of the prosecutors of Justin Bourque, accused of murdering three RCMP officers and wounding two others in Moncton. Bourque pleaded guilty, and in 2015 made Canadian legal history by being sentenced to three consecutive life sentences (seventy-five years) before being eligible for parole. The official theory of the role of the Crown prosecutor, according to court decisions and the Canadian Bar Association, is not to secure a conviction, but to fairly place before the court (either jury or judge) all relevant evidence connected to an alleged crime. Crown prosecutors are expected to be restrained, dignified, and moderate, and during the Oland trial, Veniot was almost a textbook example of this approach.[20]

Veniot's opening address to the jury, despite its serious content and implications, was delivered in a fairly straightforward and non-emotional manner. He spoke of the victim's difficult personality and high expectations of, and tight-fisted approach towards, his own family as contributing factors behind the murder. The jury was told that Richard, one of the wealthiest men in New Brunswick, and who was planning to buy a new multi-million-dollar sailboat, allotted his wife of more than forty years a monthly allowance of roughly $2,000 (if she provided receipts). This and other evidence as to the character and behaviour of Richard certainly put a new gloss on the image of "Team Oland." Veniot described Dennis as belonging to a family where "you were not given things." He continued: "as time went by.... the relationship between Richard Oland and the accused...evolved into one more like a client and a banker rather than father and son." The senior prosecutor spoke of Richard's extramarital affair, of which Dennis did not approve. In describing the crime scene, Veniot noted that there was no sign of a break-in and nothing was reported as missing except the victim's iPhone.[21]

Veniot stated that the Crown would prove Dennis was the last known person to see the victim alive and was in dire financial circumstances: "The accused, we submit, was a man living behind his financial means." Veniot pointed out the bounced postdated cheque which Dennis had written as part of his deal with his father. The court would hear that on the day of the murder, the accused's main bank account had less that $300; the next day it was more than $600 in overdraft. His other debts included more than $30,000 on a credit card (in overdraft) and nearly $164,000 on a line of credit. His investment account had been depleted in March and his RRSP had only $20.13. In terms of regular expenses, he owed his ex-wife $4,300 in monthly alimony and child support and his father $1,666 in monthly interest. These commitments alone amounted to roughly $68,000 a year. At the time of the murder, Lisa, who was not working, was allegedly $90,000 to $120,000 in debt. The senior Crown also relayed to the jury that Dennis had told police he was wearing a navy jacket on the day of the murder, but security-video footage showed him in a brown blazer: "On that jacket, four areas of blood were found. DNA scientists will testify that at each of those locations, a DNA profile was found—it matched that of Richard Oland."[22] Veniot concluded: "We submit that the manner and cause of death point to an act committed by a perpetrator who, in a rage, intended to kill Richard Oland. But not in a simple, senseless act of one, two, or three strikes to the head—Richard Oland suffered no less than forty blows. The perpetrator continued way beyond what was required to cause death. We submit that Richard Oland, whatever faults and shortcomings he had, did not deserve to die in such a gruesome manner."[23]

Many who heard the Crown's opening were immediately convinced that the defence would have an uphill battle. But the handful of people in the room who had attended the lengthy preliminary inquiry in 2014 sensed that the situation was actually reversed. According to the legal procedure, this was supposed to be the case anyway. Nothing Veniot had yet said was a "fact." In addition to the key challenge of convincing a jury that Oland was guilty beyond a reasonable doubt, the prosecution was hampered by the lack of a murder weapon or witnesses to the actual attack, major gaps in its forensic evidence, an impressionistic theory of motive, and a possibly inadequate police investigation. And then there was what many had referred to as Oland's legal "dream team" of Gold and Miller, two veterans knowledgeable in the law and well versed in courtroom tactics. With a circumstantial case based in part on forensic science, Gold's track record seemed a particularly good fit. And the defence, through disclosure, had all of the documents, reports, photos, videos, and other materials on which the Crown had built its case.[24]

Christie Blatchford was the first to raise what other media people were already wondering about: were exhibits being entered into evidence going to be made available to reporters? During a break in the proceedings, she broached the issue to one of the lawyers and soon it was taken up by the judge, who apologized for not dealing with it before the formalities began. He announced that exhibits would be released to the media at the end of each day, although later there was a discussion of whether this would exclude disturbing photographs of the crime scene. The feeling seemed to be that media outlets would exercise caution and not publish or post online images that would offend the community. Many of them released photos, videos, and even documents, which ended up on media websites where they can be viewed to this day.

With the completion of the Crown's opening address, the direct examination of its witnesses began. The goal of this process is to have evidence entered into the record and to paint a "mental picture" of the case for the jury.[25] The first witness, who would be on the stand for almost three days, was Maureen Adamson; she explained that she had worked with the victim since the 1980s, starting with Brookville Transport. Adamson was an important witness and her testimony deserves special attention. She was the second-last known person to see the victim alive, was aware of both his family and mistress, knew his daily habits, and had an intimate knowledge of the office. She also had discovered the body. Adamson had a responsible position, worked long days, and often took work home. In fact, she continued working with Far End Corporation after the murder but retired in 2014. This meant that she had actually worked with the accused, Dennis Oland, in the very office where the Crown believed he had murdered his father. The hearsay rule of evidence prevented the prosecution from asking Adamson if Dennis ever discussed his father's death after the fact (although Veniot attempted to do so before meeting an objection from Gold). At any rate, she testified that she had not even spoken of the events of July 2011 to her husband. In addition to assisting Oland with his investment and real-estate pursuits, she was involved in planning skiing and yachting trips (and trips with his mistress) as well as tasks relating to his new sailboat. Adamson was also aware of the monthly interest payments from Dennis to his father made by postdated cheques.[26]

In his examination of Adamson, Veniot started by revealing her early morning office routines on July 6, 2011, such as turning on the air conditioner, and the specifics of that day, such as the insurance meeting with Gordon Graham and Barry Prosser. Her testimony also served to give the jury the basic layout of the office. There was an empty suite next to Far End Corporation where remodelling work was being done; she was not familiar with the third floor where rock bands practised at night. The court heard that Adamson had no key to the back door, but that it was open from time to time and that she always checked to ensure it was locked at the end of the day. On July 6, as she was preparing to go home, her boss advised her to leave the air conditioner running as he planned to keep working for a while. That afternoon she prepared a memo regarding the recent meeting on the cathedral-restoration project, looked into upcoming yacht races, and prepared a memo to owners of boats of a similar class as *Vela Veloce*. She testified that Dennis appeared, apparently without prior notice, around 5:30 P.M. Adamson had no memory of him carrying a bag or books but recalled that he was wearing, on a hot day, a brown sports coat. They had a brief chat about his daughter's basketball tournament in Newfoundland and she asked him to take the camp log and CDs home to his mother. Richard had seemed happy to see his son, and when Adamson left they were absorbed in a discussion of family history. Her last memory was of Dennis standing over his father who sat at his desk, looking at documents. When she departed at c. 5:45 P.M. to meet her husband who was parked on the street below, she did not lock the outer door as this was customarily the responsibility of the last person to leave for the day.

Adamson next recounted the following morning, when Oland's body was discovered. She explained that the street-level door, the door at the top of the stairs, and the door to the office all had locks, with different keys. Arriving just before 9:00 A.M., she was surprised that the second door was not quite closed. When she reached the third door, which connected the foyer to the inner office, it was closed but she was not sure if it was locked, having automatically placed her key in the lock. When she entered the office, she encountered "a terrifically vile odour" and put the coffee and papers she carried on a desk. Then she saw "two legs protruding on the floor" from under Oland's desk and "panicked." Beside the body was an overturned wastebasket. She recalled hurrying to Printing Plus for help, going back to the office with Preston Chiasson and then waiting for and speaking to the police. She also called Robert McFadden and, without providing details, told him to come directly to Printing Plus.

The witness was asked more specific questions about the victim, his financial arrangement with the accused, and (with the aid of photos displayed on screens) specific items in the office. She explained that her boss was a "techie" and tended to update his iPhone late each afternoon by connecting it to his computer. Adamson testified that Oland did not leave the office that day when she was present and that it was not his habit to drink alcohol at work. Many of the objects in the images displayed in court were stained with blood droplets. The items displayed or discussed included a Canon camera, a printed investment report on the victim's desk, and an empty pizza box. Another item on the desk was a publication of the New York Yacht Club, which Oland was considering joining. She did return to the office several days after the crime to do a walk-through with police, but could not notice anything missing.

Adamson testified that she returned to work roughly two weeks after "the incident," as Far End Corporation carried on in the unoccupied office next door until the crime scene was cleaned up and the office repainted. Until she retired, she worked with McFadden, who was now the president of Far End. In 2011, many of her duties involved settling the estate of Richard Oland. The other change was that Dennis, using the previous office of McFadden, occasionally worked in the office as a director of the company. She was also asked about travel she had helped arrange for Oland. These included ski and yacht-racing trips. She had made arrangements for Richard, Robert McFadden, Oland's daughter Jacqueline and her husband, and Diana Sedlacek. She first became aware of Sedlacek in 2008 when the former mistress was handling draperies, paint, and furniture for the Olands' home renovation. Sedlacek was "frequently in the office" during this period and would drop off CDs or DVDs and would also call Oland. That year, Adamson booked a trip for Sedlacek to go to Toronto to shop for furniture (Oland made the trip as well). Up to a dozen trips, to Toronto, Montreal, the United States, and Spain, were booked. According to other evidence, the affair between Oland and Sedlacek had started well before 2008. If so, hiring his mistress as the interior decorator for his home on Almon Lane was like something out of a soap-opera plot.[27]

Gary Miller began his cross-examination of Adamson on September 17, using the opportunity to bolster his client's alibi that he had been in Rothesay at the time of the murder and that the DNA transfer evidence was totally explainable. This was done with a series of video clips from July 6 that depicted Dennis's movements and photos of Richard in social settings. She was asked various questions: Was Richard Oland a drinker? Did he wear a hearing aid? Did he have a skin condition on his scalp? Although no medical evidence was entered about this alleged condition, Adamson stated that Richard did have scalp sores that appeared to be bloody from time to time. She was also queried about his habit of standing close to people and touching them when he was speaking to them. Miller asked about Oland's work habits and trips taken prior to his death. In terms of visits by Dennis, Adamson admitted that it was not unusual for him to drop in without calling first. Miller ran the video clips of a casually dressed and seemingly relaxed Dennis shopping in Rothesay with his wife and speaking to his aunt within an hour or so of leaving his father's office. As Blatchford wrote in the *National Post*, the Crown was suggesting that Dennis had been transformed from an enraged murderer to a suburban "happy shopper" in "68 minutes."[28]

Miller spent some time on the issue of the camp logbook that Adamson had given to Richard on July 6, 2011. She told the court that she knew it had to be returned to Mrs. Oland as her brother was in town. Her memory was that she left it close to a typewriter on the end of the table near the victim's chair. In a show-and-tell exercise, Miller entered the actual log as a defence exhibit and also brought the small Brother typewriter to court in order to demonstrate how much space the book would have taken up on a table. He showed the court a crime-scene photo of the table dated July 12, 2011, with circles depicted on the surface. Adamson agreed that if the book had been present on the table on July 6, it would have covered the circles (the circles depicted blood spatter, and one inference from this exchange was that the book had not been on the table during the bloody attack).

Additional cross-examination explored whether the father had ever complained about Dennis—Adamson thought only if he was absent from Wood Gundy when Richard called—or if at the time of the murder he had been aware of the bounced cheque from Dennis. She replied that Richard was unaware of the cheque problem. Rather than a loan or a debt, Miller spoke of the $500,000 in aid to Dennis as an advance on his inheritance. His questions attempted to show the generous side of Richard, such as an incident a decade earlier when Dennis had been allowed to skip a major mortgage payment to his father in connection to property he had purchased adjacent to 58 Gondola Point Road. Miller asked if Oland had more money at his disposal after he sold his shares in Moosehead, to which she answered in the affirmative. At the same, he remained obsessive and somewhat controlling with the monthly expenses Mrs. Oland incurred in running their home. Miller also asked questions about the genealogy hobby of the father and son, and how their research challenged some of the pretensions of the Halifax Olands. One crime-scene photo displayed on the court monitors was a family history document on "W. O." of Marshfield, Gloucestershire, which Dennis allegedly had brought to the office on July 6, 2011. It was marked by blood spatter.[29]

On September 18, Maureen's last day in the witness box, her husband, William, also testified. Examined by Derek Weaver, he repeated what he had told police in 2011. He had been parked in his Saturn Astra on Canterbury Street facing south near the end of business hours on July 6, waiting to pick up his wife. He testified that at roughly 5:20 P.M., as was his custom, he sounded his car horn to alert Maureen. He saw Robert and Galen McFadden leave the building and acknowledge his presence. Sometime after this, he noticed a man approaching along the east side of the street from the direction behind his left shoulder. He could not identify this person but told the court that he carried a red reusable grocery bag and wore a brown sports coat. William Adamson, cross-examined about the bag by defence counsel Jamie McConnell, evoked some laughter when he admitted to parking in a loading zone.[30]

The first witness on September 21 was Preston Chiasson, who had responded to Adamson's call for help on the morning of July 7, 2011. This friend of John Ainsworth, on-site since 8:00 that morning, testified about encountering Richard "on the floor, slaughtered," calling 911, and then helping a distraught Adamson down the stairs. This witness had a difficult time in court, especially when examining photos of the victim.

It was clear that he thought highly of Richard, whom he used to visit in his office. The next witness was Constable Duane Squires, one of the first officers on the scene, who was asked about his timeline and movements that day. He described the arrival of several officers by 11:07 A.M., his role in the removal of the body, and the canvass of the neighbourhood later. He was cross-examined by Gold, speaking in front of the jury for the first time (and in a loud voice), who asked about blood and whether the attacker would have gotten close to the victim. The cross-examination introduced two recurring defence themes: the back door and the actions of Const. Davidson. Squires was followed by Constable Trinda (Fanjoy) McAlduff, who had arrived with Squires. McAlduff, a cadet at the time, had been sent to locate the victim's BMW and help in the exterior search. Gold also asked her about the back door and Davidson. The final witness for the day was Constable Stan Smith, who was asked about his role in asking for security-video footage at Pizza Hut and Thandi's. Cross-examined by Miller, he too was queried about Davidson's actions at the scene.[31]

On September 24 the Crown examined Constables Don Shannon, Ben MacLeod, and Shanda Weir, paramedics Phil Comeau and Chris Wall, and funeral directors Adam Holly and Sharlene MacDonald. Their testimony revealed how the body had been first encountered, the state of the inner office, how the body had been removed, and how officers had searched the area. Shannon, who had also checked the unoccupied third floor, testified that officers were trained to avoid contaminating a scene. He also reported conducting initial interviews with Adamson and Chiasson. Comeau, who had responded to dozens of crime scenes, testified that they had been told they were dealing with "Code 2 trauma: gunshots, penetrating and stab trauma." Defence questioning continued with its now-established theme: was the rear exit door open? Were gloves and other protective gear worn? Weir testified that she saw the door open at 2:45 P.M. on July 7, 2011. The paramedics, who had been in the inner office for only one or two minutes, had worn protective gloves, as had the funeral directors.[32]

On September 25, the sixth day of the trial, Constable Michael Horgan of the canine unit testified about searching the back alley and other areas on July 7 with his dog, Leo. He told the court that "no evidence was found as a result of the search." Horgan's appearance was used by the defence to promote its theory that the unexamined back door, and the alley way, was most likely the route of the real killer. The officer was shown photographs of the rear area taken by the defence in June 2014, nearly three years after the crime, and was unable to recall many details about the area other than the door itself. Gold stated (again, this by itself could not be considered evidence) that the exact exit route of the killer was not known. Const. MacLeod, who had testified that his task on July 7 was to watch over the crime scene, came on duty in the early evening and stayed in the foyer area until after 6:00 A.M. on July 8. In his memory, the back door was open during his entire shift. When prodded by Gold, he admitted: "it dawned on me that the killer could have left through that door and any other door in the building" but reminded the court that he was not an investigator was only there to guard the scene.[33]

The Crown's first expert witness, Payman Hakimian of the RCMP Technological Crimes Unit (J Division, Fredericton), appeared on September 28. A tech-crimes analyst, he investigated computer crimes such as hacking and assisted other units with recovering and forensically examining digital evidence from computers, tablets, cellphones, recorders, and cameras. Hakimian explained that activity on computers was like "footprints left behind" for forensic investigators. The first step is creating a "forensic duplicate" of a seized device's information that will allow investigators to restore deleted email messages and texts, analyse user patterns, and determine the time of "last use." The original digital data remains untouched. On the basis of his experience and training, he was accepted by the court as an expert witness, having served in this capacity a number of times since 2008. Hakimian testified that together with Sergeant Pierre Bourguignon he responded to a request of the SJPF on July 7, 2011, arriving at 52 Canterbury Street at 6:55 P.M. (when Dennis Oland was being interviewed at police headquarters). The RCMP investigators met Sgt. Smith who advised them that he was still processing the crime.[34]

After checking on their legal authority to search and seize electronic devices, the tech specialists began their work at 9:00 P.M. At the request of Smith, they wore gloves and booties. Every computer in the office was still turned on, just as police had found them several hours earlier. Oland had a Dell computer and monitor on his desk and immediately to the left was a table with six additional computer screens, presumably to monitor financial information. In total, a dozen devices were seized for transport back to the RCMP tech lab in Fredericton. They included an iPad, cameras, a number of computer CPUs, and an external hard drive. Once at the lab, each device was analysed using software such as Write Blocker and Forensic Tool Kit. One item seized near the victim's desk-computer keyboard was a USB cord for an Apple product, presumably for the missing iPhone 4. The phone had been backed up on the main computer at 4:44 P.M. This established a key fact: the iPhone was in the Far End Corporation office late on the afternoon of July 6, 2011. Given that Oland did not appear to have left the office that day, this was highly significant. Apparent human activity on most of the office computers, according to Hakimian, stopped at 5:30 P.M. just before Dennis arrived to speak to his father about genealogy. Oland's main computer, according to his examination, logged no new activities past 5:39 P.M. The last apparent activity of the victim was looking at sites dealing with yacht racing.[35]

Cross-examination by Gold raised the issue that some user-generated activities on computers, such as closing a browser or reading certain files, do not necessarily leave a trace. He also questioned whether the RCMP had analysed the victim's computer-use patterns for other dates, suggesting that Hakimian's evidence did not prove that July 6, 2011, was not a typical day in the Far End Corporation office. The exchange between the two men on the first day was often testy. Hakimian refused to comment on how his report differed from that of his colleague Sgt. Bourguignon. Gold also used this witness as an opportunity to suggest that the detailed examination of Oland's computers had failed to reveal any concerns about his son's financial status. Hakimian explained that the contents of files and email messages was outside of his purview. In November 2012, he conducted forensic testing of the three computers seized from the home of Dennis Oland. The SJPF had asked him to check for internet searches, email activity, and file and digital image content. The testing revealed that other members of the household also used the computers. The expert did not analyse the data but turned it over to the Saint John investigators.[36]

The Crown's second expert witness, Neil Walker, a techno-logical-crime expert with the RCMP in Halifax, presented evidence on the victim's text messaging prior to the murder. He told the jury how he had assisted the SJPF in 2012 with two questions: when was the iPhone last disconnected from Oland's computer, and when did his email program time out? He reported that Adobe Acrobat had been opened at 5:28 P.M. (for viewing PDFs) and the browser Firefox at 5:38 P.M. Although the iPhone disappeared, most likely taken by the killer or killers, Walker was able to access a backup program on the desktop computer: the phone had been disconnected at 4:44 P.M. What was entered into evidence was a series of texts between Richard and Sedlacek. Although the often-embarrassing messages were further proof of infidelity, the reason they were entered as a Crown exhibit was their potential in reinforcing the prosecution's theory of timeline. In cross-examination, Gold attempted to establish that Oland did not always respond promptly to text messages from his mistress (to explain his lack of response to her on the evening of the murder). The defence, arguing that Oland had attempted to keep the affair secret, entered as an exhibit the contact image linked to Sedlacek's incoming calls. Rather than Diana, it displayed a picture of male friends. Gold's cross compelled both experts to admit that not all human interaction with computers could be tracked.[37]

According to Professor Nicole O'Byrne, the Oland case turned on one material issue: did the accused commit the crime?[38] By the time September ended, the Crown had introduced important ele-ments of its case, but there were two months and many witnesses to go. The "dream team" had one goal: subject witnesses, especially police and expert witnesses, to vigorous cross-examination in order to raise doubt in the minds of the jury about the professionalism of the SJPF and the overall strength of the Crown's case. During the preliminary inquiry, Miller had described the case as a "defence counsel's dream." And by October, in the view of many observers, the ground was shifting in its favour.

NOTES: CHAPTER 6

1. Rick MacLean, André Veniot, and Shaun Waters, *Terror's End: Alan Legere on Trial* (Toronto: McClelland & Stewart, 1992), 298.

2. CBC, "Bill Reid is 'comfortable' with Oland murder investigation," CBC New Brunswick News, April 22, 2015.

3. *R. v. Dennis James Oland*, 2015-11-24, Laboratory Testing Results.

4. *R. v. Dennis James Oland*, motions meeting, Feb. 2, 2015.

5. Mike Landry, "2,500 people could be summoned for Dennis Oland trial jury panel," *Telegraph-Journal*, March 31, 2015, B1.

6. *R. v. Dennis James Oland*, *Voir dire*, April 5, 2015.

7. Court of Queen's Bench of New Brunswick, Trial Division, Judicial District of Saint John, *Between Her Majesty the Queen and Dennis James Oland* (Hon. Mr. John J. Walsh), April 7, 2015, paragraph 35.

8. Court of Queen's Bench of New Brunswick, Trial Division, Judicial District of Saint John, *Between Her Majesty the Queen and Dennis James Oland*, Ruling #2, (Hon. Mr. John J. Walsh), June 10, 2015, paragraphs 94-95, 156, 206.

9. *Ibid.*, paragraphs 209-10, 227-30, 243-70.

10. Court of Queen's Bench of New Brunswick, Trial Division, Judicial District of Saint John, *Between Her Majesty the Queen and Dennis James Oland*, Ruling #3 (Hon. Mr. John J. Walsh), July 29, 2015.

11. Court of Queen's Bench of New Brunswick, Trial Division, Judicial District of Saint John, *Between Her Majesty the Queen and Dennis James Oland*, Ruling #4, (Hon. Mr. John J. Walsh), Sept. 2, 2015.

12. Court of Queen's Bench of New Brunswick, Trial Division, Judicial District of Saint John, *Between Her Majesty the Queen and Dennis James Oland*, Ruling #5, (Hon. Mr. John J. Walsh), Sept. 10, 2015.

13. Court of Queen's Bench of New Brunswick, Trial Division, Judicial District of Saint John, *Between Her Majesty the Queen and Dennis James Oland*, Ruling #6, (Hon. Mr. John J. Walsh), Sept. 10, 2015.

14. Interview with David Lutz, March 8, 2016.
15. Regina Schuller and Neil Vidmar, "The Canadian Trial Jury," *Chicago-Kent Law Review*, Vol. 82 (2) (2011): 497–535.
16. Bobbi-Jean MacKinnon, "Jurors in Dennis Oland murder trial at risk for PTSD," CBC News New Brunswick, Sept. 26, 2015.
17. Eric Andrew-Gee, "Sex, class, family discord fuel Saint John's fascination with Oland trial," *Globe and Mail*, Dec. 13, 2015.
18. Christie Blatchford, "Trial of Dennis Oland, accused of murdering millionaire father, reveals dysfunctional family," *National Post*, Sept. 16, 2015.
19. Canadian Resource Centre for Victims of Crime, *If the Media Calls: A Guide for Crime Victims and Survivors*, 2015; Andrew-Gee, "Sex, class, family discord."
20. *Boucher v. The Queen* [1955] S.C.R. 16.
21. *R. v. Dennis James Oland*, Opening Statement, Sept. 16, 2015
22. *Ibid.*
23. Chris Morris, "Oland trial into 10th week," *Telegraph-Journal*, Nov. 16, 2015, A1, A2.
24. Adam Huras, "City man part of Oland's legal 'dream team'," Fredericton *Daily Gleaner*, June 2, 2014, A1.
25. Ray Moses, "Direct Examination—Building a Dramatic Story," Direct Examination in Criminal Cases, http://crominaldefence.homestead.com/direct.html.
26. Chris Morris, "Oland suffered no less than 40 blows, murder trial hears" *Telegraph-Journal*, Sept. 17, 2015, A1–2.
27. Testimony, Sept. 16-18, 2015.
28. Testimony, Sept. 16–18, 2015; Christie Blatchford, "Could Dennis Oland have gone from killer to happy shopper in 68 minutes?" *National Post*, Sept. 17, 2015.
29. Testimony, Sept. 16–18, 2015.
30. Testimony, Sept. 18, 2015.
31. Testimony, Sept. 21, 2015.
32. Testimony, Sept. 24, 2015.
33. Testimony, Sept. 25, 2015; Chris Morris, "Officer says no evidence found of killer's route from Oland murder," *Telegraph-Journal*, Sept. 26, 2015, B1– 2.

34. Testimony, Sept. 28–29, 2015.
35. *Ibid.*
36. *Ibid.*; Chris Morris, "Prosecution at Oland murder trial brings in computer expert," *Telegraph-Journal*, Sept. 29, 2015.
37. Testimony, Sept. 29, 2015, A1.
38. Interview with Nicole O'Byrne, March 9, 2016.

CHAPTER 7

DID YOU KILL YOUR FATHER?

October 1–December 2, 2015

T he first witness for October was Const. Davidson, who had been named lead investigator in the fall of 2011. He recalled attending the scene and conducting initial interviews. He could not remember which day he exited through the rear door but was adamant that it had been locked when he first encountered it on July 7. He testified that he unlocked then locked the deadbolt mechanism and, like a surprising number of officers, probably did not wear gloves. The rest of his testimony dealt with attending at the victim's residence to notify his family and interviewing Jacqueline (Oland) Walsh between 3:47 and 5:07 P.M.

That afternoon, Sergeant Mark Smith of the Forensic Identification section was in the witness box. Wearing his dress uniform, he came across as professional, confident, and fair minded. Given his importance in examining the crime scene and testing various exhibits, Smith would be examined and cross-examined for several days. His testimony was also used by the Crown for entering more exhibits into evidence. Although he had noted the rear exit, by the time he returned from escorting the body to the hospital, the door had been opened and contaminated. Smith explained how he had examined and photographed the scene. The jury saw a large blood pool near the victim's head and "hundreds of spatter stains." Smith took measurements, sketched a floor plan, and collected blood swabs for DNA typing. He and Const. MacDonald also forensically examined the victim's clothing and body prior to the autopsy on July 8, 2011. For the first time, the jury was exposed to the severity of

Richard Oland's injuries, which were displayed on large screens. Walsh warned that the images were graphic. According to journalist Chris Morris, Dennis did not look at the disturbing photos, and family members averted their gazes or left the room.[1] Smith testified about examining the camp logbook for blood, examining the victim's BMW, and taking part in another search of the office on July 9.[2]

When court resumed on October 5, there was an issue with a juror. On the first day of the trial, it had been determined that one juror had an unreported relationship with Cox and Palmer, the law firm involved with the defence. That juror had been dismissed and one of the alternates took his place on the jury. Now, the defence informed Walsh that another juror had contacted another person associated with the firm. Walsh erred on the side of caution and in an understanding manner, dismissed the fourteenth juror. Smith's testimony continued with an explanation of how exhibits such as frozen DNA extracts were handled and stored in police custody.[3]

Cross-examined by Miller on the sixth, Smith explained that by the time he processed the second-floor washroom on July 9, 2011, it had been used by police officers. Traces of blood in the sink matched the DNA profile of Galen McFadden (who had provided a voluntary sample). The failure to secure the bathroom was a breach of basic crime-scene protocol.[4] Given the modern emphasis on forensics and the chain of custody of evidence, the actions of the SJPF damaged the reputation of the entire department but also possibly compromised the prosecution's case.[5] Miller questioned Smith on his meticulous search of the VW Golf and its contents, including the red bag. Various chemical tests had been conducted for the possible presence of blood. As the jury would hear more than once, there was no trace evidence in the car or in or on the bag.[6]

Further cross-examination focused on the bloodiness of the scene and Smith's examination of the camp logbook.[7] Smith was shown the video clip of Dennis walking outside Thandi's on July 6 at 6:12 P.M. As with other police witnesses, he refused to positively identify the person in the images as the defendant. Questioned about the rear exit, he testified that he had been asked by the Crown to photograph the door in July 2015. This led to a related issue the defence used in an attempt to discredit the investigation: the height and width of the back stairs. Miller asked whether a person who had bludgeoned someone to death would have visible trace evidence of blood on their person. Smith agreed but qualified this and many of his answers. The cross-examination concluded on October 8, with Miller raising the issue of Davidson's appointment, despite his relative inexperience, to lead investigator. Miller ended by complimenting the officer on his thoroughness, with the exception of his neglect of the rear exit.[8]

Smith was followed by Dr. Ather Naseemuddin, the pathologist who performed the autopsy. Much of the evidence was graphic in nature and members of the jury were disturbed by autopsy photographs. In addition to photographs, the doctor relied on his autopsy report, a sketch, and his notes. Matching other testimony, he reported that the autopsy revealed thirty-five sharp-force or "chop-like" wounds on the head, six blunt-force injuries, and fourteen skull fractures. In a Fredericton newspaper, journalist Chris Morris noted that the defendant "routinely looks away when photos of Oland's body are shown in the court room."[9] The pathologist explained that the impact of such wounds would have been "rapidly fatal," with the victim succumbing within five to ten minutes. He could not estimate the time of death. The six wounds on Oland's hands seemed to be defensive in nature. Oland was probably struck many times as he was unconscious on the floor: "There are so many injuries… which are terribly incapacitating, I would think those would have come after the victim was able to make any defensive motion."[10] The Crown, remembering earlier defence questions, asked if the pathologist had noticed any skin condition on the scalp. Naseemuddin replied in the negative, although how anyone could have detected evidence of pre-attack blood traces on the head of such a traumatized victim was not explained.[11]

Under cross-examination, the doctor agreed with Gold that the victim, "a healthy, robust man," had been "physically quite capable of defending himself." Asked about a possible weapon, all Naseemuddin could offer was that the injuries had been caused by two surfaces, one that was roundish, three centimetres wide with a cross-hatching pattern, and a second with an edge sufficiently sharp to penetrate bone. There was more trauma on the left side of the victim's head, with a series of blows creating an indented area up to two centimetres in depth. Gold asked the witness if the attacker would have been covered in blood. Naseemuddin stated that the weapon would have been covered, but he could not give an opinion about the assailant's clothing. When Gold brought up contradictory testimony from the preliminary inquiry, the doctor agreed that substantial blood would have been present. The lawyer also asked about the level of alcohol in the victim's urine, blood, and vitreous fluid. Justice Walsh gave the jury some rare weekend homework, asking them to read the autopsy report.[12]

The next witnesses were Constable Tony Gilbert, retired Staff Sergeant Mike King, and Deputy Chief Glen McCloskey. Gilbert, Davidson's partner in 2011, was asked about his role in the early investigation, which included monitoring the interviews of Dennis and Lisa Oland and Lisa (Oland) Bustin and tracking down security-camera footage.[13] Things took an unexpected turn with the testimony of King, who had retired in April 2015. His evidence generated headlines and intense discussion in the community and the promise of a departmental investigation. Examined by Patrick Wilbur, King alleged that McCloskey in 2014 had asked him not to tell anyone that he had entered the inner office to view the victim's body. King claimed: "I said I never lied on the stand in thirty-two years and I wasn't about to start. I don't care if it was a murder or a traffic ticket, I was telling the truth." The tale became even stranger when King recalled being sent by McCloskey to a midnight rendezvous in an East Saint John parking lot. He met an individual he assumed was a Mountie and then travelled to the RKYC in Millidgeville. He testified that if he received a call from dispatch, he was to ignore it. As Gold suspected, the point of this instruction was to avoid detection at the yacht club. This turned out to be an RCMP operation unrelated to the Oland matter. King claimed that he had spoken to Davidson, whom he considered to be friend, prior to the trial and that the younger officer felt that he was "being made to look bad," presumably by the Oland defence team, and was actually contemplating quitting the MCU because of the stress. The retired officer also alleged that he had spoken with Davidson about the alleged conversation with McCloskey and that Davidson had stated that the matter was potentially serious.[14]

On October 14, both King and McCloskey, who had been friends and who had served in Moncton in 2014 during the Justin Bourque shootings, were in the witness box. King told Gold that he had retired because of health issues. Following this testimony, McCloskey told the court that he had never requested King to lie under oath. He explained that King, before he retired, had been upset about SJPF staffing policies. McCloskey admitted that on July 7, 2011, he had ventured into the inner office twice, the first time to view the body and the second time because he was curious. Prompted by Gold, he explained that he had called Constable Greg Oram "an idiot" because he had told other officers about the second visit. Gold pressed McCloskey on the issue of the rear exit. There was mention of a steel gate or fence that had blocked off part of the alley in 2011, but no picture of this barrier was ever entered into evidence. The deputy chief admitted that he may have opened the door but was not entirely certain.[15]

On October 14, Chief John Bates confirmed to the media that the department's professional-standards unit was initiating an internal investigation into the allegations against the deputy chief and that he had informed both the Saint John Police Commission and the New Brunswick Police Commission. This was a potentially serious issue in its own right because if King were truthful, the man who was now second in command of the largest police service in the province had asked a veteran officer to commit perjury. Bates, who had only been on the job for two months, refused to comment on a case that was still before the courts and promised that the SJPF would continue to provide "a first-rate policing service to this community each and every day." He expressed his "full confidence" in the force and claimed it enjoyed "the confidence and respect of the greater Saint John community." The provincial police commission was reported as following the King allegations but was not actively involved in any investigation of police misconduct.[16]

After this strange side trip, the trial was back on track with expert witness RCMP Sergeant Brian Wentzell, the bloodstain-pattern analyst.[17] Ideally, this type of analysis takes place when the victim's body is still present, but Wentzell had to rely on Smith's photos, the victim's clothing, and his analysis of the dried blood at the scene. On July 11, he and Smith worked on the scene for several hours without taking a break. They divided the room into sectors and photographed and documented the spatter stains in each one. After measurements were taken, a computer program was used to analyse the bloodstain patterns. Wentzell instructed the jury in the physics of blood spatter, explaining that patterns are determined by the relative positions of the victim and attacker and the degree of force employed.[18]

Wentzell's testimony detailed not only his work at the scene but also his examination of seized clothing after he returned to Nova Scotia. He recalled inspecting the Hugo Boss jacket in late 2011 and late 2012 for bloodstains.[19] Under Gold's cross-examination, the officer agreed that the VW Golf appeared to display no signs of a cleanup. Gold spoke of the ferocity of the attack, which resulted in brain matter resting on Oland's back. Wentzell reported that there was "no distinct void" in the 360-degree circle of spatter centred on the attack (a void is created when blood splashes back on an attacker). He agreed in theory that the attacker would have been "a perfect target for spatter" and would have been in close proximity to Oland. Yet, his answers were usually guarded and qualified.[20] Wentzell testified that he had been asked to examine fifteen marked areas on the jacket but identified only four small stains. Gold asked the same questions about the logbook and blood spatter that Miller had asked. Wentzell responded that spatter on the table suggested the book may not have been there during the attack. The cross-examination concluded with the sergeant stating that he had not been asked to test the rear-exit door.[21]

The next witnesses, Anthony Shaw and John Ainsworth, and their earwitness testimony, were crucial to the outcome of the trial. Their statements to police and testimony, if similar to their direct evidence at the preliminary inquiry, were a problem for the Crown as they corroborated the defendant's alibi evidence, which at this point consisted only of video clips from two retail outlets in Rothesay.[22] Shaw did not alter his testimony from the preliminary inquiry, which was good news for the defence, as he placed the "loud and unusual" sounds from the second floor as occurring between 7:30 and 8:00 P.M, or more specifically, 7:45–8:00 P.M. He was certain of "a loud crash and several thumping sounds" prior to the appearance of an after-hours customer at 8:00 P.M. (The defence also entered, as evidence, a Thandi's video clip which showed a young man parking a car on the street around this time.)

Ainsworth, the owner of Printing Plus, had some health problems and, of all the non-police, non-expert witnesses, he was the least likely to give short, factual answers. His testimony was potentially damaging to the defence. Although he agreed with Shaw on the nature and number of sounds, he was less specific as to when he heard them. Ainsworth recalled "an initial thump" from the second-floor office, followed by "eight to ten thumps," over a period of several seconds. During his direct examination he spoke of an alternate path out of the back alley. This "escape route" had been entered into evidence by the defence during the preliminary inquiry in 2014 in the form of a video, which showed a law student walking to the southern end of the alley, boosting himself up over a cement retaining wall, then walking across a small back yard until encountering a narrow alley between two brick buildings. The student (followed by the videographer) proceeds to the end of the alley, unbolts a wooden door, and steps onto the sidewalk on the west side of Germain Street, the street uphill from Canterbury. This semi-secret passageway, together with the back door, was a key part of a possible other-guy-did-it defence. The problem for the Oland defence was there was no plausible other guy. The video was not entered as a defence exhibit in 2015.[23]

Gold was unable to shake Ainsworth from his less exact estimate of the time during which the pounding sounds occurred (anytime between 6 and 9 P.M.). The witness replied that Oland "very rarely" worked on weekends and nights, largely because of the unpredictable schedules of the rock bands. Circling back to the key issue of timing, the lawyer attempted to show inconsistencies between Ainsworth's informal statement to police at the crime scene, his formal written statement and response to police queries, his testimony at the preliminary inquiry, and what he was telling the court that day. Gold asked the witness if he had been "truthful" with the police in 2011. Ainsworth was unapologetic, citing the stress of the situation and the difficulty of remembering specifics of an incident that took place when he was absorbed with a frustrating work task.[24]

Later that day, the jury began to view the videotaped interview of Dennis Oland (the associated 114-page transcript, Walsh explained, was not the actual evidence). As soon as the interview video was released to the media, it ended up on YouTube and other websites. It was entered by Const. Davidson, who was back on the stand. On the screen, Davidson leaves the room four times: after asking Oland to write his statement; at 7:30 P.M. to consult with the monitoring officer; at 7:58 P.M. to speak to officers Copeland and Gilbert, and finally at 8:22 P.M., following a knock on the door. The jury continued watching the video the following morning, and all eyes in the courtroom were on its computer screens and monitors. For the first time, jurors were hearing, from not only a family member, but one accused of murdering the victim, about Richard's difficult personality, his treatment of his family, his affair with the "dragon lady," and his not totally altruistic financial assistance to his son. They were not only listening for the details being discussed, but also assessing Oland as a credible witness. After the lunch break on October 21, the two sides agreed that Dennis became a suspect in the death of his father at 8:22 P.M. on July 7, 2011, and was made aware of this fact.[25]

The remainder of Davidson's testimony concerned his other activities in the investigation, such as helping to search 58 Gondola Point Road, acquiring video-surveillance files from a number of businesses, and helping to interview Derek Oland on July 19, 2011. In addition, he explained a series of test calls (two-hundred-and-ten calls from twenty-three locations in Saint John and Rothesay) he made with an iPhone 4, the same type as Richard Oland's, in 2012. Along the same lines, Davidson reported on more than a dozen driving tests he conducted in 2013, attempting to gauge the suspect's travel time to Rothesay.[26]

On October 23, Davidson faced Miller's expert cross-examination on a number of issues, such as the scientific validity of the cellphone tests, the officer's reported comments on the preliminary inquiry, and whether he had been able to track down any information on the Hugo Boss jacket. Davidson had tried, but with no luck. Possibly to the embarrassment of the Crown, Miller entered as a defence exhibit a VISA statement from 2009 indicating that Dennis had purchased the jacket for $1,079 CDN in Orlando. (What the casually dressed male members of the jury thought about this was another question). Miller used his remaining time with Davidson to show the jury twenty-eight grainy video clips that purported to show Dennis Oland at various times on July 6, 2011.

The defence saw no need for the Crown to bring in the next expert witness, Grant Fredericks, from Spokane, Washington. Fredericks was a forensic video specialist contacted in 2012 to assist the SJPF. In his analysis of security videos and photographs, he refused to positively identify Oland or various articles of clothing; instead he spoke of "similar features" such as buttons and the cut of the garments. He refused to be drawn into an on-the-spot expert analysis by Gold, and explained that he had not been asked to review images of the VW Golf. Fredericks's testimony did prompt Justice Walsh to speak to counsel about asking various witnesses questions that were beyond their expertise.[27] Walsh instructed the jury that it was entirely up to them to identify any "person, place, or thing" in video evidence.[28]

Following Fredericks, Davidson returned for further cross-examination on video segments, including the 6:12 P.M. clip of Dennis walking north on Canterbury Street. Miller was attempting to show that his client was truthful and had merely forgotten where he had parked. Davidson was also asked if the police had any proof that the defendant owned a drywall hammer. Apparently, the theory of a drywall hammer as the murder weapon "was passed around" in police circles after the autopsy. Davidson explained that he had searched for examples of the specialized tool online and examined them in a building-supplies store, but had not bought one. He did not show any hammer to the pathologist who had testified that the victim had been attacked either by two weapons or by an object with a sharp axe-like edge and a round blunt surface.[29] Miller had one more go at Davidson's memory of the rear exit in 2011, especially his testimony that he had "jumped down" several feet to reach the ground. The building owner had testified that the stairs, which were steep, had been in place for years.[30]

The last two trial dates for October featured Constable Shawn Coughlan, retired lead investigator Rick Russell, Staff Sergeant David Brooker, and Constable Jay Henderson. Coughlan explained his role in the acquisition of cast-off DNA from Robert McFadden, Scott Laskey, and Derek Oland, and in placing Dennis under surveillance prior to his arrest.[31] On October 28, a juror sent a note to the judge, which momentarily caused a stir of excitement in court. The juror asked it was "prudent" for Mr. Oland to be texting on his phone during the proceedings. This meant that one or more jurors possibly thought that the defendant was not taking his own murder trial seriously. Justice Walsh explained that Oland was communicating with McConnell and that this was not only permitted but the "most unobtrusive way to communicate with his lawyers." In the past, the judge explained, defendants would send notes to their lawyers during court.[32]

Brooker testified about finding Oland's cellphone number, sending a production order request to Rogers Communications, and about the details of the house search of July 14. Henderson explained his role in that search, where officers had been told to look for a blue and a brown blazer. Part of his testimony included the discovery, on a dresser, of a receipt for VIP Dry Cleaners dated July 8, 2011. One of the last matters in October was entering an agreed-upon statement of fact. This was the statement of Barbara Murray and Douglas LeBlanc who had been parked at the Renforth Wharf between 5:30 and 7:00 P.M. on July 6, 2011. There were slight discrepancies in their testimony, as described in a previous chapter.[33] The news that the SJPF had seized cast-off DNA from the victim's brother, Derek, came as a surprise to many. The sample came from a drinking glass and a fork seized at the Bourbon Quarter restaurant on April 5, 2015, by a member of the SJPF and the Rothesay Regional Police Force.

Derek had been having dinner with Dennis and Lisa Oland and an unidentified woman. Derek issued a statement explaining that he would have co-operated with police if asked. He also had been vacationing outside of Canada when allegedly under surveillance.[34] It was just another of those strange little twists associated with the Oland case.

On November 2, Constable David MacDonald, a forensic officer, testified about being the "seizing officer" during the search of the defendant's residence. He recalled changing latex gloves after handling each exhibit (in contrast to lead investigator Russell who had touched the brown jacket with a bare hand). MacDonald also described visual and chemical tests of various items such as Dennis's shoes, the logbook, the BlackBerry, and the jacket. Without the jury in the room, the defence conceded the continuity of evidence in terms of exhibits being sent to and from labs. But Gold argued that the integrity of the evidence itself still needed to be proven. Following this testimony, Walsh instructed the jury on the legal defence of an inadequate police investigation and explained that he would deal with it in detail at the end of the trial.[35]

For the next two days the witness was accountant Robert McFadden, the victim's right-hand man at the Far End Corporation. He had worked for McCain Foods and Baxter Dairies before joining Brookville Transport where he became chief financial officer. He told the court that after the trucking company was sold in 1997, he worked on a per-diem basis for Oland on various projects and by 2006 was working for his former boss full-time. The court was not told that in 1998 McFadden sued Brookville Carriers, the company's new owners, for wrongful dismissal and "mental distress, upset and embarrassment." This was when Oland was still associated with the company. McFadden recalled the events of July 6, 2011, and said that Oland usually kept his iPhone 4 close at hand and backed it up regularly on his computer. By the time he and his son left for the day, Dennis had not arrived. McFadden thought that Dennis visited the office four to five times a year. He also described the events of July 7, including telling Constance Oland by phone, in so many words, that her husband was dead.[36]

McFadden explained the details of Richard's assistance to Dennis, which McFadden helped realize, during Dennis's divorce. The evidence offered insights into the mentality of the father, who appeared to be making business deals even when helping his son. This included a $120,000 cash settlement with Dennis's ex-wife, Lesley Oland, $303,000 to pay off the mortgage on the ancestral home in Rothesay, and $115,000 to pay off a line of credit. During the trial, the $538,000 sum was described either as a loan, a mortgage, or an advance on an inheritance. Starting in 2009, Dennis was obliged to pay Richard $1,667 a month, supposedly to avoid allegations of special treatment compared to his sisters. Richard asked his son to enter into a domestic contract with his soon-to-be-wife, Lisa, and that Kingshurst Estates be given a mortgage on an adjacent farm property and first option to buy the house. McFadden testified that none of these agreements were ever signed.

As mentioned earlier, following Oland's death, McFadden and Dennis were the executors of his estate. The former received the lion's share of the executor's fees and both were paid $50,000 as trustees. The will allowed the executors to tap into the trust on behalf of the widow. McFadden became president of Kingshurst Estates and Far End Corporation and Dennis president of the deceased's holding company. McFadden testified that the office had to be not only cleaned but partially remodelled, as "the blood seeped through four layers of flooring to the ceiling below."[37] The witness acknowledged that he was aware of the affair with Diana and that Dennis had asked him to speak to his father about it. Like Dennis, McFadden seemed unable or unwilling to directly confront his boss on the issue. One could simply "follow the money," he explained, such as travel itineraries and airline tickets, to see evidence of his employer's adultery. In addition, by virtue of his access to Richard's phone and email account, he had seen messages from Sedlacek. In cross-examination, McFadden testified that he had never heard the victim complain about his son's financial situation or express antagonism towards Dennis: "It was more fun building sailboats."[38]

The second witness that day was Jin Hee Choi, originally from Korea, who, with her husband, operated VIP Dry Cleaners in Rothesay.

On the morning of Friday, July 8, 2011, the brown jacket and other items had been dropped off in the name of Lisa Oland less than twelve hours after Dennis's police interview ended. Choi, testifying through a translator, explained how clothing was tracked at the business, including how items were identified with tags. She remembered that Lisa had picked up the order on Saturday as Dennis waited in the car.[39] Twelve days later, the court heard from her husband, Yang Gwan (Steve) Nam, who did the actual washing, dry cleaning, and ironing. Also speaking through an interpreter, he said that the customer had given no special instructions about stains and that he remembered telling police he had detected no blood or other stains as part of his routine inspection prior to cleaning the garment. In another example of an investigatory lapse, the SJPF did not fully interview Nam until February 2015. Part of Gold's cross-examination dealt with the chemical products used in the dry-cleaning process.[40]

The next three days were devoted to financial matters, which, according to the Crown, were central to motive. Michelle (Taylor) Lefrancois, formerly of the CIBC, explained that Dennis had obtained a $75,000 line of credit secured against his house in 2010, and that by March 2011 it had increased to $163,000. CIBC financial adviser David Cosman described Richard Oland as a "high-value" customer. John Travis, the accused's supervisor at Wood Gundy, had worked for Richard at Brookville Transport and considered him a mentor. Introduced into evidence was an email message to Travis wherein Dennis claimed he had convinced his father and another investor to bring $10 to 20 million to the company. In a June 1 message, Dennis cited cash-flow difficulties and asked for an advance on his expected earnings. Travis, who had floated the idea in May 2011, agreed to advance him $8,000 a month for June and July. (Oland told his wife this was "pay"). Later, he expressed concern about a delay in the advance on the day his loan and child-support payments were being deducted. The jury heard that Dennis was forced to leave Wood Gundy in late July 2011 as clients had begun to depart because of the controversy. He was given a financial settlement. Travis estimated that Dennis's clients had invested $20–25 million and explained that when an adviser left the firm they sold their client book to other advisers.[41]

The next witness was Eric Johnson, a senior forensic account-ant with Public Works Canada contacted by the SJPF with the task of summarizing and analyzing the suspect's financial records. His testimony focused on Oland's finances as of January 2011. The rec-ords indicated trips to Italy, Hungary, Florida, and England between November 2010 and April 2011, which added $21,000 to his credit-card debt. Dennis's main bank account for January 1 to July 7, 2011, was often in overdraft. In this same period, he withdrew more than $28,000 from an investment account and his credit-card debt rose to more than $31,000. During this time, Oland's employment income was $34,000, yet he was on the hook for almost $52,000 a year for child support and $20,000 a year for his father's loan. The Crown, for whom motive was a combination of money issues and ill will over the victim's adultery, was attempting to show that the defendant, although a financial adviser, was living beyond his means. It may have also been attempting to send a message about his character.[42]

On November 10, the court was packed to capacity: "the mis-tress," Diana Sedlacek, who now lived in British Columbia, would deliver her testimony. Wearing large sunglasses and a head scarf, and accompanied by a younger woman, she braved the media gauntlet and entered through the same security gate as any other visitor to the justice complex. Examined by an excessively diplomatic Veniot, Diana (who had been called a "bitch" and a "whack job" by Dennis) was relaxed and clear on the stand. She testified that she would visit Oland at his office, "perhaps once a month," often on Sundays fol-lowing church. They had been in a "romantic relationship" for close to eight years, and her spouse had not known. Much of her testi-mony centred on the text messages entered earlier as evidence. The messages of July 6 reflected her frustration with Richard's lack of a response. Her last text that evening was to the point: "Pathetic." By the morning of July 7, her messages were more frantic: "What has happened? Please, I love you...God be with you my love....Praying. Praying." Calls to Oland's office also produced no answers. On that morning, she testified, she drove past Oland's office and saw his BMW in his parking spot. When she saw police towing the car away, "I knew that something terrible had happened."[43]

The main purpose of Diana's testimony and associated cell-phone evidence was to show that she and the victim were in constant contact, usually via text message, and that Richard's failure to respond to her texts and calls starting at 6:44 P.M. on the evening of the murder indicated that something was wrong. Who knew the victim's routine better than his mistress of several years? Her testimony was also used to counter recurring defence questioning about Oland's alleged scalp condition (the inference that blood and DNA could have been transferred by the "close-talking" Richard to his son and others). The jury did not hear about Sedlacek's polygraph test or that her phone records suggested she had been at home on Darlings Island the night of the murder. She was familiar with Oland's iPhone 4 and explained they had a routine for calls and texts. Like Dennis taking orders at CIBC Wood Gundy, she was expected to respond immediately to Richard's messages.[44]

On a previous day in court, Gold had remarked that the defence was "not sure what to expect" from Diana's testimony and even the Crown had worries. Many court watchers and journalists anticipated that the cross-examination of Sedlacek would be a dramatic moment. For example, Gold stated that the defence would question her about some of her "unpleasant" text messages to Oland. The second-biggest surprise of the trial was the decision, announced after the noon break, that the defence would not be cross-examining Diana. This suggested that it did not consider her a suspect and /or feared that she could reveal negative aspects of the father-son relationship.[45]

Diana was followed by now ex-husband, Jiri, who was eighty-seven and lived in Hampton, New Brunswick, to the east of Darlings Island. Sedlacek, well dressed, urbane, and calm, spoke in an East European accent with an English inflection. He totally charmed the courtroom when he told Alan Gold, "I'm delighted to see you." Sedlacek explained that in his final years at Bata headquarters in Toronto, he was director of corporate planning when the firm was operating in eighty-eight countries and had eighty-thousand workers. He had married Diana in 1987 when he was fifty-nine and retired the next year. He denied to Patrick Wilbur that he had any involvement in Oland's death and claimed that he had been completely unaware of the affair until he heard the allegation in a media report more than two years after the murder. (This conflicted with Diana's testimony, which suggested he had found out two years earlier.) Sedlacek told the court that he and his wife had socialized with Mrs. and Mr. Oland. He thought that the last time he had spoken to the victim, an interesting and "worldly" man, was at Our Lady of Perpetual Help Church in Rothesay at Christmas mass in 2010. Jiri testified that he had spent the evening of July 6, 2011, at his home on Darlings Island, where he had been busy gardening.[46]

The other-guy-did-it strategy can be useful for the defence to amplify reasonable doubt about the prosecution's evidence, but it cannot solely be based on speculation. It can be devastating when one or more key prosecution witnesses has a history of criminal activity or conflict with the victim. Jiri Sedlacek was questioned twice by the SJPF but had been ruled out as a potential suspect. The cross-examination of a witness whose wife had been having an affair with the victim was completely necessary, but many court watchers described Gold's questioning of a man who was eighty-three years old at the time of the killing as one of the trial's low points. The aggressive cross-examination came across as excessive and generated animated pen tapping from a grim-faced Justice Walsh. Gold began by flattering the witness about his education, manners, and career, asking him if he was "an honourable man." He then more or less accused him of lying. Jiri agreed with Gold that he "probably" would have been angry if he had learned about the affair. Gold continued to ask him what he had known, indelicately reminding the aged man that his wife "had sex with this man." Sedlacek reiterated that he had been in the dark about his wife's infidelity. Next, Gold asked him if the police had asked for his phone records and bank statements (which presumably could have provided leads connecting the cuckolded husband to a contract killer). Jiri replied no. The seven-minute cross-examination revealed a side to Gold that may have alienated members of the jury. Tellingly, the Crown asked for no redirect.[47]

Week ten of the trial opened with the cross-examination of forensic officer MacDonald (who never visited the scene). Under Gold's questioning he agreed that the handling of the Hugo Boss jacket "could have been done better." Gold asked if any of the evidence from the jacket, which had been rolled up and folded in a bag, could have migrated after it was seized. MacDonald responded that it was a "dry" exhibit. He then detailed how he had examined various exhibits with special lights, conducted presumptive tests for blood, and taken swabs. The defence used this opportunity to have a SJPF forensic specialist tell the jury what the Crown did not have: any blood, DNA, or other trace evidence—other than possibly the jacket—to link Dennis to the crime. And the evidence sites included the crime scene, the victim's body and clothing, the *Loki*, the VW Golf, the red bag, the logbook, the BlackBerry, the suspect's clothing (including a J. Crew shirt he allegedly had worn on July 6), shoes, various items from his residence, and even the lint trap of the clothes drier (sometimes a fruitful source of forensic evidence in sexual assault and homicide cases).[48]

The next two Crown witnesses were Sylvie Gill, a Rogers Communications investigator, and Joseph Sadoun, a radio-frequency engineer who specializes in the design and operation of cellphone towers. Gill had received a judicial order for the victim's cellphone records on July 9, 2011. Examined by Crown prosecutor Derek Weaver, Gill used spreadsheets indicating incoming and outgoing calls and texts from Richard's iPhone, and the cell towers associated with this activity, for July 6. According to Gill, the last incoming text—"You there?"—to the missing cellphone pinged off a tower in Rothesay at 6:44 P.M. that evening. Subsequent texts (which never arrived on the victim's phone) pinged off the Quispamsis tower between Saint John and Sedlacek's Darlings Island location.[49] When Rogers attempted to locate the iPhone 4 in its system on July 9, the response code was "roaming error." The jury was informed that this meant one of three things: the phone was on "a foreign network" that had no agreement with Rogers, the location was unknown because of an "unspecified reason," or it was a case of an "absent subscriber." The last explanation could have meant that the device was turned off or was out of the coverage area. The court did not hear evidence on the latter issue, but in 2011 one did not have to travel too far from Saint John or Rothesay in order to lose Rogers's cell coverage. For example, St. Martins, a coastal village which is a thirty-minute drive from Rothesay, did not have Rogers coverage.[50]

Sadoun was recognized as an expert witness and submitted a twenty-one-page report on cell-tower coverage for the Saint John and Rothesay areas. The Crown's evidence was that the incoming text at 6:44 P.M. had registered on the tower at 2524 Rothesay Road, close to Renforth Wharf. He told the court that cellphones generally register with the tower geographically closest because it has the strongest radio signal. Anticipating the defence theory that Richard's phone was in uptown Saint John at 6:44 P.M. because he was still alive, Weaver asked Sadoun about the probability of an incoming signal to uptown Saint John pinging off a tower in Rothesay. Sadoun replied that this was "minimal" and his evidence indicated that in addition to two towers in Saint John's central business district only a block from the murder scene, there were other cell towers in East and West Saint John.[51] The other part of Sadoun's testimony dealt with his review of the test calls conducted by the SJPF. The point of these calls was to establish the cell towers that were most likely to connect with the wireless signals. Gold had compelling cross-examination questions on the accuracy of the software program used to predict tower-coverage areas (many of the actual tests calls had not connected as predicted) and on whether the elevation of the test calls and the time of both year and day would affect their accuracy. Gold also had Gill admit that the victim had allowed his earlier voice messages on July 6 to go to voice mail, implying that there was nothing suspicious about his failing to answer between 6:30 and 7:30 P.M.[52]

The last two Crown witnesses, both qualified as DNA experts, were Joy Kearsey and Thomas Suzanski. Kearsey, formerly of the RCMP crime lab in Halifax, had testified more than forty times in court and had worked on the Robert Pickton serial-killer case in British Columbia. The first part of her testimony, led by Wilbur, educated the jury on the basics of DNA typing and how samples were extracted and analysed. She explained that 99.9 percent of "the blueprint of life" is similar between people but that forensic analysts focus on the remaining 0.1 percent and that the chances of the DNA of two people matching was virtually impossible. Kearsey was an excellent witness, but her subject matter was somewhat intimidating in its complexity. Following the tutorial on DNA, she testified as to the findings in the Oland case based on eleven separate reports. Her evidence was that the Hugo Boss jacket contained three areas of blood-staining and that within these areas were DNA samples matching the victim's. The stains on the jacket were tiny, but scientists require less than a nanogram (one billionth of a gram) of genetic material to test with accuracy.[53]

Here was the key forensic evidence on which the prosecution was based. The areas were the outside right sleeve, the upper left chest, and the lower part of the back of the jacket. The probability that the samples would match another Caucasian male, based on the Canadian database, was 1 in 510 billion. Although blood was not confirmed inside the right sleeve, there were two areas of mixed origin, with the major component similar to the victim's DNA. (In this case, the odds of the DNA not being Richard Oland's was 1 in 180 million.) Kearsey agreed with Gold that it was impossible to determine how the DNA was transferred to the jacket or the length of time it had been present. Gold suggested that DNA can be transferred when people cough or touch one another, and Kearsey agreed. He also raised the issue of the jacket being rolled into a paper bag and stored away for several months before being tested. Kearsey responded that dried blood tends not to "migrate" from one surface to the next but that it can flake.

Suzanski, based in Ottawa, had worked for the RCMP as a forensic biologist since the late 1980s. His involvement in the case was relatively late, having contributed two lab reports in May 2015 based on the newer Identifier Plus amplification kit, which tests for fifteen areas ("loci") within a DNA sample. He told the jury that he had analysed the DNA samples taken from the bloodstained areas of the jacket and calculated that the estimated probability of selecting an unrelated individual at random from the Canadian Caucasian database was 1 in 20 quintillion (a quintillion being a prime number followed by eighteen zeros). He described the stained areas as "clearly interpretable" despite the fact that the garment had been subjected to dry cleaning before it was seized. Gold asked the witness if it was possible to know with certainty how the DNA was deposited on the jacket.

Suzanski agreed with Kearsey that in his expert opinion it was "rather unlikely" that Richard's DNA was deposited through any other biological substance than his blood.[54]

The following day, one month before Christmas, on day forty-four of the trial, Miller rose to start the case for the defence. He explained that not only the accused, but also two expert witnesses, several members of the Oland family, and a friend of the family would be testifying. The veteran barrister, now sixty-seven, told the jury that the Crown had not satisfied the burden of proof and that the only logical outcome was a verdict of not guilty. His client's testimony, he explained, would explain his whereabouts and movements on July 6 and 7, 2011, including his electronic communications. Miller also suggested that the defence would challenge the Crown's assertion that Dennis was last person to see his father alive. The defence denied that the Crown had entered convincing evidence that Dennis's financial situation and resentment over his father's affair were motives for murder. Miller rejected assertions that there had been bad blood between the father and the son over money, the affair, or anything else, and promised that his witnesses would bring no evidence of this nature. These would include the defendant's mother, his sister Jacqueline, who supposedly saw Dennis after his arrival home on July 6, 2011, and his wife, who would be questioned about her dry-cleaning errand on July 7.[55]

The defence called only two expert witnesses. The first was Patrick Laturnus, formerly a forensic specialist for the RCMP and now a consultant, who had been an observer during part of the 2014 preliminary inquiry. Basing his analysis on crime-scene photos, he theorized that the killer would have stood over Oland, repeatedly bludgeoning him, and would have ended up with significant amounts of blood on their hands, upper body, and even face. This challenged the testimony of Sgt. Wentzell (whom Laturnus had taught). Gold used crime-scene photos to remind the jury about the severe trauma to the victim's head. The witness also opined that if the brown jacket had been worn during the attack, there would be blood spatter in photographs visible to the eye. He also advised the court that "no analyst with any certainty" could determine how the bloodstains were transferred to the jacket. In cross-examination, he was asked about the contradiction between evidence of no bloody footprints or "blood trail" leading from the scene and his opinion that the killer would have been soaked in blood.[56]

The second expert witness for the defence was Geoffrey Fellows, a forensic-data expert and former police officer based in Great Britain. His task was to challenge the Crown's suggestion as to why the victim's computers fell silent soon after his son's visit. The Crown was pushing the period 5:45–6:30 P.M. as the time of the murder. Yet it had failed to prove that July 6 was an atypical day for Oland's computer use. Fellows, who had examined the data from three computers at the crime scene, told the jury that, based on patterns from June 13 to 17, 2011, there had been no sign of human interaction with the devices after 6:00 P.M. (or earlier). The point here was to reinforce in the minds of the jury that there was nothing sinister about the apparent lack of computer activity a few weeks later. Fellows agreed with Crown prosecutor Weaver that the June 13–17 data was not necessarily a "true reflection" of computer activity on those dates. Miller had announced that his client would testify, as would members of his family, as they had "lived under intense media coverage and scrutiny for over four years" and wanted to tell what they knew. The hint here was that family members might shore up the defendant's alibi, or at least help reinforce his positive character to the jury. Either way, court watchers and members of the media eagerly awaited hearing from the family.

According to one expert on juries, "appearance counts in the courtroom."[57] If this is the case, the defence appeared on December 1 to have a witness with many positive qualities. Dennis was well dressed, well mannered, and well spoken, seemingly likeable, and had no criminal record. But there was just one problem: he was on trial for murder. Although one can find media stories wherein legal experts refer to the positive side of defendants testifying in murder trials, it can be excessively risky and is not common in New Brunswick.[58] This is the opinion of veteran criminal defence lawyer David Lutz, who is based in Hampton, New Brunswick, and has taken part in one-hundred jury trials, more of a third of them murder cases. Exceptions would be cases where the defence is relying on provocation or self-defence.[59]

Combined with his July 7 police interview, the testimony of Dennis Oland would be the crucial personal evidence in the trial. At the end of the preliminary inquiry, the defence had complained that despite what Justice LeBlanc concluded, there was not enough evidence to justify a trial. Now that the Crown had concluded its case, the defence, despite Miller's remarks in late 2014, must have changed its mind about not only about the weight of that evidence but also the credibility of the Crown witnesses, because it was agreeing to its client's request to go into the witness box. Prior to the testimony, there was a *voir dire* on a new defence exhibit: a time-line document which attempted to track the defendant's activities, through evidence already entered as exhibits, from 6:55 A.M. on July 6 to 1:28 P.M. on July 7. Over the objection of the Crown, the judge admitted the document on the understanding that it would be an aid for the jury, not new evidence. Veniot pointed out that Oland was "probably the most important witness of the trial" and that "the sequence of events" was extremely important. Before Oland testified, the judge explained that the absence of his family members from court that day did not mean they had abandoned him. Rather, as they were scheduled to testify after Dennis, they has been banned during his testimony by order of the court.

One guide on direct examination advises lawyers to start with general background questions to establish the credibility of the witness. But Miller chose a dramatic opening: "We'll start at the end. Did you kill your father?" His client replied: "No, I did not."[60] The goals of Miller's direct were fourfold. The first was to allow Oland to explain anything that could appear incriminating or odd about his activities and whereabouts on July 6. The second was to bring out a human side to someone who, in three months, had spoken only two words in front of the members of the jury (before they were chosen and sworn in): "not guilty." Next was damage control: the 2011 police interview, which stressed a negative father-son relationship, was a large part of the prosecution's argument on motive. The defence had to convince the jury that the father and son had a more positive relationship than was depicted in the interviews of Dennis, his wife, his mother, and his sisters in 2011. Finally, the defence had to establish to a jury of average citizens that Oland, despite his background and lifestyle, and any inconsistencies in his story, was a credible witness.[61]

Oland's account of his timeline for July 6 and 7, and cellphone and surveillance-camera evidence that appeared to reinforce it, has been discussed in some detail in previous chapters. Miller examined his witness with the help of large maps depicting the uptown area centred on Canterbury Street, Oland's alleged driving routes home, and the area of Rothesay between his residence and Cochran's market. Miller also made liberal use of the grainy video clips that depicted Dennis leaving work, parking, driving and walking on Canterbury Street, and shopping and buying gas in Rothesay and Saint John on July 6 and 7. There was also an interesting use of the witness to identify himself and his own vehicle in the clips (he claimed he spent a week viewing surveillance footage). For the most part, Dennis appeared confident and relaxed and did not act like a person on trial for killing his father. The courtroom was packed and local media was reinforced by journalists from outside the province.

Dennis stuck to his initial account with one important exception. Despite what he told police on July 7, 2011, twenty-four hours after the events, he now explained that he had made not two visits to the office after work that day but three. In other words, he was now agreeing with the timeline suggested by the Crown during the preliminary inquiry. He told Miller that he had "a great time" discussing family history issues with his father, then left to go home. The Dennis of 2015 portrayed a much more positive image of his father than the Dennis of 2011. He explained that the 6:12 P.M. clip showed him walking back after making a wrong turn coming out of the main door. Around this time, he sent the text to his sister by mistake. He repeated his claim from 2011 that he had crossed the street away from his car because he was thinking about going to the drugstore on King Street. A few minutes later, his vehicle, as noted earlier, was captured on security camera heading east on King Street and three minutes later driving once more down Canterbury Street. It was at this point that he made the illegal turn on Princess Street and parked in the gravel lot. He now told the jury that he went back to retrieve the logbook, which he had forgotten. Dennis insisted that he and his father "would have gone through several pages." The witness cited an entry from August 1956, when his parents were dating: "Dick Oland had to go home to shovel shit," which provoked laughter in court. He testified that when he returned, the logbook was "at the end of the long table by the typewriter" and that Richard had been standing beside Maureen's desk. Miller had his client note on a map of the office projected on the interactive screen where the log allegedly was positioned. After he left around 6:30 P.M., he received the corroborated call from his wife: "I knew she had a cold and we had to get some medication."[62]

Given that it would take two minutes to reach the office from the parking lot, and that Dennis was on his phone at 6:36 P.M., if he was being truthful there would not have been time for much conversation during this alleged third visit. Especially as he now testified that he had not taken his BlackBerry to the office on his final visit, which meant that it was back in the car. There were no security cameras covering the lot or the stretch of the east side of Canterbury that connected it to number fifty-two, so two other unknowns are whether Dennis, who appeared in an earlier clip to have taken off his jacket, put it back on, or carried his trusty red "man purse."[63]

Having been asked by Miller to mark on a large map the routes of his three trips to the Far End Corporation, Oland used markers on another map to illustrate his route home, which started with a somewhat circuitous drive south to the end of Canterbury, where he turned left on Broad Street and followed on to the Highway 1 access ramp. He made the stop at the Renforth Wharf supposedly to see his children: "It's not easy when you go through a divorce and you don't see your kids...to this day I find a way to run in to them, I do." He did add one new bit of evidence: when at the wharf, he noticed broken glass on the ground (ironically from Moosehead bottles) and picked them up and put them in the red bag. He could not remember if he disposed of the glass at the park or at home. His account of the rest of the evening was similar to what he had told police in 2011 and was largely corroborated by surveillance-camera footage: trips to the drugstore and grocery store around 7:30 P.M. and a run for milk at 10:30 P.M. in Rothesay. There was no corroborating evidence of his whereabouts after 10:30 P.M.[64]

On December 2, Miller continued the direct examination of his client, the purpose of which appeared to be to portray a more positive version of the father-son relationship and to offer other theories as to how the victim's blood could have been transferred to the jacket. Dennis described his response to the question on July 7, 2011, about which jacket he had been wearing the previous day as a mistake, influenced by the fact that earlier on the day of the murder he had been wearing a navy blazer. He claimed to have realized "in the following days" after his interview that he made three trips to the office. Dennis also described the family's frustration at not being given any information about his father's death on July 7, 2011. Under questioning, he described his father's habit of biting his fingernails down to the cuticles, his scalp condition, and his preference for close-in handshakes, all of which could raise reasonable doubt about the Crown's theory of the bloodstained jacket. Oland testified that when work was being done on his house in 2010, he and his family had temporarily moved into the Almon Lane home when his parents were on vacation. During this time (which included a period when his parents were back in the house), the Hugo Boss coat allegedly had been kept in Richard's clothes closet. The accused also recalled visiting his father in his workshop and taking off the coat before lending a hand. When he left that day, the jacket remained behind and his father supposedly had picked it up. Miller had key questions about Dennis's visit to his father's office: had he spoken to his father about the bad cheque, his financial problems in general, or Diana Sedlacek? The answer to all three queries was no. Then there was a series of questions and answers that portrayed Richard in a more positive light and suggested that the two men shared a love of tinkering and fixing things, skiing, and, of course, the family history project. Richard was an "old school" and at times judgmental father perhaps, but he was also an adventurous and interesting mentor who did not hold a grudge. Miller's final questions to his client were whether he loved and missed his father. Oland, shedding tears, responded "yes" to both questions. His examination had lasted about four-and-a-half hours. Miller had completely sidestepped any questions about his client's financial situation.[65]

It was now up to veteran prosecutor P. J. Veniot to ask his most important questions of the trial. Compared to prosecutors in movies or television shows, he was non-confrontational and non-emotional—some would even say non-aggressive. A number of court watchers believed that the cross-examination was not only too gentle but also not sufficiently detailed. In fact, despite the experience at the Crown's table, a number of tactical errors were made that would be mentioned, as required by law, during the judge's final charge to the jury. On the other hand, Veniot did push Oland on his financial situation in 2011 and the years leading up to that period, and on how he had changed his story about his visits to 52 Canterbury between 2011 and 2015. His cross-examination lasted roughly three-and-a-half hours, punctuated by breaks.

Veniot began by asking Oland if he thought he was a suspect when he began his police interview on July 7, 2011, and whether he had been truthful. Dennis explained that he handled 10–20 percent of his father's investments and denied asking his father for financial aid in 2011. He was surprisingly nonchalant about his financial situation, although he did admit that his income was below his monthly expenses in early 2011 and his debts had totalled $700,000. He saw no need to tell the bank about the loan from his father and explained that since 2011 he had borrowed money, and that his house was now worth $650,000. He offered a cyclical theory of his income, claiming that the market—and his income—would have improved in the fall of 2011.[66]

The prosecutor next asked questions about the visit to the Far End Corporation. Dennis had not informed anyone in advance. Interestingly, he claimed that the rear exit had been closed. During an exchange on Oland's criss-crossing route at 6:12 P.M., Veniot informed Oland that the Lawtons drugstore was closed by this point. (Dennis had explained his irregular route on a contemplated trip to the pharmacy.) He denied having any role in taking the clothes to the dry cleaners and could not remember if he had actually worn the jacket during the week of the funeral. In terms of the inconsistencies between his 2011 statement and his new testimony, Dennis explained: "I was nervous, in shock and sad." (Readers should watch the interview online to make up their minds on this issue.) The reason why he had worn his blazer on the wharf on a hot summer night was because he was "old-fashioned." Veniot's final question related to one of the quirkier moments of the interview, when Dennis, alone in the interview room, spoke out loud, attempting to retrace his steps: "Did you know you were on camera?" Oland replied that he would have "assumed so." Most court watchers, and one veteran lawyer looking on, thought that Dennis had acquitted himself fairly well.[67]

When court reconvened on the morning of December 3, Miller arose, addressed the judge, and simply stated: "We see no need to call any other evidence." As one observer noted, with this low-key announcement, "You could feel the oxygen being sucked out of the room." Court watchers were both puzzled and disappointed as they had looked forward to hearing from the Oland family members and one friend. Constance Oland, Lisa (Andrik) Oland, Jacqueline Walsh, Jack Connell, and Mary Beth Watt would not be testifying on behalf of the defendant. The issue no doubt had been intensely debated by the defence team on the previous evening. Almost immediately, people speculated that Dennis had performed so well in the witness box that there was no need for alibi or character witnesses. The other theory was that the defence feared that family members, especially if opened up to cross-examination, even by the respectful Veniot, would make a bad situation even worse. The decision remains one of the most-discussed tactical aspects of the case to this day, especially as it occurred just before the jury was sent home for a well-deserved break.[68]

Justice Walsh announced that court was adjourned until December 14 and advised the jury to take advantage of the time to attend to pre-Christmas errands. In the meantime, the judge and the two legal teams would be hard at work on issues relating to his final charge to the jury. As he had already explained, the drafting of the charge would be a collaborative exercise and the document would be lengthy. As people left the Law Courts that day, one question was on their minds: where would Dennis Oland be spending Christmas?

NOTES: CHAPTER 7

1. Testimony, Oct. 1, 2015.
2. Testimony, Oct. 1–2, 2015.
3. Testimony, Oct. 5, 2015.
4. Testimony, Oct. 6, 2015
5. United Nations Office on Drugs and Testimony, *Crime scene and physical evidence awareness for non-forensic personnel*, New York: United Nations, 2009, 10.
6. Testimony, Oct. 6, 2015.
7. Testimony, Oct. 7, 2015.
8. Testimony, Oct. 8, 2015.
9. Chris Morris, "Richard Oland's skull 'completely broken in attack,' court hears," Fredericton *Daily Gleaner*, Oct. 10, 2015. A3.
10. Bobbi-Jean MacKinnon, "Richard Oland survived only 'minutes,' murder trial hears," CBC News, New Brunswick, Oct. 9, 2015.
11. Testimony, Oct. 8–9, 2015.
12. MacKinnon, "Richard Oland survived."
13. Chris Morris, "Senior Officer Tried to Hush up Visit to Oland Death Scene, Court Told," *Telegraph-Journal*, Oct. 14, 2015, A1.
14. Testimony, Oct. 13–14, 2015.
15. Testimony, Oct. 14, 2015.
16. Karissa Donkin, "Chief orders investigation into deputy chief," *Telegraph-Journal*, Oct. 15, 2015, A1–2.
17. Bobbi-Jean MacKinnon, "Oland murder blood stain analysis 'limited' by delay, expert testifies," CBC New Brunswick, Oct. 15, 2015.
18. Testimony, Oct. 15–16, 2015.
19. Testimony, Oct. 16, 2015.
20. Testimony, Oct. 19, 2015.
21. Mike Landry, "Expert says attacker would have been 'perfect target' for spatter," *Telegraph-Journal*, Oct. 20, 2015, B1.
22. Testimony, Oct. 20, 2015.
23. *Ibid.*

24. *Ibid.*
25. Testimony, Oct. 20–21, 2015.
26. Testimony, Oct. 21-23, 2015.
27. Testimony, Oct. 26, 2015.
28. Chris Morris, "No proof Oland owned drywall hammer," *Telegraph-Journal*, Oct. 28, 2015, B1.
29. *Ibid.*
30. Testimony, Oct. 27, 2015.
31. Mike Landry, "Police tried to get DNA from Moosehead boss, jury told," *Telegraph-Journal*, Oct. 29, 2015, A1-2.
32. Testimony, Oct. 28–29, 2015.
33. *R. v. Dennis James Oland*, Exhibit P-103.
34. Bobbi-Jean MacKinnon, "Derek Oland says he was out of country when police surveilled him," CBC News New Brunswick, Oct. 30, 2015.
35. Testimony, Nov. 2, 2015.
36. Testimony, Nov. 3, 2015.
37. Testimony, Nov. 3-4, 2015.
38. *Ibid.*
39. Testimony, Nov. 4, 2015.
40. Testimony, Nov. 16, 2015.
41. Testimony, Nov 5–6, 2015.
42. Testimony, Nov. 5–6, 9, 2015.
43. Testimony, Nov. 10, 2015.
44. *Ibid.*
45. *Ibid.*
46. *Ibid.*
47. *Ibid.*
48. Testimony, Nov. 16, 2015.
49. Testimony, Nov. 17–18, 2015.
50. *Ibid.*
51. Testimony, Nov. 18–19, 2015.
52. *Ibid.*
53. Testimony, Nov. 23–24, 2015.
54. Testimony, Nov. 25, 2015.
55. Testimony, Nov. 26, 2015

56. *Ibid.*

57. Stephen J. Adler, *The Jury: Trial and Error in the American Courtroom*, Crown, 1994, 194.

58. Bobbi-Jean MacKinnon, "Dennis Oland testifying in his own defence 'not that unusual'," CBC News New Brunswick, Dec. 1, 2015.

59. Interview with David Lutz, March 8, 2016.

60. Ray Moses, "Direct Examination—Building a Dramatic Story," Direct Examination in Criminal Cases, http://crominaldefence. homestead.com/direct.html.

61. Interview with Nicole O'Byrne, March 9, 2016.

62. Testimony, Dec. 1, 2015.

63. *Ibid.*

64. *Ibid.*

65. Testimony, Dec. 2, 2015; Chris Morris and April Cunningham, "Dennis Oland Describes His Loving Relationship with Slain Dad," *Telegraph-Journal*, Dec. 3, 2015, A1-2.

66. Testimony, Dec. 2, 2015.

67. *Ibid.*

68. Testimony, Dec. 3, 2015.

CHAPTER 8

HOW COULD YOU DO THIS?

December 2015–February 2016

As the jury rested or engaged in pre-holiday activities, Justice Walsh and the two legal teams remained busy, meeting on three separate occasions to discuss issues relating to his charge to the jury. These sessions were open to the public and Dennis Oland was present, but the deliberations were under a publication ban. Walsh had provided counsel with a draft charge and requested summaries of the key points in their cases. On the third day, December 9, a fire in a room housing batteries for backup lighting forced the closure of the entire Law Courts building as air quality had been compromised. The conference continued at another location. Former lead prosecutor John Henheffer was present, sitting in the public benches along with police officers. Most family members and court watchers did not attend these highly technical sessions. The detailed and collaborative nature of this legal horse-trading seems to have been unprecedented for the New Brunswick court. One of Walsh's goals was to render a charge that was less likely to open to an appeal.[1]

In the interest of brevity, a few examples of these delibera-tions will be discussed. The defence raised the *Brown v. Dunn* rule, which established that one party in a prosecution could not use contradictions in testimony to their advantage if they had failed to cross-examine on those details. In other words, if the Crown had failed to cross-examine Oland on contradictory testimony, then it could not use this point in its summation. One example was Oland's ability in 2015 to recall the "workshop incident" from c.

2010 but not remember in 2011 which sports coat he had worn the previous day. Walsh agreed that he would give the jury a *Brown v. Dunn* instruction on the workshop-incident evidence (and provided the actual wording to counsel) but also explain that it was up to them to assess Oland's credibility on this and all matters.[2] In another ruling, he refused to classify the SJPF's decision not to seek the phone and banking records of Mr. Sedlacek under the heading "inadequate police investigation." The judge agreed with the Crown that it would have been difficult to find probable cause to seek a warrant and considered the decision reasonable.[3] On December 4, he criticized the Crown for failing to ask the pathologist directly about a potential murder weapon and the police for mishandling the bathroom and the rear-exit door. There were some basic lapses in Crown cross-examination—for example, prosecutors never bothered to ask the defendant if he and his father had ever argued over money or the mistress.[4]

On Monday, December 14, the jury returned for closing arguments. Walsh explained the process and that the jury would be sequestered as soon as the charge concluded. He reminded the panel, "You are judges," and advised them to keep an open mind and to make their decision after hearing the closing submissions and his charge. Closing arguments at this level of court are formal affairs, with the lawyers standing at a podium in front of the jury and reading their documents. The defence argument was delivered by Alan Gold, who on one level was a logical choice because of his experience and expertise. Yet as he quickly acknowledged, he was a "CFA," a come-from-away. Gold told the jury that "you" (either Saint John residents or New Brunswickers) were the politest people he knew. He spoke of working with Miller in the past and described the jury as the cornerstone of the justice system. In his view, the jury was no closer to knowing who killed Richard Oland that day than it had been when it assembled three months earlier. Gold reminded the jury of the two guiding principles of reasonable doubt and the burden of proof. He admitted that "the police don't charge just for the fun of it," but cautioned that these principles, especially in a circumstantial-evidence case, placed a heavy burden on the Crown. If they believed his client's testimony, then they must acquit. If any evidence raised reasonable doubt, they must acquit. One of his lines was: "Never have so many searched so long to find so little."[5]

Gold spoke for three hours and addressed motive, opportunity, and means. In terms of the first factor, he pointed out that although his client's income had fluctuated in past years, in 2011 he had a good-size client book and his job had not been in danger. His house was worth $600,000 and encumbered with a mortgage of $167,000. There was no evidence of credit being denied or of Richard being concerned or even knowing about the bounced monthly interest-payment cheque. The victim's will did not benefit his client directly. Finally, there was no incriminating financial or personal information on the phones and computers of Richard, Dennis, or Diana. Another defence theme was the inadequacy of the police investigation, which supposedly had allowed "the true killer or killers" to escape detection. Gold cited the mishandling of the back door, Davidson's inexperience and untrustworthy memory of the early investigation, and the failure of RCMP experts to examine the victim's computer-use patterns over a longer period. Gold even mentioned the King-McCloskey controversy. Other examples that raised reasonable doubt included Dennis's visit to the office when Maureen Adamson was present, the lack of evidence as to how the attack actually unfolded, and the testimony that Shaw and Ainsworth had heard noises when his client was eighteen kilometres away in Rothesay. Dennis, furthermore, had been "candid and thorough" on the stand, admitted his mistakes, and said that he loved and missed his father. Although the inconsistencies in his client's initial interview were not important, that interview had "made him a suspect."[6]

The defence had to neutralize the evidentiary value of the jacket, which it had attempted to block from the trial. Gold asked why his client would lie about which jacket he wore on the previous day when he knew there was security-camera footage and that the police could secure search warrants. The brown jacket was taken to the cleaners by his wife, and Dennis made no attempt to hide his clothing and shoes. The stains on the garment were small and faint and had been subjected to dry cleaning. (Gold contrasted photos of the bloody crime scene with those of the jacket.) If Dennis was the murderer, why would he leave the jacket, the dry-cleaning tag, and even the receipt in his bedroom for police to find? He downplayed the significance of the DNA findings on the jacket, which would be "good evidence" if the accused were a stranger. He also declared that there was neither any proof the spots were "spatter," nor of the age of the stains or how they were deposited. Cast-off DNA was "a perfectly normal feature of modern life." Gold stated that both the attacker and the weapon would have been covered in blood by the end of the attack.[7]

Gold pointed out that there was no trace evidence either from Dennis on the body of the victim or from the victim on or in the VW Golf, BlackBerry, the red bag, the logbook, the *Loki*, or on the pants, shoes, and shirts of the accused. And the logbook, which revealed no blood spatter, was strong evidence that Dennis had left the office prior to the murder. Video clips of Dennis from 6:12 to 7:30 P.M. on the evening of the crime indicated a "perfectly normal" person, not someone who had just committed murder. Similarly, would a person really answer his phone at 6:36 P.M. if he had just killed someone? Given that Richard did not always respond to texts and calls on his iPhone, Gold argued that he was killed after 7:30 P.M. He also noted that the "unexplained" alcohol in the victim's system suggested that he may have left the office after 6:30 P.M. Gold also attacked the Crown's cellphone evidence: the predictive cell-tower evidence was not conclusive, the field tests of the iPhone 4 were flawed, and the "roaming error" message was not properly pursued.[8]

In his closing address Veniot spoke for two-and-half hours and identified financial issues, the brown jacket, and cellphone records as key evidence. Although the evidence was circumstantial, the Crown benefited from a framework or narrative that told a simple (if incomplete) story that jurors could easily understand. Veniot spoke of the need to assess "the whole of the evidence." The killer had to be the accused, who reached out to his wealthy father for help and was the last person to see him alive. Dennis was known to drop in only four or five times a year to see his father at work. The crime took place sometime between 5:44 and 6:36 P.M. During that evening, Shaw and Ainsworth were engrossed in a difficult task and there was no evidence that Shaw looked at his watch when he heard noises. The victim supposedly kept his iPhone 4 close by at all times and had backed it up prior to 5:00 P.M. He did not respond to texts and phone calls from 6:44 P.M. onwards because he was dead. Veniot did not know why the phone was taken, but calls to it later that night went to voice mail. It was most likely that the phone communicated with the cell tower at 2524 Rothesay Road when Dennis was nearby.[9]

As for weaknesses in the case, the police did make mistakes, but there was no proof that any relevant evidence had been lost, only speculation. As for the failure to show the pathologist a possible weapon, he had never seen the cross-hatched pattern wound before and had not wanted to speculate. The suggestion that alcohol in his system indicated that the victim had left the office before the crime was also speculation. This was a crime of passion, "born of an enraged mind," and not a robbery gone wrong. With second-degree murder, the Crown does not have to prove motive, but it can be useful in building a case. Oland's initial statement to the police suggested the difficult nature of the victim and the strained relationship between father and son. Added to this was animosity about his father's adultery and a stressful financial situation. The victim, who was worth $36 million, had in the recent past helped his son with his divorce. But assistance from Richard Oland came with a price, including a monthly interest-only payment and certain conditions governing the family property on Gondola Point Road. Despite this help, and two collateral mortgages, Dennis Oland, by 2011, was taking overseas trips and living beyond his means. Facing mounting debts and diminished income, he had even secured advances on his pay from his employer and was promising CIBC Wood Gundy that he could deliver investments of $10–20 million within a few months. Veniot went over the accused's bank account and credit-card information in detail to paint a picture of financial desperation as of early July 2016.[10]

As he had in 2009, Dennis supposedly attempted to resort to "the bank of Daddy," but unsuccessfully. The Crown doubted that the logbook or family history motivated the visit to Far End Corporation that day. Veniot painted Dennis's hesitant moves after leaving his own office on July 6 as "odd." The reason why he walked in the wrong direction to his car after the second visit was that he was "disturbed and distraught." One implication was that the father had rebuffed his request for help and possibly did so in an inflammatory fashion. Another was that Richard had just been murdered. Veniot pointed out that Dennis, with a sick wife at home, stopped at the Renforth Wharf, and, wearing his sports jacket, carried a red bag allegedly to pick up broken glass and then walked to the end of the wharf. After telling police three times on July 7 that he had worn a blue blazer the previous day, he was informed that he was a suspect in his father's death and that his wardrobe would be confirmed by security cameras. The next day the jacket was dropped off for dry cleaning and the shirt he had worn for laundering. Sgt. Wentzell's expert opinion was that it was difficult to be exact in determining the amount of spatter on an attacker. Laturnus, the defence expert, had not been to the scene and relied totally on photographs. As for the hairs clutched in the victim's fingers, the reason there was no positive DNA match with Dennis Oland was because they lacked their roots. Veniot cited Kearsey's testimony about dried blood not transferring to other surfaces, thereby defending the integrity of the jacket in storage and transit. DNA typing provided "strong evidence" (Veniot did not say "proved") that Dennis killed his father. As for the defence argument that the victim was a "close talker," the Crown pointed out that no DNA of a female or females was found on the jacket. Veniot described the back door to the Far End office as "nondescript" and "easy to miss." Mocking the phantom "third-party-killer" theory, he declared that there was no evidence linking the back door to the crime. The weapon was carried out of the office. Mr. Sedlacek was, in theory, a possible suspect, but he had not known about his wife's affair. Veniot told the jury that the "inescapable conclusion" was that Richard had been murdered by his son.[11]

In the Canadian legal system, trial judges not only ask witnesses questions of clarification, they also sum up the major evidence of a trial in their charge to the jury. Both of these practices are in contrast with American practice and reflect British influences.[12] Walsh began his charge to the jury on Tuesday, December 15. In his view, at two hundred pages, this was the longest charge in New Brunswick history.[13] He began by reminding the jury of its duties, the general rules of court, and the special rules relating to this case. And in a largely circumstantial case, he explained the difference between direct and indirect evidence. He also reviewed the specific points that the Crown had to prove beyond a reasonable doubt. Walsh reminded the jury to base its decision on the evidence presented in court and not to be influenced by the media or "sympathy, prejudice, or fear." The key question for them to answer was whether the Crown had proven, beyond a reasonable doubt, that the accused had killed his father.[14]

Walsh provided an extensive review of the evidence and reminders for assessing its probative value. He explained that DNA "genetic profile estimates are not intended to be precise" and reminded the jury that there was no direct evidence on the impact of dry cleaning on bloodstains or that the weapon had been a drywall hammer. Walsh also clarified that the Hemastix test was not a confirmatory test for the presence of blood, just a screening test. A key (perhaps *the* key) question for the jury was if the DNA found in spots AA, AC, and AO on the jacket was derived from blood as opposed to other biological material such as skin cells or saliva (especially as an area on the inside cuff of the right sleeve had DNA consistent with the victim but no blood). Walsh also cautioned the jury against relying too much on the cell tower–propagations maps produced by expert witness Sadoun when attempting to ascertain the location of the victim's missing iPhone. As required by law, he noted possible examples of an inadequate police investigation, such as failing to properly secure the scene, including the bathroom and the rear-exit door.[15]

Walsh's charge devoted several pages to the issue of the exit door, including when it was opened after police arrived on July 7, 2011, and the problematic testimony of Const. Davidson (and his lack of notes from that day). It also revealed the conflicting testimony of several officers at the scene about the status of the door. Walsh pointed out inconsistencies in the evidence of the accused, but cautioned the jury that even if Oland's 2011 statement and recent testimony "leave you with a reasonable doubt of his guilt," they were required to make their determination on the totality of the evidence.[16] He reminded the jury of the special instruction he had already given regarding Anthony Shaw's testimony on the timing of the noises from the second floor. If that testimony raised reasonable doubt, then they must acquit the defendant. Although the Crown did not have to prove motive, Walsh reviewed the relative evidence. On the afternoon of December 16, as Walsh was approaching his conclusion, the Law Courts building was hit by another technical glitch. As a result of a power failure, the courtroom and floor of the building had to be temporarily evacuated. Ninety minutes later, the power was restored and Walsh concluded. He urged jurors "to keep an open mind but not an empty head."[17]

Following the charge, Walsh watched as the clerk of the court, Amanda Evans, and Sheriff George Oram carried out a necessary function: the discharge of the thirteenth juror. They did this by placing ballots in a wooden box and drawing a number at random. This was likely the same box that been used for jury draws at the old Saint John County Courthouse for decades. The judge reminded the soon-to-be surplus juror that they were under the same code of silence as the jury and expressed his "personal, heartfelt thanks" for their devotion to their civic duty. The juror whose number was drawn was a woman; Justice Walsh thanked her as she left. The jury that would decide the fate of Dennis Oland consisted of four women and eight men. It departed for the jury room at 3:30 P.M. In an interesting display of collegiality, the lawyers on the two sides, including John Henheffer who initially had been first chair for the Crown, shook hands and congratulated one another. The youngest counsel on both sides embraced one another.

The jury started its work before supper and deliberated for at least a couple of hours that evening before retiring to a hotel for the night. They were supervised by members of the sheriff service who made sure they had no telephone or electronic contact with family or friends and refrained from reading, watching, or listening to media reports of the trial. Following the intense three-and-an-half-month trial period, activity in the court complex seemed to slow down, particularly on the floor containing courtroom twelve. The jury reported each day to its room next to the courtroom, equipped with wash-room facilities, coffee, key exhibits, and equipment for viewing video clips. One juror was a smoker, and the rules required that sheriff staff escort all twelve outside to the cool early-winter air for each cigarette break. During the days, local, regional, and national media hung out on the chairs and at the large, wooden former jury-room table from the old county courthouse, worked on their laptops, texted and emailed, and swapped the occasional story about other trials and assignments. Many reporters, perhaps anticipating a quick not-guilty verdict, remained on-site after supper, when normal court business is suspended. The press was updated by email by Dave MacLean, the provincial government communications person who also remained on-site for long hours. The jury watch extended into Thursday and Friday. On those evenings, the jurors stood down before 9:00 P.M. On December 17, the first full day of deliberation, a friend posted the fol-lowing message on the Facebook page of Diana Sedlacek (now living in Victoria, BC): "Thinking of you. Hope justice will be served."

During those days, members of both the prosecution and defence teams were seen in and around the Law Courts (which houses the offices of Crown prosecutors), and it was understood that the judge and the defendant were also staying close by in case the jury gave notice it was returning. There appeared to be a strong bond of respect between the judge and jury, and given the length of the trial and the tricky issues of reasonable doubt and presumption of innocence, one theory was that it would take at least two days, roughly the length of Walsh's charge, for a decision. Another theory was that the jury, after long months of intense observation, wanted to be free before Christmas. Yet, observant court watchers doubted that this jury, which appeared to be disciplined and dispassionate, would be motivated by personal concerns. Earlier in the year, the jury in the Joseph Paul Irving second-degree trial had deliberated for less than four hours; the Cormier jury had met for six hours. In both cases, the defendants had been found guilty. By the start of the last weekend before Christmas, many busy citizens were shop-ping and running family errands, but keeping close to the radio, Facebook, Twitter, and their text and email connections. By the start of the third full day of deliberation, people were speculating that one or two jurors, not yet fully convinced of the defendant's innocence, were still holding out against the majority. There was also speculation about how Dennis and his family, with the expected not-guilty finding, would be accepted by their peers and the wider Saint John area community. Even if acquitted, would he still be associated with the murder of his father?

On the morning of Saturday, December 19, the author was the second non-staff person to enter the Law Courts, following veteran CTV reporter Mike Cameron. The jury arrived around 9:00 A.M., and the handful of court watchers wondered if this would be the day. Shortly after 10:00 A.M., sheriff staff escorted the entire jury to the elevator in the public hallway and down to the ground floor for a smoke break. They returned a few minutes later and the watchers went back to their conversations or tried to read or use their phones, tablets, and laptops. Within minutes, the Department of Justice sent an email to the media that the jury was returning to the courtroom. The defendant, his lawyers, and his family and supporters began to converge on the security gate and proceed to courtroom twelve. Many people expected that the jury would be asking a question.

As the lawyers, sheriff deputies, the defendant, the Oland family, the media, and a handful of spectators gathered in the courtroom, an ominous silence took hold. Justice Walsh appeared and the jury filed in, giving no visible indication of its intentions. The sheriff was present, suggesting that something different may be happening. Suddenly it was apparent: it was verdict time. The foreman was asked for the jury's decision. The author logged in to Facebook and prepared a message; his thumb was hovering over the letter N, to start the message "not guilty."

The verdict was read: guilty.

CBC reporter Bobbi-Jean MacKinnon, who had covered many criminal trials, reported a sound "like a wild, wounded animal." Oland, who was sobbing and physically affected, was comforted by Gary Miller. His wife, Lisa, yelled out, "That's impossible," and, in an accusatory tone, asked, "How could you do this?" Dennis collapsed into his chair on the side of the court. The convicted man exclaimed:

"Oh no! Oh no!...Oh my God...my children." One media account claimed that he "wailed."[18] The defendant and his family appeared to be totally unprepared for any verdict other than not guilty. Oland, now a prisoner, was removed from the courtroom at the judge's order almost immediately. Walsh, possibly distracted by both the verdict and the level of emotion, thanked and dismissed the jury before it was asked to perform its last duty, making a recommendation on minimum parole eligibility. The jury was summoned and a more composed Oland was escorted back to court by a deputy to watch the proceedings. Walsh explained the criteria for sentencing and while the jury deliberated in its room, a woman's cries (presumably Lisa's) could be heard from the washroom across the hall.

A few minutes later, the jury and Oland returned to the court-room. The foreman reported a unanimous recommendation of ten years, and then each juror was polled, with the same answer. Oland made no response to this, and the jury exited for the final time. Justice Walsh set a sentencing hearing for February 11, 2016, and the prisoner, who looked forlorn and defeated but acknowledged his family, was taken by sheriff staff through the side door to the internal elevator. From there he was walked through the tunnel to the SJPF lockup and either placed briefly in lockup or escorted to the underground parking garage. There he would have been loaded into a secure sheriff's van for transport to the Saint John Regional Correctional Facility, where he had been briefly incarcerated in late 2013. For a few minutes, as reporters filed to the exit of the building, readying their cameras, the Olands remained in the corridor outside courtroom twelve. This was the same area where twice a day for three months they had enjoyed coffee and conversation with Dennis when he was a free man.[19]

This Christmas, Dennis Oland would not be with his family in Rothesay. After the verdict, friends (and possibly family) gathered at the home of Bill Teed where, according to Oland neighbour Kelly Patterson, they were "totally stunned." According to friend Larry Cain, people had expected to be celebrating that evening.[20] Outside the Law Courts, the well-dressed defendant, photographed and captured on video by reporters for months, was nowhere in sight. His wife,

Lisa, carried his coat past the media gauntlet and was driven away. After the family had departed, the three Crown attorneys, dressed in their black robes, appeared outside to make a brief statement. The defence lawyers had not made any comments. A serious-looking Veniot, flanked by Wilbur and Weaver, was not gloating or in a speech-making mood. He thanked the jurors "for their careful consideration of all of the evidence" and for completing their legally bound duties. There was no reference to either the victim or the accused, and no mention of justice being served.

Chris Morris and Mike Landry, writing in the *Telegraph-Journal*, described the verdict as sending "shockwaves across the country." The conviction immediately became a national media story, with reports being filed from coast to coast in print, radio and television broadcasts, and online news sites, over the next few days. Local media attention was particularly intense. Todd Veinotte, a Saint John broadcaster, reported that many in the community were not prepared for the verdict and believed the case had all the drama of a TV movie.[21] Bizarrely, in the immediate aftermath of this somewhat unexpected win by the Crown and the police, the *Telegraph-Journal* ran an editorial cartoon mocking the SJPF. The various crusades of Brunswick News publications' editors aside, the allegations of inadequacies in the police investigation, combined with a series of allegations of officer wrongdoing in other parts of the province, fed the media's requirement to keep the Oland story alive pending any substantial news.[22]

No prominent resident of the Saint John community was cited in the media as approving of the verdict or stating that justice had run its course. But the online world was different, and email, Twitter, Facebook, and other social media, as well as the comments sections on online news sites, revealed a range of opinions. Some comments became so nasty that the *Telegraph-Journal* at one point disabled the function. One person who posted on the CBC News website had no doubt about the identity of the murderer:

Well rest in peace Father Richard Oland. Seems as there is no one on the video that shows another person of interest in this case, Dennis, spoilt, lazy, privileged, now he has certainly erased his debt to his father. The father suffered a painful death, a man who had a strong work ethic that made him a wealthy, and a respected man in the community...[23]

Another, one of many, suggested that the family was living in denial:

Sounds like the Oland family will be coming to terms with the court-based determination that Dennis murdered his father this weekend. Must be horrible to realize that your family member is not only capable of murder but so pathological and selfish as to drag his entire family into his murderous deception.[24]

A social media post by a member of the local cultural scene repeated the theme of the sufferings of the Oland family:

The only thing more shocking than the Oland verdict would be the level of lazy, smug, hateful—and, in some cases, I suspect, action-able—commentary now poisoning my newsfeed and generally polluting the twittersphere. I really can't fathom it. Where is the joy, especially in this season, in so casually venting such vitriol? Whether you think Dennis Oland is guilty or not, please remember, as you swing your own little drywall hammer in sundry acts of character assassination, that he has a family; he's surrounded by, and attached to, a whole constellation of good people that are now suffering yet another terrible blow.[25]

In the face of the conviction, the Oland family appeared deter-mined to exonerate Dennis. Derek Oland issued a statement insisting on his convicted nephew's innocence and affirming the family's faith "in the course of law." Constance Oland's statement expressed the hope that "justice eventually will be served."[26] On December 20, the day after the verdict, the ministers of St. David's United Church and St. Paul's Anglican Church in Rothesay (both located on the Rothesay Common) asked the congregation to observe a moment of silence and to keep the Oland family in their prayers. The next night, as many residents of Rothesay celebrated the official opening of a new outdoor skating rink on the Common four days before Christmas, the Oland family was no doubt still in shock.

The response of the SJPF was not as muted as that of the Crown. A statement by Chief John Bates, who started on the job in the middle of the trial, was careful to state that "no winners emerge from such a tragic event" but declared that the verdict was "a degree of valida-tion" for the police service. Bates promised that the SJPF would be dealing with professional lapses revealed by the Oland trial.[27] Lawyer Christopher Hicks, deemed an expert on the case although he lived fifteen-hundred kilometres away in Toronto, told CBC's *The Fifth Estate* that the SJPF was guilty of "substandard behaviour" in its fail-ure to secure the crime scene. Early in 2016, the Oland family issued a statement urging the NB Police Commission to make public the results of its investigation into how the SJPF had conducted the inves-tigation of the murder of Richard Oland.[28] The police commission had announced after the verdict that at the request of the Saint John Board of Police Commissioners it was planning to examine the role of the SJPF in the investigation. This was separate from the inquiry into the King-McCloskey allegations announced in October. The plan was to forward any recommendations to the provincial minister of Public Safety. (After the Oland appeal was filed on January 20, 2016, the NB Police Commission announced it was suspending all investigations until the legal process ran its course.[29]

On Monday, December 21, Gary Miller told the *Telegraph-Journal* that the defence planned to work on an appeal. This raised the possibility of a hearing to ask that Oland be released on bail, a rare outcome in Canada. Although one Toronto-based lawyer was optimistic about this outcome, University of New Brunswick law professor Nicole O'Byrne opined that a positive outcome was "highly unlikely," given the conditions spelled out in the *Criminal Code*. The release of Oland would be highly exceptional given that one of the key criteria for a reviewing judge was the public interest. O'Byrne stressed that a judge would have to carefully consider that "the release of a convicted murderer would destroy the public's confidence in the justice system."[30]

What exactly had happened? Twelve randomly selected people, from a jury pool chosen from two counties, sat through a sixty-five-day trial, heard dozens of witnesses, and found the accused guilty after three days of deliberation. Professor O'Byrne thought that the strategy of allowing Oland to testify bore great risk. She concluded that "the jury did not believe the accused's version of events and they decided to convict the accused." Despite the attempt by the defence to raise reasonable doubt by vigorously cross-examining Crown witnesses and questioning the competency of the SJPF, Dennis Oland had not been believable in the eyes of the jury.[31]

The jury deliberated for a total of thirty hours, from Wednesday afternoon till Saturday morning, which suggests a split. The final panel consisted of eight men and four women and several of them appeared to be in their twenties or early thirties. Given the *Criminal Code*'s restrictions against revealing what happens during jury deliberations, the dynamics of what occurred over those three days can only be speculated about. Given the outcome, it is plausible that the split may have been nine or ten in favour of guilt and two or three not convinced. Although common sense suggests that women are more liberal than men and therefore sympathetic to defendants, research indicates that age is a more discriminating factor. According to American research, older jurors are more likely than younger jurors to convict. Another reason why deliberations were extended is that the jury had a lot of circumstantial evidence to consider and probably watched video clips and reviewed the trial's extensive documentary record. Over the three-day period the gap narrowed, so it is likely that the panel came to an unofficial consensus on the evening of the eighteenth, and knocked off at roughly 8:00 P.M. The jury then relaxed for the rest of the evening and returned to the courthouse the next morning for the final, formal vote.

Veteran Nova Scotia defence lawyer Joel Pink, interviewed on CTV Atlantic, was "a little surprised" but viewed the outcome as "a good example of our criminal justice system." Pink thought that both legal teams were experienced and professional and reminded viewers that the decision to charge Oland would have been reviewed by the Crown. He explained that cases can appear from the outside to "lean towards the defence" but only the jury sees the "totality of the facts." Then there was the credibility of the defendant as a witness, especially in relation to the key point of the trial, the brown jacket. The defence had offered no other theory to explain the crime and obviously failed to raise sufficient reasonable doubt. Pink believed that "this particular jury was very careful."[32]

Murder, sexual assault, and child-abuse trials, with their graphic testimony and evidence of human trauma, can be incredibly stressful to jurors. Yet the *Criminal Code* prohibits jurors from speaking to spouses, family, or friends during or after a trial about the evidence, the accused, the witnesses, or the judicial process. Graphic evidence, such as autopsy photos and videos taken by sex murderers, combined with the presence of the victim's emotional relatives and friends, can take its toll on jurors and produce emotional problems similar to post-traumatic stress. Difficulties adjusting to family and work routine after trials can last for weeks or months. After the Paul Bernardo trial for the kidnapping, rape, and murder of two teenage girls, the presiding judge sought personal counselling. But jurors, because of the legal requirement for non-disclosure (which does not exist in many jurisdictions in the United States), may not be a good fit for traditional counselling. They are also forbidden from explaining how a jury comes to a particular decision—for example, identifying a pivotal moment or crucial piece of testimony. The philosophy behind the *Criminal Code* prohibition is to prevent jurors from being influenced or intimidated, and to protect the integrity of the trial, especially with the possibility of appeals.[33]

Given the length of the Oland trial, its high profile in the media, social media, and in everyday conversations in the community, the feeling of pressure and isolation among the jury must have been significant. Judge Walsh did not spend much time in his opening remarks warning the jury about what to expect. Jurors, no doubt, saw the solid front presented by the Oland family and the lack of visible supporters of the Crown in the courtroom. Lisa Oland's confrontational outburst, not to mention media reporting on reactions to the verdict, many of which expressed surprise, must have been difficult for them. Added to this was the family's continued public insistence—rare in New Brunswick court cases—that the jury had got it wrong. A few days after the ruling, the provincial government announced it was offering support for members of the jury. The details were not disclosed.

Oland's lawyers filed a notice of appeal with the Court of Appeal on January 20, 2016. The brief stated that the jury verdict was "a miscarriage of justice" and alleged that Justice Walsh had erred in his jury instructions multiple times—for example, for neglecting to remind the jury that the Crown had failed to cross-examine their client on at least three key issues. The document also alleged that the judge had mistakenly permitted inadmissible evidence relating to Richard's Oland's iPhone and Dennis Oland's jacket.[34]

On January 20, the defence also filed a notice of motion to argue before the provincial Court of Appeal that its client be released on bail pending the appeal. Affidavits of Dennis, Constance, and Derek Oland were provided to the court. Both the mother and the uncle declared that they possessed "unencumbered assets" of at least $1 million and would act as surety if the prisoner were released on bail. Derek noted that he was executive chairman of Moosehead Breweries Limited. Dennis Oland's affidavit contained information that could have proven useful to the Crown in front of a jury, as it detailed more than a dozen trips taken after the murder and prior to his arrest in 2013. One of them was a trip to Maryland in March 2013 to "look at a boat." In July, he flew to Baltimore to "pick up a boat and sailed it back to Rothesay." Dennis, if released, planned to continue to act as a director of Far End Corporation and Kingshurst Estates Ltd.[35]

February 11, 2016, was the date of Oland's sentencing hearing. The stakes were high as the maximum sentence (time served before being eligible for parole) for second-degree murder is twenty-five years. With second-degree murder, the trial judge has discretion not with the sentence but with the minimum years to be served before parole eligibility; judges ask juries for recommendations but these are not binding. In a somewhat unprecedented move, a large number of Oland supporters met for breakfast before court and planned to converge on the Law Courts in a show of solidarity with the convicted prisoner and his family. Not all the supporters, who trudged in a line through the snow, entered the building. Photos of the crowd in the falling snow outside the Law Courts appear to include Dorothy Shephard, the PC MLA for Saint John Lancaster (Lisa's former employer). According to Larry Cain, a management consultant who organized the show of support, "They were gathered because they feel the same way that I do, that justice has not been served in this case." The social prominence of the crowd inspired veteran lawyer David Lutz to describe the event as "the march of the 1 percent."[36]

As a result of the large crowd outside, the courtroom was filled to capacity with many more people (including the author) having to sit or stand in the corridor. Spectators inside the courtroom included some well-known and well-connected residents of Saint John and Rothesay such as realtor Bob McVicar, who in 2004 had run in the Saint John riding for the PCs in the federal election, and the Honorable John Wallace, a Rothesay resident who practised law before being appointed to the Canadian Senate by the Harper Conservatives. Dennis, well dressed as usual, appeared for the first time in leg shackles. His daughter Hannah, apparently in her inaugural visit to court, sat in the first row with the family.

According to the pre-sentence report, both Dennis's wife and mother gave him a positive assessment and did not report on any anger issues. Once again, Constance hinted at the entire family's stress caused by a husband who could be "very difficult and controlling." Dennis supposedly had never experienced "emotional turmoil" or had any mental-health interventions and had served on the board of organizations such as the Canadian Automobile Association and the YMCA. The pre-sentence report stated that Oland was reporting an annual income of $50,000 a year and that "his financial affairs are in order." He told the probation officer that "he cannot express any remorse for this matter presently before the Court as he is innocent."[37] The report stated that Dennis was receiving $50,000 a year as a director of his father's two companies and $40,000 a year as a co-trustee of the estate. According to one lawyer, being convicted of murdering the owner of a business may not preclude a person from being a director of their company. What this means is that if Dennis loses his appeal bid, or wins the right to a new trial and is convicted again, he could help direct Richard Oland's companies from behind prison walls.[38]

Victim Services contacted the following persons, all of whom declined to submit a victim-impact statement: Constance Oland, Jacqueline Walsh, Lisa (Oland) Bustin, Lisa (Andrik) Oland, Andru Ferguson, Derek Oland, Jane Toward, Lesley Oland, Emily Oland, Hannah Oland, Henry Oland, Maureen Adamson, Robert McFadden, and Diana Sedlacek. Interestingly, Derek Oland, Jane Toward, and Diana Sedlacek initially were interested in completing the document but changed their minds. Two individuals did file statements: Preston Chiasson and John Ainsworth. Neither man read his statement in court. Ainsworth expressed compassion for the Oland family, the victim's co-workers, "Maureen and Bob," and especially for the victim himself for "the undeserved horror he must have experienced." He described his relationship with the victim as amicable. The trauma of the murder had an impact on not only Ainsworth, but also his family, his employees, and his friends. He also spoke of lost time and claimed that the association of 52 Canterbury with this brutal crime "doesn't enhance business; rather [it is] detrimental to the bottom line, to my livelihood." He wrote that it was "demoralizing that thirty-plus years of my toil has been relegated to being inextricably linked to some-one else's brutal actions." Chiasson, who had responded to Maureen Adamson's call for help on July 6, 2011, filed an even bleaker state-ment. He reported that he had known Oland for twenty years and felt helpless that he could not help him that day. Chiasson claimed he had experienced PTSD and depression following the murder. His per-sonal relationships had suffered and he experienced nightmares and sleep problems. His statement was a simple but eloquent reminder of the collateral damage the murder of one person can inflict.[39]

A total of seventy-three character letters were filed with the court prior to sentencing but Justice Walsh excluded a number of them as inappropriate after the Crown objected. This included a letter by Larry Cain, the friend of Dennis's who had organ-ized the show of support. Some of the letters criticized not only the jury's finding, but also specifics of the police investigation.

The judge noted his displeasure at the language of a number of letters which questioned the verdict, noting that this was highly inappropriate: "It's upsetting to me as a judge that people would do that," Walsh stated, reminding the court that a trial was not a popularity contest. The Crown objected to ten letters, and after the noon break the defence withdrew seven of them. Yet, a number of the remaining letters also alluded to a wrongful conviction and probably should have been removed.[40]

The list of relatives, friends, neighbours, and associates who submitted letters included Derek Oland and his sons, Andrew and Patrick, Pat Darrah, uncle Jack Connell, Reverend James W. Golding (former RNS chaplain), Reverend Michael Leblanc, Wallace Turnbull (a former judge and RCS old boy), and people known in business circles, such as Bill McMackin, Derek Riedle, Stephen Carson, Bob McVicar, and Chris and Troy Northrup. Carson, CEO of Enterprise Saint John, described his friend Dennis as a "community leader." Uncle Derek, using Moosehead letterhead, described his nephew as "a credit to the Oland family." Despite the judge's displeasure, some editorializing on the case did slip through, for example when Andrew Oland told the judge that he did not believe Dennis had killed Richard. Lisa (Andrik) Oland's letter spoke of a special effort by her husband to help a young father of five who needed an expensive treatment for cancer outside of Canada. The letter also disputed the perception that Dennis was "the spoiled boy who was born with a silver spoon in his mouth." More than one letter suggested that Dennis was a peacemaker of sorts who tried to restore harmony within a family affected by tensions between his father and his uncle. Turnbull, a "sometime confidant of Dick's," had practised law in Saint John starting in 1964 before being appointed to the provincial Court of Appeal in 1993. He retired from this position in 2013, two years after the murder. One letter reminded the judge that the victim "was disliked or even despised by many people." In the morning, Walsh ruled that the letters from the Oland children would be placed under a publication ban to protect their privacy, but that the issue could be revisited in the hearing scheduled at the request of the CBC. The letters revealed a very positive relationship between Dennis and his children. The letter from his stepson, Andru Ferguson, was also extremely positive. The fact that sister Lisa did not submit a letter was noted by many in the community.[41]

Constance Oland's handwritten letter to the judge was more than five pages long. It may have contained information that Mrs. Oland would have relayed to court if she had testified. She described her family as having transitioned from "a very happy time in late June 2011, into a living hell." She found out from "a very peculiar phone conversation" with Robert McFadden at 12:30 P.M. on July 7 that her husband was dead. Two weeks earlier, the family had gathered to celebrate her cousin May Bourne's one-hundredth birthday. Her letter mentioned that Dick had been fond of May and also of Constance's uncle Gordon Fairweather, and that he had believed his son's personality was similar to that of Fairweather, a long-serving PC MP and an esteemed public figure. Constance explained that Dennis had been exposed to family history through his relatives and that led her to discuss the camp logbook, which belonged to her brother Jack Connell. The treasured family heirloom was described as the object of Dennis's visit to his father's office.[42]

On July 25, 2011, Constance, Dick, and visiting relatives socialized with Dennis and Lisa and were shown photos of the couple's recent visit to England where Dennis had been working on genealogy. The next morning, Dick left on his fishing trip, but, according to his wife, father and son planned to discuss family history later. Her husband returned from fishing "in a great mood and went out to dinner that night with the relatives that were still at our house." She explained that on the evening of July 6, when Dick did not show up at home, she assumed he had travelled to St. Stephen to attend "a Ganong meeting." At the time, Ganong Brothers Ltd. was "in a dire financial position and Dick had put money into the company." She thought her husband had stayed over in St. Stephen after the meeting. After the conversation with McFadden, Constance was visited by the SJPF at roughly 2:00 P.M. The family was in "total shock" at the news of Dick's death but travelled to police headquarters. Connie and her daughter "sat in a small room" with a police officer who would not tell them anything about the death: "That night, this very same individual tried to get us to go home and leave Dennis behind." When the women replied that they would wait until Dennis was finished speaking to the police, the officer Rick Russell "proceeded to jump up and down, got red in the face." The family finally left at around 11:00 P.M. "with a very low opinion of the Saint John Police dept."[43]

Constance went on to describe the days, weeks, and months that followed as a "nightmare" for the family, with her four oldest grandchildren suffering particularly. She defended the character of her son, claiming that he had a "caring personality and stood up for the 'underdog'." She gave him full marks as a parent who taught his children to sail, showed patience when helping them with homework, and helped them with their frustrations. Constance stated that Dennis "was more of a father to his stepson Andru than Andru's biological father." The letter concluded: "Dennis Oland is a good man and did not kill his father. I believe that in your heart you know this as well."[44]

The prosecution obviously had other ideas. Crown Attorney Pat Wilbur, citing the brutality of the crime, called for twelve to fifteen years before minimum parole eligibility. One New Brunswick case cited as precedent was the 2008 conviction of Adam Wade Nash for the second-degree murder of his brother. The victim had been shot in full view of their teenaged nephew, and the convicted man appeared to show no remorse. Defended by Gary Miller, Nash had been sentenced to a minimum of twenty years before parole eligibility. The appeal court later reduced this to twelve years. In 2011, the three second-degree murder convictions in Saint John, of Jason Getson, Joseph Paul Irving, and Frederick Cormier Jr., resulted in sentences of twenty, twelve, and ten years respectively before parole eligibility. Dennis Oland, as he was objecting to his conviction, expressed no remorse, according to the pre-sentence report.[45]

Although the Oland family and its many supporters obviously discounted the jury's verdict, the defence emphasized the jury's recommendation on sentencing. Miller, using various arguments such as Dennis being a good family man, tried to make the case for the minimum of ten years. One of the themes of the defence was "the sufferings of the Oland family." Miller urged Walsh to "give him the kind of sentence that allows him to get home to his family as soon as possible."[46]

When the court reconvened, Judge Walsh declared the Oland case a "family tragedy of Shakespearean proportions." He explained that his sentencing decision was guided by the character of the convicted person, the nature and circumstances of the offence, and the recommendation of the jury. He also mentioned the underlying need to maintain public confidence in the justice system. In this case, there was no prior criminal record and no evidence of underlying mental-health issues; the prisoner was a well-educated professional and family man who had worked for CIBC Wood Gundy for a decade and was the trustee of an estate and a director of two companies. His lack of remorse was a neutral factor in this case. His character references were "glowing" and the letters from his children were "simply heart-wrenching." In short, Walsh did not seem concerned about Oland's chances for rehabilitation and reintegration post-sentence. The judge, guided by the jury, the only truth-finder in the process, reviewed the facts of the case and stated that Dennis, who was in a "desperate" financial state and in a dysfunctional relationship with a difficult parent, "simply lost it" and killed him in a fit of "pent-up rage." Walsh also declared that Dennis had brought a weapon to the scene and had disposed of both it and the victim's cellphone. In closing, Walsh noted that the jury had unanimously recommended ten years and that the jury supposedly reflected "the values of the community."[47]

Taking all factors into account, he agreed with the jury and pronounced that minimum parole eligibility would begin after ten years. On a day when almost everyone appeared to be thinking of the convicted murderer, Walsh reminded those present that Richard Oland, "who was slaughtered on his own office floor," should not be forgotten. Oland was told to stand for the formal sentencing, which included a ban on owning firearms and a mandatory sample for the national DNA database. Dennis was relaxed at this point, and most of the family, with the exception of his mother, did not appear to be upset. After the prisoner was taken away, there were positive comments about the "fantastic" turnout of supporters, and Hannah and Lisa were smiling and chatting. Miller was even seen joking with former lead Crown John Henheffer. Perhaps the family and defence were buoyed by a feeling of optimism about the bail hearing scheduled for the next day in Fredericton.[48] Following the sentencing, Senator Wallace spoke to the media outside the Law Courts, explaining that he was there as a friend of the Oland family: "It has been nightmarish for them and very painful for many, many in the community who they are so close to."[49]

Oland was brought back to court a short time later for the final matter of the day: a hearing on the media ban applied to the preliminary inquiry, which included not only its proceedings but also exhibits, some of which had not been seen by the jury. David Coles, representing the CBC, was present and prepared to make arguments. Earlier, Walsh had placed a temporary ban on the character letters from Oland's three children and stepson. The Crown was opposing release of photos of the victim's head wounds and any autopsy images. The Crown conceded the release of the second half of the Dennis Oland interview, a move the defence supported, as, according to Gold, it indicated how the police had mistreated their client. Given that there were reporters in the room, this comment appeared to be aimed at the media. Despite the age of the children, the defence did not object to the release of their letters, but sections were redacted. With the exception of the photos mentioned above and the redactions, the record of the preliminary inquiry and pretrial hearings was opened up to media, which revealed certain details to the public in the days and weeks to follow. Having been scrupulously neutral during all proceedings to date, Walsh made a good-natured dig about Gold's new interest in "public relations." And Gold did say to reporters in the room, "There will be a time when we will talk."[50] The end of the ban allowed the media to report on evidence and issues raised in the preliminary inquiry of 2014 and the *voir dire* hearings of 2015, providing more fodder for those who believed either the police had fingered the wrong man or that the Crown had not proven its case beyond a reasonable doubt.

On February 12, the same day as Oland's bail hearing in Fredericton, Justice Walsh attended to his final duty connected with the trial: dealing with the more than thirty prospective jurors who had not shown up at Harbour Station months earlier. The judge heard each individual and accepted the excuses of eleven of them.

The rest were found to be in contempt of court and penalized with fines. Walsh explained that he was obliged to inflict these penalties to protect the institution of the jury, "the cornerstone of democracy, pure and simple."[51]

After his sentencing hearing, Dennis spent the night in custody and was taken by sheriff's service van to the law courts in Fredericton. For the first time, media cameras recorded him in handcuffs and leg shackles as he entered the rear entrance, just like any other convicted criminal or prisoner on remand. The bail hearing was argued before Justice Mark Richard of the New Brunswick Court of Appeal. In 1997, as a defence lawyer, Richard had won an important case, *Stillman* (as discussed in chapter 4), before the Supreme Court of Canada. Jack Walsh had acted for the Crown. According to Professor Nicole O'Byrne, the odds were against the prisoner and the defence may have made the application for other reasons. One of the criteria for bail was whether there were merits to the possible appeal. The Crown did not view Oland as a flight risk but it did argue that releasing a person convicted of murder would damage public confidence in the administration of justice. Indeed, no convicted murderer had even been released on bail in New Brunswick, and Crown Prosecutor Kathryn Gregory was aware of only twenty-one such cases from across Canada. (Most murderers have pre-existing criminal records, which works against release.) In each of these cases, the circumstances had been exceptional. The Crown, if Oland were to be released, wanted sureties of $400,000.[52] Gold claimed, based on the evidence, that the jury's verdict had been unreasonable and that the trial judge had made errors in his instructions. He argued that the prisoner should be released pending his appeal and stated that he would work with his father's companies and live at home with his wife in Rothesay. Counsel had advised the judge that the earliest date an appeal could be argued, if leave were granted, would be several months in the future (transcripts had to be completed). Richard reserved his decision until the following week.[53]

On February 17, the media was on hand, along with Oland family members and supporters, to hear Justice Richard's ruling. The judge pronounced that "the grounds of the appeal may be clearly arguable" and that Oland did not represent a threat to the public. But he used a hypothetical "reasonable member of the public" and a defence of trial by jury to deny bail in this case. He wrote that this reasonable person "would know that the jury which delivered the verdict convicting Mr. Oland of second-degree murder is presumed to have been composed of reasonable people acting reasonably" following a three-month trial where they heard considerable evidence. This was a serious offence that had been carried out with great brutality. The judge agreed with the Crown that in this case there was no "unique circumstance" to justify release and that if bail were permitted "the confidence of the reasonable member of the public in the administration of justice would be undermined."[54] The prisoner, unlike his family and friends who were on hand, appeared to take the decision well. The Oland family issued a statement in response: "Today's decision is difficult to accept. We know Dennis has been wrongly convicted and are confident our appeal will see justice prevail. His prolonged absence will be incredibly difficult and only serves to further compound the loss and anguish our family has suffered since Dick's murder. We will continue our long legal battle by pursuing every option to prove Dennis's innocence. We will not rest until he is home and Dick's killer is found."[55]

On February 19, two days after bail was denied, the CBC program *Fifth Estate* aired the episode "The Richard Oland Case: Murder in the Family," narrated by Bob McEwen. It was a basic overview of the investigation and the trial based on CBC footage. The only expert consulted was a Halifax journalism professor. The forty-four-minute-long program sacrificed important details of the investigation in order to interview neighbours and friends of the Olands. These included Larry Cain, who described the allegation against Dennis as "preposterous," Saint John businessman Dale Knox, and Rothesay neighbour Kelly Patterson. These interviews, recorded after the conviction but before sentencing, reflected the "sufferings of the family" narrative that was quite widespread in the community. The program focused on four key elements of the investigation: the son's visit to 52 Canterbury, the suspect's apparent lying about the jacket and the DNA evidence found on the jacket, the incriminating 6:44 P.M. text to the missing iPhone, and the forensic accounting evidence. The friends interviewed either explained that they were unaware of problems within the Oland family or defended Dennis. Cain, for example, explained that the nature of his friend's employment meant his income fluctuated. Patterson declared that "the killer is still at large... nobody is looking for him." Interestingly, the program featured not a single person who believed that Dennis was guilty.[56]

NOTES: CHAPTER 8

1. Interview with Nicole O'Byrne, March 9, 2016.
2. Court of Queen's Bench of New Brunswick, Trial Division, Judicial District of Saint John, *Her Majesty the Queen. v. Dennis James Oland,* Ruling # 7, Dec. 9, 2015.
3. Court of Queen's Bench of New Brunswick, Trial Division, Judicial District of Saint John, *Her Majesty the Queen v. Dennis James Oland*, Ruling #8, Dec. 9, 2015.
4. Pre-charge conference, Dec. 4, 2015.
5. Closing argument, Dec. 14, 2015.
6. *Ibid.*
7. *Ibid.*
8. *Ibid.*
9. *Ibid.*
10. *Ibid.*
11. *Ibid.*
12. Regina Schuller and Neil Vidmar, "The Canadian Criminal Jury," *Chicago-Kent Law Review* (86), 487–535 (2011).
13. Judges, in drafting their charges, are assisted by manuals such as Honourable Mr. Justice David Watt's, *Watt's Manual of Criminal Jury Instructions*, Second Edition, Carswell, 2014.
14. Jury Instruction (final). The full document can be found online at: http://s3.documentcloud.org/documents/2648059/R-v-Oland-Final-Instructions-Jury-s-Written.txt.
15. Jury Instruction (final), 134–35.
16. Jury Instruction (final), 138.
17. Jury Instruction (final), 198.
18. Bobbi-Jean MacKinnon, "Dennis Oland wails uncontrollably after guilty verdict in father's murder," CBC News New Brunswick, Dec. 19, 2015; Chris Morris and Mike Landry, "Dennis Oland breaks into heaving sobs as guilty verdict delivered," *Telegraph-Journal*, Dec. 21, 2015, A3.
19. Morris and Landry, "Dennis Oland breaks into heaving sobs"; CBC, "The Richard Oland Case: Murder in the Family," *The Fifth Estate*, Feb. 19, 2016.

20. CBC, "The Richard Oland Case," *The Fifth Estate*.
21. Morris and Landry, "Dennis Oland breaks into heaving sobs,"; CP, "Work beginning for appeal in Oland murder conviction: lawyer," *Globe and Mail*, Dec, 21, 2015.
22. [Editorial cartoon] *Telegraph-Journal*, Dec. 22, 2015, A8.
23. CBC News New Brunswick online, post in response to Dec. 19, 2015 story.
24. CBC News New Brunswick online, post in response to Dec. 19, 2015, story.
25. The author is keeping this Facebook post anonymous.
26. Chris Morris, "Circumstantial case Against Oland Hinged on Key Evidence," *Telegraph-Journal*, Dec. 21, 2015, A1.
27. *Ibid.*
28. CP, "Oland family members call on police commission to release inquiry's findings," *Toronto Sun*, Jan. 5, 2016.
29. CP, "New Brunswick police commission to probe police handling of Oland murder," *Globe and Mail*, Dec. 22, 2015.
30. Morris, "Circumstantial case," A2; Interview with Nicole O'Byrne, March 9, 2016.
31. Morris, "Circumstantial case," A2.
32. Joel Pink, CTV Atlantic News, Dec. 21, 2015.
33. CBC Radio, "After the verdict; should there be more counselling for jurors?", *Day 6*, Feb. 6, 2016.
34. Notice of Appeal, In the Court of Appeal New Brunswick between, Dennis James Oland Appellant and Her Majesty the Queen Respondent, Jan. 20, 2016.
35. Affidavits of Constance Oland, Jan. 13, 2016; Affidavit of Derek Oland, Jan. 12, 2016; Affidavit of Dennis James Oland, Jan. 12, 2016.
36. CP, "Dennis Oland sentenced to life for murder of his millionaire father," *London Free Press*, Feb. 11, 2016; Interview with David Lutz, March 8, 2016.
37. Pre-sentence report for the *Court of Queen's Bench, R v. Dennis James Oland*, prepared by Jim Peters, Feb. 2, 2016.
38. Bobbi-Jean MacKinnon, "Dennis Oland could co-direct murdered father's companies from behind bars." CBC News New Brunswick, Feb. 20, 2016.

39. Victim Impact Statement, John Ainsworth, Feb. 2, 2016; Victim Impact Statement, Preston Chiasson, Feb. 2, 2016.
40. Sentencing hearing, Feb. 11, 2016.
41. *R. v. Dennis James Oland*, Letters filed in support of Dennis Oland, Jan–Feb, 2016.
42. Constance Oland to Justice John Walsh, Jan. 16, 2016.
43. *Ibid.*
44. *Ibid.*
45. Pre-Sentence Report for the Court of Queen's Bench, *R. v. Dennis James Oland*.
46. *R. v. Dennis James Oland*, Sentencing hearing, Feb. 11, 2016.
47. *Ibid.*
48. *Ibid.*
49. *Ibid.*
50. *R. v. Dennis James Oland*, Media ban hearing, Feb. 11, 2016.
51. Mike Landry, "Thousands in fines issued for those who skipped Oland jury duty," *Telegraph-Journal*, Feb. 13, 2016, B6.
52. Interview with Nicole O'Byrne, March 9, 2016.
53. Kevin Bissett, "Oland jury got it wrong, lawyer tells appeal court as he seeks bail," *Globe and Mail*, Feb. 12, 2016.
54. Court of Appeal of New Brunswick, 2-16-CA, *Dennis Oland and her Majesty the Queen*, Bail ruling, Justice Richard, Feb. 17, 2016.
55. Bobbi-Jean MacKinnon, "Dennis Oland denied bail as he awaits murder conviction appeal," CBC News New Brunswick, Feb. 17, 2016.
56. CBC, "The Richard Oland Case," *The Fifth Estate*.

CHAPTER 9

A WRONGFUL CONVICTION?

March 2016–present

F ollowing its defeat in February, the Oland defence team continued its quest to make New Brunswick legal history: it attempted to convince a court to release a convicted murderer on bail. On March 7, 2016, three judges of the New Brunswick Court of Appeal heard arguments on the merits of Justice Richard's decision to deny Oland's release. Crown prosecutor Kathryn Gregory repeated earlier arguments about public confidence in the administration of justice and the sanctity of the jury system. Alan Gold, on behalf of his client, claimed that a jury had registered a conviction despite "an astonishing lack of evidence," that the verdict was unreasonable, and that the police were guilty of tunnel vision. The court decided it would reserve its decision. Justice Ernest Drapeau also announced that the court had set aside one week, starting October 18, 2016, to hear arguments on the merits of an appeal.[1] The results of the bail review were released on April 4. Drapeau wrote that he was "duty bound" to uphold the February 17 decision and Justices Larlee and Quigg concurred. Yet, Drapeau agreed that "the grounds of appeal appear to be serious."[2] By this time, Oland, aside from court appearances, had been in custody for three-and-a-half months. Family lawyer Teed told media that a final appeal to the Supreme Court of Canada had not been ruled out, and confirmed that the defence was hard at work preparing for the appeal of the conviction. Constance Oland issued another statement about the family's commitment to proving Dennis's innocence and finding "Dick's killer."[3]

Pending his possible appeal, Oland remained in federal custody. What the average convicted criminal experiences in prison is rarely of interest to the New Brunswick media, but one report outlined the likely conditions of his Dennis's custody. Following his sentencing, he probably remained in provincial custody, presumably in Saint John, for two weeks. Next, he was sent to the Springhill Institution, a federal facility in Nova Scotia, to be assessed for intake by a parole officer. His rating as a prisoner depended on his admission of guilt, a difficult situation for an individual insisting on his innocence. Many convicted murderers are sent to a maximum-security penitentiary such as the Atlantic Institution at Renous in the Miramichi region, but more are kept in medium- and minimum-security institutions. Corrections Canada, for reasons of privacy, does not notify the public about where it houses individual prisoners. Oland has no criminal record, is small of stature, and a likely candidate to be bullied while in custody. His lawyers describe him as a model prisoner. There were rumours that as of June 2016, Oland was either still at Springhill or at the Dorchester medium-security penitentiary, a two-hour drive from Saint John. This foreboding-looking Victorian institution, built in the 1870s, is well past its prime. In Dorchester, or any other federal institution, inmates wear prison-issue clothes, and can receive mail and visitors from the outside and place calls to approved persons; they are also permitted to have televisions in their cells (if they can afford one) and can earn a small daily allowance. Outside exercise is limited to one hour a day and all mail and phone calls (except calls with lawyers) are monitored. Family visits are permitted, but visitors can bring nothing into the penitentiary on regular visits except change for vending machines near the visiting lounge.[4] A check with Service New Brunswick in June 2016 indicated that Dennis was still a director of Kingshurst Estates Ltd. and Far End Corporation, companies founded by the man who, according to a jury of his peers, he murdered.

In early April 2016, the media reported that Deputy Chief Glen McCloskey was being investigated by the Halifax Regional Police, on behalf of the SJPF, for allegedly attempting to interfere with a witness in the Oland matter. Early in the year, a NB Police Commission investigator had concluded that the allegations against

McCloskey were beyond the provincial Police Act and required a criminal investigation. Chief Reid defended the reputation of his deputy and described the exercise as ensuring fairness and transparency, but the allegations against McCloskey, as well as examples of lapses in the Oland investigation, surfaced at a time when many New Brunswickers were troubled by the growing police-misconduct numbers. The most dramatic, also investigated by an outside police service, was the shooting of Michel Vienneau by Bathurst Police in 2015. Charged with manslaughter and other counts, two officers in February 2016 opted for trial by jury.[5] At the time of writing, McCloskey, a veteran of twenty-eight years, remains on active duty.[6]

On December 23, two days before Christmas and four days after the conviction, Constance and Lisa Oland issued the following statement through their lawyer: "We continue to be stunned and shaken by the outcome of the trial—especially given the circumstantial nature of the prosecution's case....We know Dennis has been wrongfully convicted and we will pursue an appeal as soon as the process allows." According to the family, the verdict was a wrongful conviction and the killer of Richard Oland was "still at large."[7] The family, which continued to work with at least three lawyers, was attempting to influence public opinion through the media, but because of the possible appeal was not doing interviews.

The use of the term "wrongful conviction" was interesting and in many ways highly novel given the circumstances of the case. The outcomes of trials where defendants are represented by high-profile legal teams funded with a war chest of millions of dollars usually are not classified under this heading. In the best-known cases, the term generally is reserved for people who have been convicted of murder or sexual assault on the basis of police and prosecution tunnel vision, informed by a usual-suspects type of bias: the defendants usually have been young, working-class, poorly educated individuals with spotty employment patterns and criminal records. In Canada, many of the best-known cases date from before the advent of full disclosure to the defence and the acceptance by the courts of DNA evidence.

Criminology and legal-studies literature suggests that in some instances investigators or prosecutors are simply out to get a specific individual. But in most cases, miscarriages of justice stem from a combination of incomplete police work, mistaken identity, stereotyping, and a weak defence. Identification errors can start at the scene of the crime and be amplified with police show-ups and lineups. As discussed earlier, the Reid Technique, favoured by most investigators for decades, has been criticized for provoking false confessions and false testimony by witnesses.[8] In Canada prior to 1963, and in much of the United States where the death penalty remains in place (with more than seven hundred being executed between 1976 and 2001), the reality of wrongful conviction has meant that innocent people have been executed and many more sentenced to long prison terms for crimes they did not commit. It does not appear that any of the executed, or most of the nearly three thousand Americans on death row in 2016, were or are wealthy.[9]

When these cases are reopened, usually after investigative reporting has raised public concern, a number of things can happen. New evidence or excluded old evidence, tying the actual perpetrator to the crime, comes to life. In some cases, the crime remains unsolved. Eyewitness and jailhouse informants, out of guilt or remorse, change their original incriminating testimony. New forensic evidence, notably DNA typing, is introduced to exclude the wrongfully convicted from the murder or sexual assault scene. Some of the best-known Canadian examples of overturned convictions are the cases of Steven Truscott, Donald Marshall Jr., David Milgaard, Guy Paul Morin, and Thomas Sophonow.

According to criminologist D. Kim Rossmo (formerly a member of the Vancouver Police Department), the two leading contributing factors in two-hundred-and-forty cases of wrongful conviction identified by The Innocence Project were problematic forensic science and misconduct by police and or prosecutors. Rossmo adds his own category: "faulty investigative thinking." Related to this was intuition, the "gut instinct" of investigators, which is often hasty, affected by emotion, and "prone to error." "Tunnel vision" (the practice of police focusing on a single suspect early in the investigation to the exclusion of other possible leads) and "confirmation bias" (the tendency, often the result of police intuition, to find or interpret information based on a person's pre-existing biases) were also problems. Another danger is "working backward from the suspect to the crime." In the Steven Truscott case of 1959, for example, the Ontario Provincial Police appear to have "invented" the time of death of victim Lynne Harper because of their determination to convict fourteen-year-old Truscott who seemed to match what they were looking for in a suspect.[10]

The SJPF has been associated with a number of actual or alleged cases of wrongful conviction, but not in recent years. The best known case is that of Erin Michael Walsh, featured in an episode of CBC's *The Fifth Estate*, hosted by Linden McIntyre, in 2007. In 1975 Walsh, a petty criminal, visited Saint John to try and sell speed. He was convicted of second-degree murder for the shotgun slaying of Melvin Peters at Tin Can Beach in the city's South end. The trial lasted four days and the jury deliberated for one hour before returning a guilty verdict. Prosecutor William McCarroll later became a judge.[11] Walsh's appeal attempt failed but almost three decades later he acquired the Crown's full file, not available to his lawyer in 1975, from the provincial archives. It revealed several types of information, such as the jailhouse conversations of witnesses, which could have raised reasonable doubt with a jury. With the assistance of Canada's Association in Defence of the Wrongfully Convicted, he applied to the federal Minister of Justice for a review of his case. The minister referred the matter to the provincial Court of Appeal which in 2008 quashed the conviction. A year later, Walsh, who had been suing the provincial government and the City of Saint John, reached a deal on compensation. In 2010, he died of cancer.[12]

The second example, in this case an alleged wrongful conviction, was the trial of Bobby Mailman and Wally Gillespie for beating George Leaman with a shotgun butt and axe and setting him on fire in 1983. In 1984, the defendants had been represented by Wilber MacLeod, who, fourteen years later, pointed out that in the 1980s defendants did not benefit from full disclosure, such as statements given to the police. The first trial produced a deadlocked jury; a second trial ended with a conviction. Mailman, who had been prosecuted for murder three times in one case and for the attempted murder of a police officer and acquitted each time, was the type of offender the authorities wanted behind bars. In 1994, the Supreme Court of Canada denied the defendants leave to appeal. One of the complicating factors in reopening the case was that a number of exhibits from the trial had been destroyed.

By 1998, Mailman and Gillespie were pursuing their case from prison. They had refused to admit guilt in order to be released earlier and had passed lie-detector tests. Two witnesses for the Crown, in a case where there was no forensic evidence linking the accused with the crime, claimed they had lied at the trial. Both had been given money by the SJPF—one to act as an informant—and the Crown dropped murder charges against the adult witness in return for her testimony. The provincial Justice Department and the police refused to release the files on the investigation and the provincial minister explained that the only hope for Gillespie and Mailman was to appeal to the federal Minister of Justice under section 690, the "last chance" clause, of the *Criminal Code*.[13] Investigative reporting on the issue produced a somewhat unprecedented public statement by SJPF Chief Butch Cogswell, who had been a polygraph officer in the 1980s. Cogswell denounced coverage of the controversy in the *Telegraph-Journal* as characterized by "falsehood, misrepresentation and distortions" and tried to rebut various evidentiary issues identified by the convicted men, including the credibility of the two witnesses. The Crown attorneys in the original case also stood by the prosecution. The SJPF refused to release investigation files to the media or public but it did co-operate with the lawyer working on behalf of the Criminal Conviction Review Group of the federal Department of Justice. In 1998, the NB Court of Appeal refused to hear the new testimony of the male witness, who had been only sixteen at the time of the murder. Although both men were later released on parole, they were never exonerated.[14]

The third example of a possible wrongful conviction by the SJPF was the attempt by George Pitt to reopen his 1994 conviction for the murder and sexual assault of six-year-old Samantha Dawn Toole. In 1993, she was found on the bank of the St. John River in the Indiantown area of Saint John's North end. The girl, who had been sexually assaulted and suffered from trauma on her head, later died from drowning. Although her mother, Gloria, first called 911 at 12:48 P.M., it took the SJPF nearly four hours to respond. Police eventually arrested Pitt, her boyfriend. Gloria testified that when she returned from a night of drinking at 4:00 A.M. Pitt was laundering a comforter from the girl's bedroom. Both George (who had a troubled upbringing and a record for assaulting women) and Gloria had been drinking. DNA from the victim was found in a bloodstain on the comforter, which also had particles of grass and leaves, suggesting it had been outside. Blood was also found on Pitt's housecoat, pillows, and other items in the apartment. Pitt, who hid from the police before being arrested, said he had taken off because he was on probation and afraid of being penalized for welfare fraud. He was convicted by a jury after eight hours of deliberation. The chances of an appeal seemed promising when Butch Cogswell, then a senior officer, found a witness whose testimony could have shifted suspicion to Pitt's friend Steve Miller. That witness changed her story, however, and the NB Court of Appeal dismissed the case (Gary Miller was involved in the appeal). In 1997, the Supreme Court of Canada refused to hear an appeal. In 2004, the Association in Defence of the Wrongfully Convicted became involved. It drew attention to hairs collected from the victim's body and rape-kit type evidence, which, incredibly, had never been tested. DNA testing had advanced considerably since 1994, and in 2005 Justice Hugh McLellan ordered the testing of the hair samples, the victim's nightgown, and vaginal and rectal swabs. The only DNA evidence detected from swabs of the body was that of the victim (who had been in the river before being discovered). The effort to exonerate Pitt came to a halt, and he remained in penitentiary.[15]

The point of the three cases discussed above is not simply to uncover further evidence of the dark side of Saint John, but to indicate the typical case of proven, and alleged, wrongful conviction in our justice system. In each instance, the convicted person was criminally involved or had a police record; they were also poor and known to abuse drugs and alcohol. There may be examples of members of the economic or social elite being mistakenly convicted of murder or other serious crimes in Canada, but they have yet to be documented.

There are two levels to understanding the claim of a wrongful conviction in the case of Dennis Oland. The first is that he is innocent and that someone else carried out the crime. Given the circumstances of the murder, this person was known to the victim and is out in the community. The second is that there was insufficient evidence to convict Oland, beyond a reasonable doubt, of one of the most serious offences in the *Criminal Code*, where the penalty can be up to twenty-five years in prison. When people attempt to solve mysteries as armchair detectives, they focus on forensic evidence and other physical clues. Yet in a criminal trial, especially one involving a jury, two factors that are not always quantifiable but hugely important are the perceived credibility and character of the witnesses, especially the defendant. Ultimately, because of legal rules that prohibit jurors from disclosing the reasons behind their verdicts, we will never know what the jury thought of Dennis on the stand. But given the verdict, balanced against the judge's reminders of reasonable doubt and the burden of proof, it must have found major problems with his testimony on December 1 and 2, 2015, particularly compared to his original police statement. Although many observers considered him confident, sympathetic, and believable in the witness box, the verdict suggests otherwise. The defendant's changed account of the number of visits to the office, the recollection of the workshop incident as an explanation for the victim's DNA on his jacket, as well as the more positive spin he placed on the dysfunctional father-son dynamic, ending with the declaration that he "loved" his emotionally abusive father, may have been too much to bear. Perhaps the defence sensed that Oland's lifestyle and perceived character were also on trial, which might explain its surprise decision to not call family members as witnesses. One important clue is found in a *voir dire* from November 2015, when Robert McFadden was in the witness box. With the jury absent, the defence objected to the Crown's attempt to introduce evidence of Dennis Oland's financial situation from 2009 as irrelevant and even prejudicial to its client because it was possible "evidence of bad character," and related to motive. In fact, this was a core element of the Crown's strategy, which was based not simply on Oland's money problems, but the combination of inconsistent income, a pattern of living beyond his means, and a reliance on a temperamental father, who was also having an affair.

The outcome raises the possibility that the Oland verdict may have been influenced by reverse class discrimination. The public (and presumably members of juries) can have an aversion to privileged defendants; this appeared to be the case with Americans Lyle and Erik Menéndez, convicted of the 1989 shooting deaths of their wealthy parents. The defence argued that the young men, twenty-one and eighteen at the time of the crime, had been physically and sexually abused by their parents. The motive for murder appeared to be greed, suggested by the brothers' extravagant lifestyle after the crime. The first trial, broadcast on Court TV, resulted in deadlocked juries, but in 1994 a second prosecution succeeded. In 1998, an appeal court upheld the Menéndez brothers' life sentence for first-degree murder and conspiracy to commit murder. While interviews indicated that jurors had some sympathy for the young men, their callousness and self-centred desire for a luxurious lifestyle were thought to be factors in the jury's decision. The jury forewoman called them "spoiled brats."[16]

If the jury verdict is correct, then there are a number of disturbing implications in the Oland case. The first is the obvious one, that Dennis not only committed murder, but killed his own father and the grandfather to his three children. And if the visit to the wharf was an attempt to dispose of incriminating evidence, he used the excuse of visiting his children as a cover story. Two, given that there was no evidence of any weapon at the Far End Corporation office prior to the attack, it must have been brought to the scene, suggesting an element of planning, as investment advisers normally do not carry tools such as hammers on their person. Three, the defendant lied to his wife, his mother, and the rest of his family who have been so public in their claims of his innocence. In fact, if guilty, he spoke to Lisa on his cellphone within minutes of carrying out a brutal crime, then went shopping with her, speaking to his aunt, and sister of the victim, possibly one hour after the attack. Four, he benefited financially after the murder by serving not only as an executor of the victim's estate, but as a trustee of his estate and director of two of his companies and president of a third. Five, he actually went to work in the very office where the crime had taken place, sitting at a desk just a few feet from where he had brutally murdered his father. Six, knowing since July 7, 2011, that he was the prime suspect in the murder, he not only appeared to live a normal life, he somehow, without having a full-time job, stabilized his financial situation, went on trips, and bought a new boat. Seven, far from keeping a low profile, he helped out at his wife's new clothing store and socialized with friends, particularly on the river in the summer months. Eight, after he was arrested, it is reasonable to infer that he relied on support either from his mother, who had inherited the interest on a $36-million estate, or from other family members, to fund his legal defence. If the verdict is correct, then we are speaking of a macabre situation where a murderer possibly used his victim's money to pay for his legal defence. The ninth implication is that loyal and well-meaning family members, friends, and associates have stood by a man who slaughtered his own father in a fit of rage. This includes close relatives who are associated with the Moosehead beer brand. As his character letters indicated, Oland is well thought of, and well connected. How many convicted murderers have senators show up at their sentencing hearing or remain, from behind prison walls, a senior member of the local yacht club—in this case, the same club where the victim's sailing trophies are on display?

Any major criminal investigation, and resulting trial, contains a number of difficult, contradictory, and unanswered questions. As criminologist D. Kim Rossmo reminds us, not all crimes, including many murders, can be solved.[17] The rest of this chapter will focus on a series of problematic questions or issues, most of them interrelated, that can aid the reader in making up their own mind about the case. A number of these questions are not as relevant if Dennis Oland was not the actual killer.

THE PURPOSE OF THE
JULY 6, 2011, VISIT

Starting at the beginning, what was the purpose of Dennis Oland's visit to his father's office? There is no record of him contacting Richard or Maureen Adamson in advance and according to Robert McFadden he only visited four or five times a year, despite working close by. Given his recent trip to England, where he had collected materials related to family history, it is plausible that Dennis, who appeared to leave at least one document in his father's office, did drop by to discuss genealogy. Maureen's testimony also supported this explanation. If so, the red bag was used to carry materials (and possibly to carry out the logbook and CDs), although there is no evidence to that effect other than the defendant's testimony.

The explanation that Dennis visited the Far End Corporation to pick up the island camp log for his uncle is less convincing. As noted in Justice Walsh's charge to the jury, the log was an important part of the explanation in Oland's trial testimony but not in his 2011 statement. It was mentioned only twice in his initial statement (roughly at the one-hour-and-ten-minute point), and the transcript reads as though he was asked to take it home by Maureen Adamson (who did not know he would be visiting) after he arrived at the office. Maureen did testify that she asked Dennis, after he arrived, to take the book with him. Constance Oland told police that at some point Dennis had spoken to Jack Connell about picking up the logbook, but there was no record on court exhibit D-80 (the timeline) of any contact between the two on Dennis's cellphone on July 6. (He may have used his home phone or his office line.) Additionally, Adamson left the items with Richard and did not give them to his son when he appeared at the office. The importance of the logbook as a reason for the visit may have been inflated by its usefulness to the defence for showing that its client left the office before the crime occurred.

According to the Crown, the real purpose of the visit was for Dennis to use a genealogy discussion as a pretext to revisit the "bank of Daddy." There was absolutely no proof at the trial that the two men discussed financial matters that day. Friends interviewed for *The Fifth Estate* professed to be ignorant of Dennis's financial situation, and it also seemed not to be on the radar of family members interviewed by the police. The financial issues behind motive were a real challenge for the defence. One was the figure itself: it was possible, although not entirely fair, to view the defendant as owing more than $700,000 as of July 6, 2011, with a negative cash flow, and ongoing automatic deductions for alimony and child support. Richard had helped his son in the past, but a discussion about money may have triggered an argument. Finally, the fact that Dennis was living beyond his means rather than altering his lifestyle, and downplaying his predicament under cross-examination, affected his credibility, a central factor in any determination of guilt.

Yet the financial issue, if valid, may have had another layer. What the police appeared not to know in late 2011, and what the jury never heard, was that Dennis and Lisa Oland at some point that year had been in the process of buying a building on Germain Street, behind 52 Canterbury. As noted earlier, the rear alley behind what was then Bustin's Fine Furniture allows fairly easy passage to 115-17 Germain, the building where in 2012 Lisa opened her used-clothing business, The Exchange. A second alley, featured in a defence video from 2014 (which the jury never saw) and described by John Ainsworth at trial, passes along the south side of the building, which for decades housed the Canadian Bible Society. This passageway, fronted by a locked wooden gate, is on the north side of the building that houses the law firm Gorman Nason.

In addition to the fact that the rear of 115-117 Germain is proximate to the rear of 52 Canterbury, the timing of these transactions raises some interesting questions. The numbered company owned by Dennis and Lisa Oland did not acquire title to the property until late 2011, more than four months after the murder. When did people first become aware that the building, whose title passed to the Canadian Bible Society two days before the murder, was going on the market? How did the couple, who had their backs to the wall financially, expect to purchase, maintain, pay taxes on, and renovate a building worth nearly $300,000? If the Crown was correct in its theory that Dennis really went to see his father to seek financial assistance, was it for his cash-flow problem or was the pressing issue to discuss a plan to set up the couple with a business? Another possibility, related to the testimony of John Travis, was that Dennis had asked his father to invest a substantial amount through CIBC Wood Gundy. The question becomes more intriguing when one remembers that Lisa (Andrik) Oland supposedly was c. $100,000 in debt at the time.

PREMEDITATION VERSUS CRIME OF PASSION

As Justice Walsh explained to the jury, the burden of the Crown was to prove beyond a reasonable doubt not only that Dennis killed his father, but also that he "had a state of mind required for murder; that is, he either meant to kill Richard Oland or meant to cause Richard Oland bodily harm that Dennis Oland knew was likely to kill Richard Oland and was reckless whether Richard Oland died or not."[18] The trial judge pointed out that the degree of overkill in the attack left little doubt as to the intent of the assailant. Yet the preliminary inquiry judge could find no motive in the evidence presented to him. The Crown had laid a charge of second-degree murder in this case because it could not prove premeditation or planning. In terms of trial outcomes, second-degree murder usually outnumbers first-degree degree convictions. All three homicide offenders sentenced in Saint John in 2011, for example, were convicted of (one had confessed to) second-degree murder. And there have been murder prosecutions in New Brunswick where the accused pleads guilty to manslaughter (which, under Canadian law, is a homicide committed without intention to cause death). The specific reason or motive behind the murder, as Walsh also explained, did not have to be proved by the Crown, but in this case the prosecution had stressed financial pressures. The defence argued that its client had no reason to kill his father, and that neither physical nor electronic evidence indicated a motive.

During the trial, the defence asked why, if there had been intent to murder, why would Dennis arrive at the office when Maureen Adamson (and possibly Robert McFadden) was still on-site? Of course, the Crown was not arguing that the crime was planned. There was no sign of forced entry or robbery, and common sense dictates that the victim knew the killer. As criminologists explain, most murders are not committed for the logical (if twisted) reasons depicted in mystery novels or crime dramas. They are "expressive—that is motivated by rage or anger and they typically involve friends, relatives of acquaintances."[19] Psychological studies suggest that murderers often have bad tempers, drug and alcohol problems, and a history of violence, or have been psychologically damaged by childhood trauma. One can find media reports of people who kill, then appear to calmly walk into a store or go home to their families with no apparent sign of emotion. There seems to be, for perfectly understandable reasons, little research on how murderers act following the commission of their crime. Yet, the fact that no weapon was discovered may suggest a degree of premeditation, as the defence once mused when the jury was not in the courtroom.

THE WEAPON

If the killing of Richard Oland was a crime of passion, with the accused "losing it" and striking out at a lifelong object of frustration, where did the weapon come from? Robert McFadden testified that there were no tools in the office except a small screwdriver, and no evidence about construction work in the building or any report of missing tools from nearby sites was entered at trial. The rules of evidence forced the judge in his charge to the jury to declare that the theory of the drywall hammer was pure speculation. Yet the weapon had to be some type of tool carried in to the scene and not one of opportunity, such as a pair of scissors, easily picked up in an office during an altercation. Why would an investment adviser (even one who was handy and accustomed to fixing things) be carrying a drywall hammer or similar tool, especially on a workday? Taking it back a step further, if he had initially gone to his father's office to ask for financial assistance, why would he be carrying a weapon? Oland, if the jury is correct, brought a weapon to the crime scene and, as the judge declared at sentencing, carried it with him when he left. This inference had major implications for the timeline (discussed on the next page). Of course, if the murder was carried out by an unidentified person, in keeping with the theory of the defence, the killer could have brought a weapon to the office and disposed of it later. Mention of another suspect begs a further question: who else would have had a motive to do harm to Richard Oland other than "almost anyone" (in the words of his daughter)? The only plausible motives could have been financial or sexual revenge, which could include an irate investor, someone to whom the victim owned a substantial amount of money (there were rumours), or a jealous husband. If Oland was cheating on his wife when in his sixties, it is likely he was doing it earlier as well. Yet, there was no evidence, at least revealed in the preliminary inquiry or at trial, of recent disputes involving the victim.

It would have been necessary to dispose of the weapon after the crime. If, as the jury believed, Dennis were the guilty party, he could have hidden it in a bag or some type of covering. The fact that he admitted to and was filmed carrying a red bag between 5:45 and 6:12 P.M. on July 6 does not mean he took it back to the office on his final trip, or that he had only one bag. One possibility is that the weapon was taken out the back door and disposed of later, but returning to the scene of the crime later that evening (post 10:30 P.M.) would have been extremely risky. Other than Dennis's own testimony, there was neither any evidence of his whereabouts after the trip to the convenience store later that night nor of him and his wife owning a second vehicle. The safest place for a killer to dispose of a weapon contaminated with blood would have been in water, and the most accessible bodies of water, given Oland's timeline from 6:36 P.M. on July 6 until he showed up at the police station on the afternoon of July 7, were the Kennebecasis and St. John Rivers. Of course, the hypothetical other killer would have a greater range of options, including the nearby Saint John Harbour.

THE TIMELINE

From the 1983 JoAnn Wilson murder in Saskatchewan to the 2013 killing of Reeva Steenkamp in South Africa, defence counsel have often argued that the prosecution's timeline of events is not feasible. This was not an overt argument in the Oland defence, largely because of its theory that the victim probably had been killed between 7:30 and 8:00 P.M. when Shaw and Ainsworth were at work below. The Crown's theory was that Dennis, after Maureen Adamson left, had asked his father for assistance and there had been a confrontation. Dennis, upset and confused, had walked in the wrong direction to his car, "distracted and distraught," and sent a text message to his sister by mistake.[20] He had then found his car, driven around the block one more time, made the illegal turn, and parked in the dirt lot. From here (beyond the range of security cameras) he had walked back to kill his father. Given that there was no evidence of a hammer in the office and it was unlikely that one was picked up on the street, if Dennis did commit the crime, the weapon must have been in his vehicle.

As with any crime of this nature, the killer would have needed time to carry out the murder and complete any other tasks. If the Crown is correct and the attack took place during the second full visit, the timeline was tight, as a Thandi's security camera depicted a light-coloured car moving south along Canterbury at 6:21 P.M. If Dennis was the culprit, then he parked his car in the lot on the corner with Princess Street and walked back to the Far End office (which takes about two minutes) and killed his father with more than forty blows from a weapon. Just before 6:37 P.M., when Dennis was either still in the office, on the street, or in his vehicle, he spoke to his wife, Lisa, who had called from their home, for less than one minute. If he was not the killer, he may have returned to retrieve the forgotten logbook. Yet innocent Dennis would have been pressed for time if he reviewed the book with his father, as he testified. Guilty Dennis, after the attack, would have had to clean up, possibly change out of protective covering, place the bloody weapon and any other incriminating articles in a bag, grab his father's cellphone, compose himself, and then walk down the stairs and out on to Canterbury Street as if nothing had happened. In this type of situation, the attacker's adrenalin levels would have been high, especially as the almost six-foot-tall victim, judging by the wounds on his hands, at first tried to fend off the attack before being driven to the floor by incessant blows. But once the victim had been incapacitated, it would have been possible to inflict forty blows to his head in less than two minutes. In other words, the actual murder could have been carried out in three or four minutes.

Another problem with the timeline is that if Dennis Oland was still in the vicinity of Printing Plus when on the phone with his wife at 6:36 P.M., it would have been impossible to be physically at Renforth Wharf by 6:44 P.M. when the Rothesay cell tower communicated with the victim's iPhone (unless his BlackBerry had a Bluetooth connection when he was in transit to Rothesay). One possible discrepancy between the timeline document and Oland's 2011 police statement and courtroom testimony is his explanation that he stopped at Renforth Wharf to see whether his kids, whose mother lived nearby, were swimming. Given that he had texted both daughters several times throughout the day and was running late, it is odd that he did not try to contact them first. Second, his eleven-year-old son, Henry, was spending the day at New River Beach, west of Saint John, and as of 5:05 P.M., as Dennis knew, was not home. Third, Emily was not kayaking in the afternoon as she had been scheduled to have braces removed, as is indicated in various text messages. On the other hand, children are known to swim after supper, especially on hot summer evenings. And the stop at the wharf may have been simply a coincidence; as the preliminary inquiry judge noted, if Dennis had not told the police about this incident "they may never have known about it."[21]

One piece of evidence that could have proven useful to the defence was a police statement from a lawyer who had been walking down Princess Street on the evening of July 6, 2011, at roughly 7:20 P.M., on her way to a 7:45 P.M. restaurant reservation. This placed her near the corner of Princess and Germain. In the company of her university-student daughter, she claimed to have heard two unseen men having a loud argument in the neighbourhood. The sounds seemed to be coming from within the block of buildings to the right (in other words, the north), which contained the Printing Plus building. Combined with the testimony of Anthony Shaw and, secondarily, John Ainsworth, this would have been potentially compelling evidence for the defence. Yet although the defence was aware of this statement and even raised it during the preliminary inquiry, the woman was not asked to testify at the trial.

BLOOD EVIDENCE

The defence, through its expert witness and cross-examination, attempted to raise reasonable doubt by arguing that any attacker who bludgeoned the victim repeatedly would have been covered in blood. Despite detailed examination and testing of many exhibits, including the VW Golf, the only trace evidence linking the victim and the accused had been four tiny spots on Dennis's Hugo Boss jacket. Whether the DNA in the three spots that tested as blood was derived from blood or another biological substance was a question for the jury to decide. Other than Patrick Laturnus, the only qualified blood-pattern expert at the trial was Sgt. Wentzell, whose opinion was that sharp-force wounds do not always force blood back in the direction of the assailant. The common-sense reaction to the crime-scene photos and the autopsy report was that this was an assault of extreme violence and the victim's blood would have splashed on the attacker. The lack of bloody footprints and handprints and a drip trail in the building, not to mention the absence of blood on clothing and footwear seized from the accused, on his cellphone, in and on his vehicle, and in and on the red grocery bag, is one the great puzzles of the case. One possibility is that the assailant donned gloves and a disposable coverall, the type used by painters, which can be purchased for $10. Yet, even these coveralls are not foolproof; the sleeve area, for example, is vulnerable to contact with paint and other substances. Another possibility would be a plastic raincoat, poncho, or other item of foul-weather gear that sailors favour. If guilty Dennis wore some type of protective covering or clothing, where did it come from and what happened to it? The more complicated the imagined scenario, the more the crime passes from one of passion to one of premeditation.

THE JACKET

Dennis Oland's brown Hugo Boss jacket was the key piece of evidence in the trial and will be the major issue in any appeal. Without it, as the Crown admitted in 2015, there would be no case. There are a number of questions revolving around this garment. If Dennis was the culprit, did he wear it on his last visit to the office (after appearing to take it off when he had reached his car earlier)? The defendant, as security videos indicated, had worn a navy blazer earlier in the day on July 6, 2011, so it is entirely plausible that he honestly forgot about changing into the brown jacket later. In addition, when Dennis's police interview began the next day he had only known about Richard's death (if he was indeed innocent) for several hours and despite his outward aura of calm, may have been upset, frustrated, and nervous. The failure of the defence to ask its client in front of the jury why he wore two jackets at work on the same day is a curious omission.

If the jacket was worn during the murder, as the Crown theorized, why was it not covered in visible blood stains, as Laturnus would have expected? People who commit crimes in the heat of the moment generally are not thinking about consequences such as blood spatter. Most of the blows to Richard's head appear to have been inflicted when he was on the ground, so it is plausible (especially given Wentzell's opinions) that an attacker may have been spared from major spatter. Yet, given that a person of average height and arm length would have been within two feet of the victim, there had to be some backward and castoff spatter, even if the blows were delivered from a sideways angle.

The SJPF forensic unit and the RCMP crime lab caught two stains of significance, on the outside right sleeve and the upper left chest. The area marked AO, on the outside back near the bottom, was detected by another lab. These spots were all deemed to be blood, and random probability estimates suggested they contained the DNA profile of the victim. A fourth area, on the inside right sleeve, had a DNA match but no blood. There was no evidence entered at court to determine whether the defendant was right or left handed. The shirt that Dennis allegedly had worn on July 6 was also tested, with no incriminating results. The Crown had to argue that the coat was worn during the murder, as this would explain the DNA in the fabric (which the defence said was not spatter). But there is another possible explanation for the presence of blood, at least on one sleeve. One forensic text recalls an American case where a man called 911 and told police that someone had stabbed his wife and three children to death. When police arrived he was washing his hands. In this case, "the force of tap water on the bloodstained hands...certainly could have deposited small splatters of diluted blood...on the sleeves and not be apparent to the naked eye."[22]

If Dennis was guilty, could he have detected the miniscule stains on the jacket (possibly made fainter by dry cleaning)? Const. MacDonald had to overexpose photographs of the stains and magnify them by 500 percent before he discovered them. As the preliminary-inquiry judge stated, a guilty person would be more likely to dispose of bloodstained clothing rather than have it taken to the dry cleaner the morning after he had been accused of murder by the police. This was essentially the argument adopted by the defence. On the other hand, if a man "lost" his $1,000 Hugo Boss sports coat on the same day his father was murdered, his spouse would be bound to be suspicious. The defence also suggested that only the most careless of offenders would leave a dry-cleaning tag on the jacket and the receipt from VIP Dry Cleaners on his dresser after being warned that the police would be applying for search warrants. There is no corroborated evidence as to who actually dropped off the dry cleaning and laundry on the morning of July 8. Dennis said it was his wife, but Lisa in the end did not testify and the jury heard no other testimony on the issue.

THE BACK DOOR

According to the judge, the Oland defence viewed the back door as "the least conspicuous, most surreptitious escape route for the killer."[23] There were only three ways for a person to exit the second floor of 52 Canterbury: the staircase to the street level exit, the elevator into Printing Plus, or the rear door into the back alley. The two men working in the printing business from 6:00 P.M. onward did not hear the elevator operating. By the end of the trial, it was unclear whether the exit door had been locked or unlocked at 8:55 A.M. on July 7. Maureen Adamson testified that she checked it before 5:45 P.M. when she left on the day of the murder. It was occasionally open during hot summer days in order to allow in fresh air, and Robert McFadden testified that he sometimes used it as a shortcut to Germain Street to the east. Although clearly marked as an exit, the back door, given its location, may not be an obvious way to leave the building for first-time or occasional visitors who may have assumed it led to a fire-escape stairway. This was obvious when police officers (who had been on-site for several hours) and funeral-home employees ignored the rear exit and instead carried the victim's body down a narrow stairwell to the Canterbury Street entrance.

Justice Walsh instructed the jury that the failure of the SJPF to process the back door handle and lock was an example of an inadequate police investigation. Const. Davidson's confusion about the stairs outside the door, especially with the contradictory evidence of building owner John Ainsworth, added to the defence's negative portrayal of the "rookie" detective (Davidson had claimed that on July 7, 2011, there were no stairs outside the door, and that he had jumped three feet to the ground). By noon of the first day of the investigation, at least a dozen officers had been on the second floor, and the constable in charge of scene continuity until at least 2:35 P.M. had no memory of the door being open. Davidson testified that he had unlocked and locked the deadbolt (presumably before 10:30 A.M.) but had nothing on this in his notes or written report. Davidson's partner, Gilbert, did not remember the door being open. Sgt. Smith, who arrived at 10:06 A.M., visually examined the door but did not touch or photograph it. Inspector McCloskey (on scene from 10:52 A.M. to 2:35 P.M.) testified that he may have opened the door. A constable who was then a cadet observed the exit open at 2:45 P.M. and just over an hour later Sgt. Smith saw it half open.

If someone exited through the door, it could only be locked from the outside with a key. The key holders were limited in number and none were considered suspects. So if the door was locked at 8:55 A.M. on July 7, it has no significance to the investigation. But if it was not locked, this fact could strengthen the defence theory about the "real" killer. During his police interview, Dennis (who wears a hearing aid) told Const. Davidson that he may have heard a door open when he was visiting his father. He testified that he knew of the exit door but had not used it. The only doors in the general area were the double doors leading to the foyer, the door at the top of the stairs, and the rear exit, which had once been a loading door. Of course, the theory of the Crown was that Dennis was the killer and that he entered via the front door, committed murder, and walked back out through the front to his vehicle. At one point during the proceedings, a prosecutor, after listening to another defence assertion that the "real killer" had used the back door, remarked that this hypothetical person would have had a difficult time as he would keep running into Dennis Oland. The verdict obviously indicates that the jury did not see the back-door theory, or evidence of investigatory lapses, as creating sufficient reasonable doubt to acquit the defendant.

THE IPHONE

Three questions come to mind concerning the victim's iPhone 4: Why was it taken? What is the significance of the 6:44 P.M. text message? What happened to the phone? In a case where robbery was ruled out as a motive, no reason was ever offered during the trial for why the phone disappeared. Was it taken during the actual attack, or did the killer seize the phone as a potential loose end? Perhaps it was grabbed on instinct or in the heat of the moment; an attacker who was capable of the explosive violence inflicted on Richard Oland was probably not acting too rationally.

Cellphone and cellphone-tower evidence is becoming increasingly important in criminal investigations, yet it is not without its problems.[24] The Crown's cellphone evidence, based on the jury's decision, must have been compelling for placing Dennis in Rothesay at the same time that his father's stolen iPhone was in range of the nearest cell tower. It also undermined compelling alibi evidence, the testimony of Anthony Shaw, and to a lesser extent John Ainsworth, that suggested the murder took place between 7:30 and 8:00 P.M. For the defence, the cellphone evidence was flawed and yet another unfortunate coincidence—along with the "everyday" DNA evidence on the jacket, its client's visit to his father, and the dry cleaning of the jacket—exploited by the Crown. The defence also attempted to show that the victim did not always immediately answer his texts or cellphone calls, especially from Diana, to suggest that he was still alive after 6:30 P.M. Yet from early July 4, 2011 (his first day back in Saint John), until noon on the day of his murder, Richard usually responded to text messages from his mistress. In fact, the longest time between one of her texts and a text or phone response from Richard was thirty-two minutes.[25]

The police and divers searched the water and area surrounding the Renforth Wharf on more than one occasion, presumably for a murder weapon and the missing iPhone 4. Given that the phone was still alive for more than twelve hours after the attack, it obviously was not in the water. Although her texts did not get through, calls from Diana Sedlacek between 7:19 and c. 11:12 P.M. on July 6 and on the morning of the July 7 went to voice mail, indicating that the missing phone was still functional. An iPhone normally can hold a charge for up to two days. The results of the forced registration by Rogers Communications on July 9, "roaming error," could have meant that the phone was still alive but outside of the provider's network. The defence also questioned the accuracy of the cell-tower propagation maps entered into evidence and the supporting cellphone field tests conducted by the SJPF. If there is ever a new trial, the entire issue of the cellphone and cell-tower evidence will no doubt be revisited, with the defence finding an expert witness to counter Crown evidence. As the 2000 conviction of Adnan Syed (featured in the podcast *Serial*) suggests, there can be a lack of certainty regarding cellphone evidence and this can lead to wrongful convictions.

THE FUTURE

On April 29, 2016, Bill Teed released a statement confirming that his client had applied to the Supreme Court of Canada following the New Brunswick Court of Appeal bail decision. The defence team saw the Oland case as "a potential opportunity for the Supreme Court of Canada to clarify this point of law." According to a defence brief, "The answer…will fundamentally define the liberty interests of all convicted persons in custody awaiting an appeal." The document also argued that eight months was a long time for a person to remain in custody pending the start of an appeal.[26] Alan Gold, in the appeal of Justice Richard's ruling, had repeated the defence claim that the conviction had been based on an "astonishing absence of evidence," as the grounds for release on bail at this level are the merits of an appeal of a conviction. Professor O'Byrne was doubtful that Canada's highest court, with its onerous schedule, would look at the Oland bail matter and reminded the media that the "standard for review" was a real challenge for the defence, particularly in light of a 2015 Supreme Court of Canada decision.[27] But on June 30, 2016, the Supreme Court, to the surprise of many, agreed to hear an expedited review of the Oland bail ruling. The defence had argued that the issue at hand, whether a person convicted of a serious crime can be released pending appeal, was of "national importance." The date for arguing the appeal of the bail ruling was set as October 31, 2016, more than nine months into Oland's custodial sentence and two weeks after the beginning of his possible appeal before the New Brunswick Court of Appeal. These announcements gave the family hope and produced one of the first public comments on the case from Alan Gold, who described the decision as "a first step towards Dennis regaining his freedom."[28]

If Dennis Oland does not win a new trial, or if a new trial also finds him guilty, the earliest he can be released from prison on parole would be 2025, when he will be close to sixty. Corrections Canada, where facilities exist, does permit private family visits in apartments located on penitentiary grounds. The spouses, children, and even parents of prisoners can visit every two months. In terms of any future inheritance from the trust of Richard Oland, case law would seem to prevent Dennis, unless he is ever exonerated, from inheriting his third of his father's fortune. Of course, this would not stop other beneficiaries from simply giving him a share.

The Supreme Court of Canada has ruled that jury verdicts are all but unassailable, but there have been exceptions. In 2013, the Supreme Court cautioned appeal judges to remember that a jury is "a trier of fact" and that higher court should "not act as a 13th juror."[29] For the defence, appeal arguments will focus on the one key alleged error: Justice Walsh's decision to allow the evidence based on the testing of the jacket. The defence had argued before the trial that the warrant had authorized only the seizure of the garment. Therefore, the testing of the jacket (which revealed the only incriminating forensic evidence of the case) had been an unlawful seizure. An appeal would also focus on the judge's charge to the jury. Section 24 (2) of the Canadian Charter of Rights and Freedoms compels courts to exclude any evidence "obtained in a manner that infringed or denied any rights or freedoms guaranteed by this Charter" on the grounds that it would imperil public confidence in the justice system. Yet, the key issue is how courts, in particular the Supreme Court of Canada, interpret these rights. A court reflecting an expansive theory of rights could, in theory, find fault with Walsh's 2015 rulings on evidence.

Professor O'Byrne is not convinced that an appeal, given the current legal climate, would succeed. Up until 2009, in her explanation, courts generally expanded the rights of persons in conflict with the law with rulings on disclosure, the right to a speedy trial, and the right to be considered innocent until proven guilty. Alan Gold and Gary Miller spent most of their careers in this era of expanding rights. But according to O'Byrne, who teaches criminal law, since 2009 the Supreme Court appears to be moving in another direction, with decisions that benefit the state over the individual. The key ruling, in her view, was *R. v. Grant* (2009), where a majority of the court dismissed the appeal of an Ontario man caught near a high school with drugs and a handgun. One of the outcomes was a new test for determining whether evidence is seized illegally. With the Oland case, an appeal court would have to apply the Grant test to the following question:

Did the sending of the jacket, already in the custody of the SJPF, to the RCMP lab in Nova Scotia bring the administration of justice into disrepute? O'Byrne's opinion is that the 2009 decision has the effect of giving the police more leeway.

At this point, there are a number of unknowns: if the Oland appeal in New Brunswick is denied, will the defence appeal to the Supreme Court of Canada? If the Crown loses after a new trial, will it appeal? Canada's highest court is under no obligation to review lower-court decisions, but *R. v. Oland*, being a murder case, may catch the attention of the justices (who have already indicated their interest in the bail issue). If that is the case, the murder of Richard Oland could continue to make history.[30]

NOTES: CHAPTER 9

1. Chris Morris, "Court reserves decision in Dennis Oland bail request," *Telegraph-Journal*, March 8, 2016, A1–2.
2. Court of Appeal of New Brunswick, *Oland v. R.*, 2016, NBCA 15, Review of decision denying bail pending determination of appeal against conviction for second degree murder: Feb. 16, 2016 (April 4, 2016).
3. Bobbi-Jean MacKinnon, "Dennis Oland's fight for bail pending appeal could go to Supreme Court," CBC News New Brunswick, April 4, 2016.
4. Mike Landry, "Dennis Oland–A Picture of Prison Life," *Telegraph-Journal*, Feb. 26, 2016, B1.
5. Mike Landry, "Saint John deputy police chief now under 'criminal' investigation over testimony at Dennis Oland trial," *Telegraph-Journal*, April 6, 2016.
6. Bobbi-Jean MacKinnon, "Saint John deputy chief under criminal investigation in Oland trial," CBC News New Brunswick, April 6, 2016.
7. CTV News Atlantic, "Family issues statement on Dennis Oland murder conviction," Dec. 23, 2015.
8. CBC, "The Interrogation Room," *The Fifth Estate*, Nov. 21, 2014.
9. David Von Drehle, "More Innocent People on Death Row Than Estimated: Study," *Time Magazine*, April 28, 2014; "The Nation's executed mostly poor, uneducated," *Nation*, June 20, 2001.
10. D. Kim Rossmo, "Criminal Investigative Failures," Texas State University, 2005, 1–2, http://www.qp.gov.sk.ca/Publications_Centre/Justice/Milgaard/PublicDocuments/04262006/Kim%20Rossmo/337674.pdf.
11. CBC, "If Justice Fails," *The Fifth Estate*, Oct. 17, 2007.
12. Sarah Harland-Logan "Erin Walsh," Innocence Canada, https://www.aidwyc.org/cases/historical/erin-walsh/.
13. Gary Dimmock, "Justice Department refuses to let men see files," *Telegraph-Journal*, March 12, 1998.
14. n.a. "Chief Defends Police Work," *Telegraph-Journal*, March 28, 1998.

15. CP, "N.B. judge approves DNA testing on evidence in 12-year-old murder," *Telegraph-Journal*, 2006; Christopher Shuglan, "Framed?" *Toro*, April 2006, 79–86; R. v. Pitt, 1996 4830 (NB CA).

16. Associated Press, "Menéndez jurors say boys were just 'spoiled brats'," *Utah Desert News*, April 21, 1996.

17. Rossmo, "Criminal Investigation Failures."

18. Jury Instructions (final), 26.

19. Larry J. Siegel and C. R. McCormick, *Criminology in Canada: Theories, Patterns and Typology* (Nelson Education, 2015), 344.

20. Jury Instructions (final), 188.

21. Ruling following a preliminary inquiry, 48.

22. Stuart H. James and William G. Eckert, *Forensic Interpretation of Blood Evidence at Crime Scenes* (New York: CRC Press, 1999), 109–10.

23. Jury Instructions (final), 194.

24. Rob Tripp, *Without Honour: The True Story of the Shafia Family and the Kingston Canada Murders* (Toronto: Harper Collins, 2012), 341–42.

25. *R. v. Dennis James Oland,* Exhibit D-26, Richard Oland's iPhone Communications with Diana Sedlacek, July 4–6, 2011.

26. CP, "Dennis Oland seeks early bail while appeal is in the works," *Toronto Star*, May 3, 2016.

27. Interview with Nicole O'Byrne, March 9, 2016; Chris Morris, "Dennis Oland Bail Fight Continues," *Telegraph-Journal*, April 30, 2016, B1–2; *R. v. St. Cloud*, [2015 SCC 27].

28. Christopher Hicks, "Oland appeal using Supreme Court in novel way," http://www.advocatedaily.com/Christopher-Hicks-oland-appeal-using-supreme-court-act-in-a-novel-way.html; Alan White, "Dennis Oland's bid for bail appeal granted by Supreme Court," CBC News New Brunswick, June 30, 2016.

29. Jacques Gallant, "Rare move by Ontario appeal court overturns jury verdict," *Toronto Star*, April 29, 2015.

30. CP, "Work beginning for appeal in Oland murder conviction: lawyer," *Globe and Mail*, Dec. 21, 2015; Interview with Nicole O'Byrne March 9, 2016.

INDEX

M

N

Richard H. Oland
(1941–2011)